DITCH
LIFE

F.U. PRESS

EDITOR & ASSOCIATE PUBLISHER: ERIC REYNOLDS
DESIGN: AMY LOCKHART
PRODUCTION: PAUL BARESH
PUBLISHER: GARY GROTH

F.U. PRESS IS AN IMPRINT OF FANTAGRAPHICS BOOKS

7563 LAKE CITY WAY NE·SEATTLE, WA 98115
fantagraphics.com/fupress/

ISBN 978-1-68396-303-5
FIRST F.U. PRESS EDITION: OCTOBER 2019
PRINTED IN KOREA
FU033

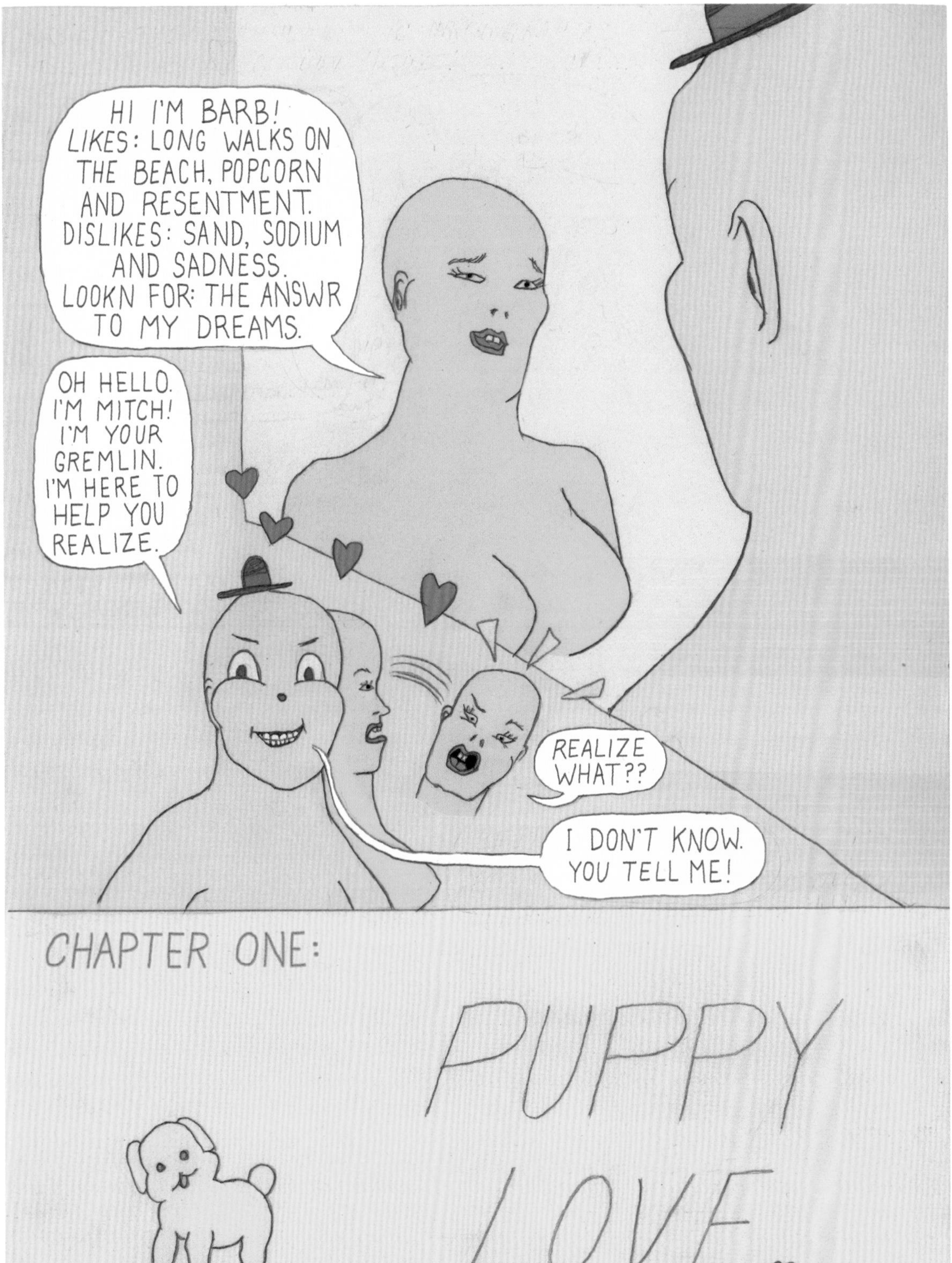
HI I'M BARB! LIKES: LONG WALKS ON THE BEACH, POPCORN AND RESENTMENT. DISLIKES: SAND, SODIUM AND SADNESS. LOOKN FOR: THE ANSWR TO MY DREAMS.
OH HELLO. I'M MITCH! I'M YOUR GREMLIN. I'M HERE TO HELP YOU REALIZE.
REALIZE WHAT??
I DON'T KNOW. YOU TELL ME!
CHAPTER ONE:
PUPPY LOVE.
STARRING TWO DITCH DWELLING DEGENERATES & A DOG

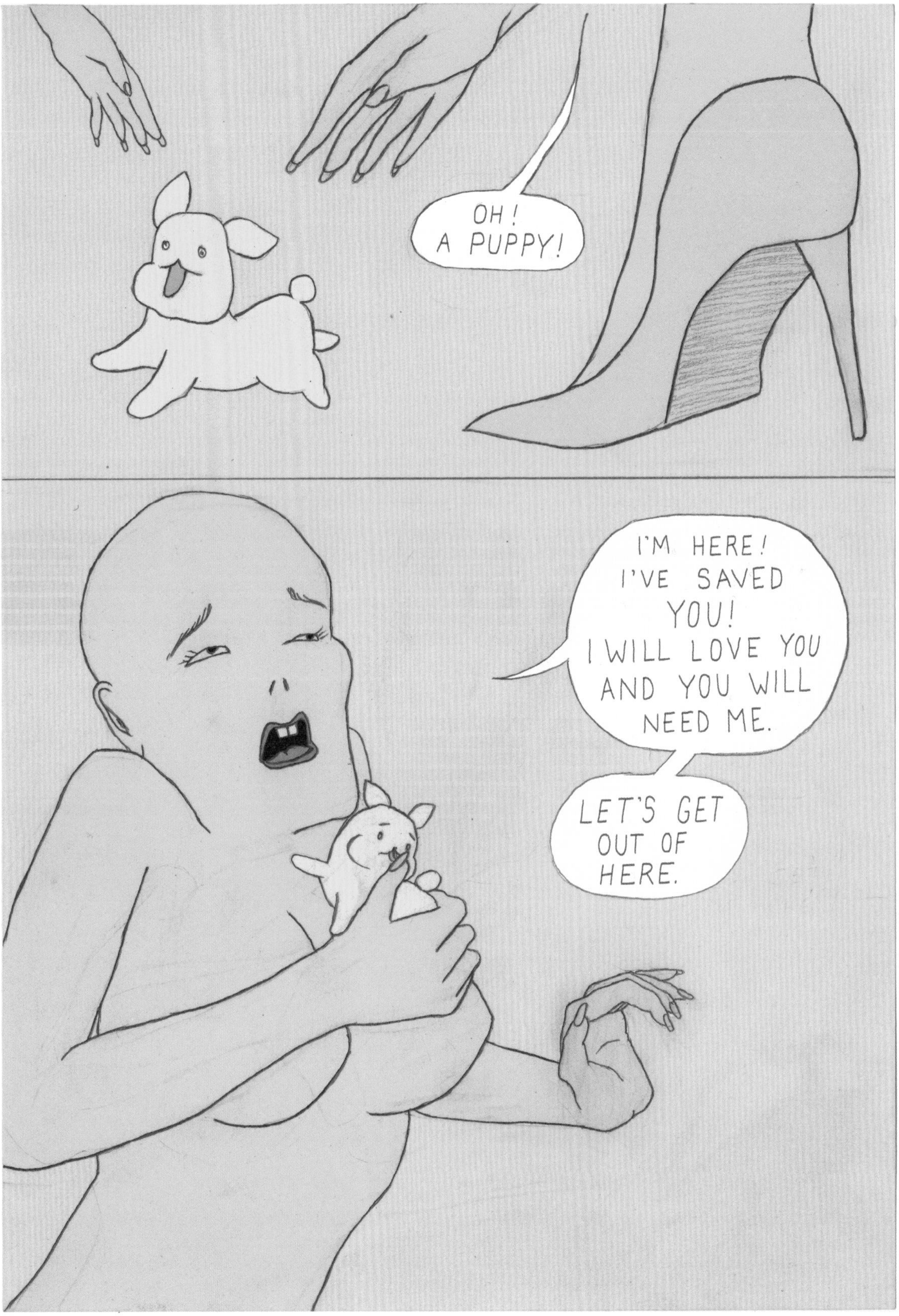
OH! A PUPPY!
I'M HERE! I'VE SAVED YOU! I WILL LOVE YOU AND YOU WILL NEED ME.
LET'S GET OUT OF HERE.

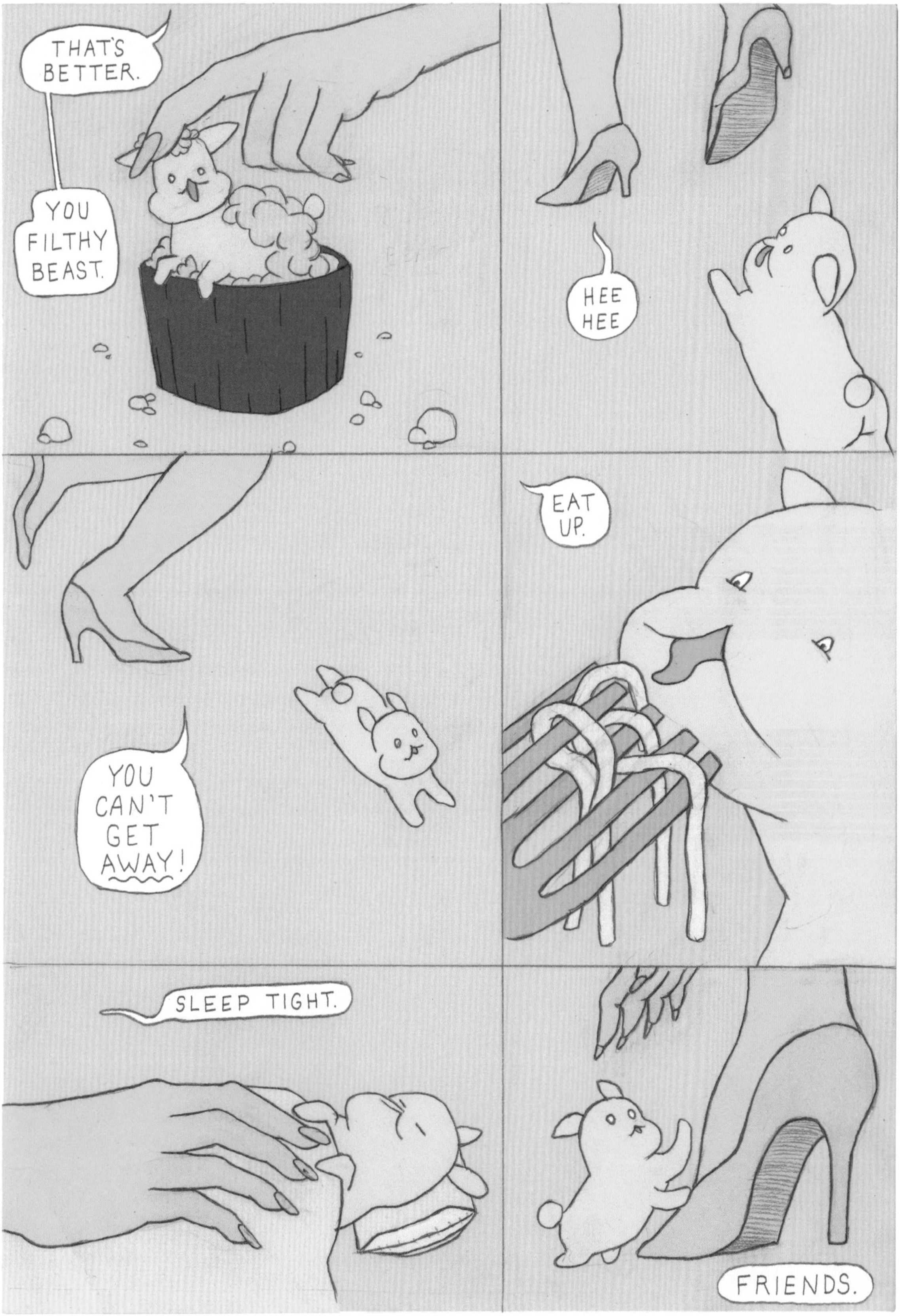
THAT'S BETTER.
YOU FILTHY BEAST.
HEE HEE
YOU CAN'T GET AWAY!
EAT UP.
SLEEP TIGHT.
FRIENDS.

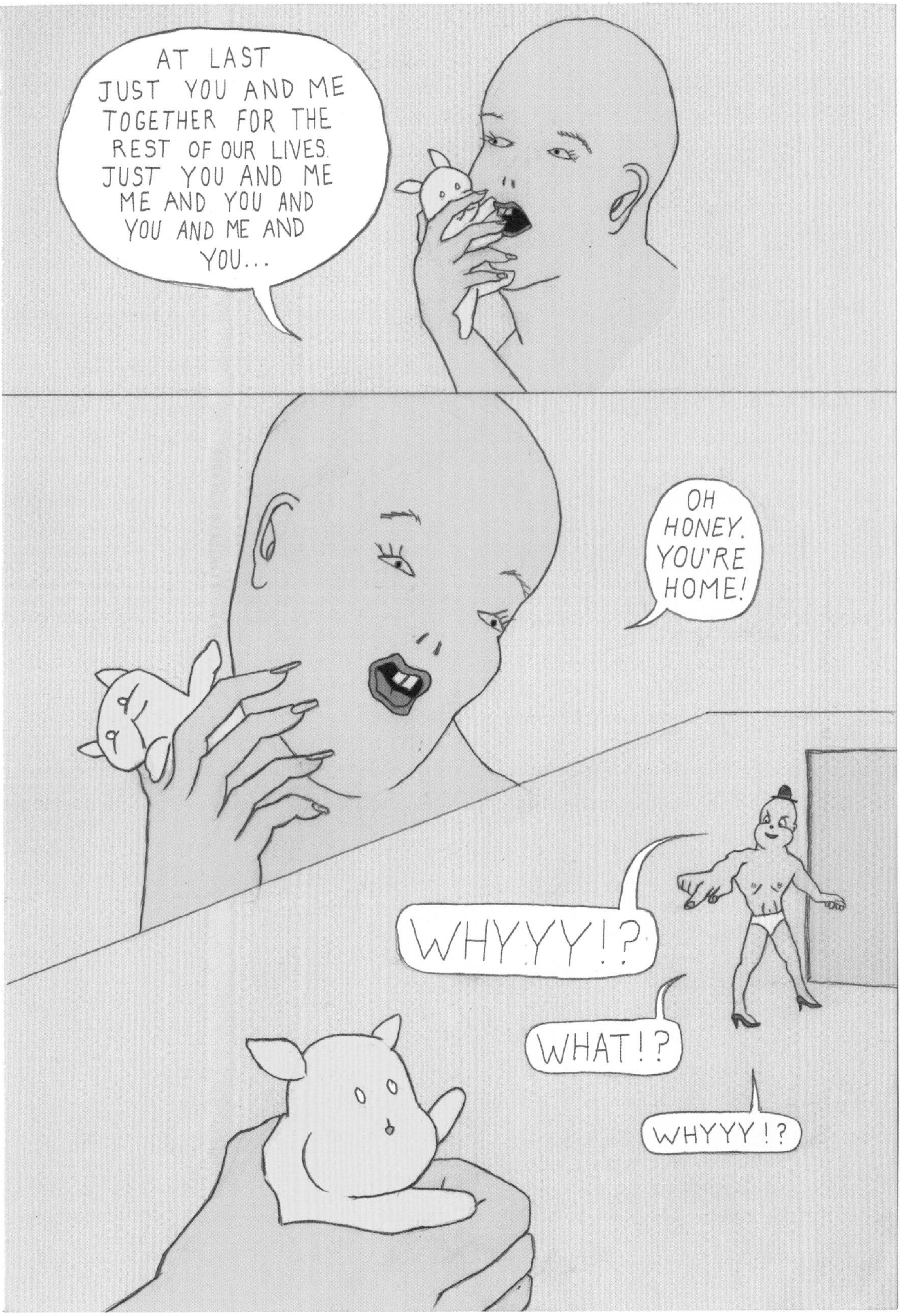
AT LAST JUST YOU AND ME TOGETHER FOR THE REST OF OUR LIVES. JUST YOU AND ME ME AND YOU AND YOU AND ME AND YOU...
OH HONEY. YOU'RE HOME!
WHYYY!?
WHAT!?
WHYYY!?

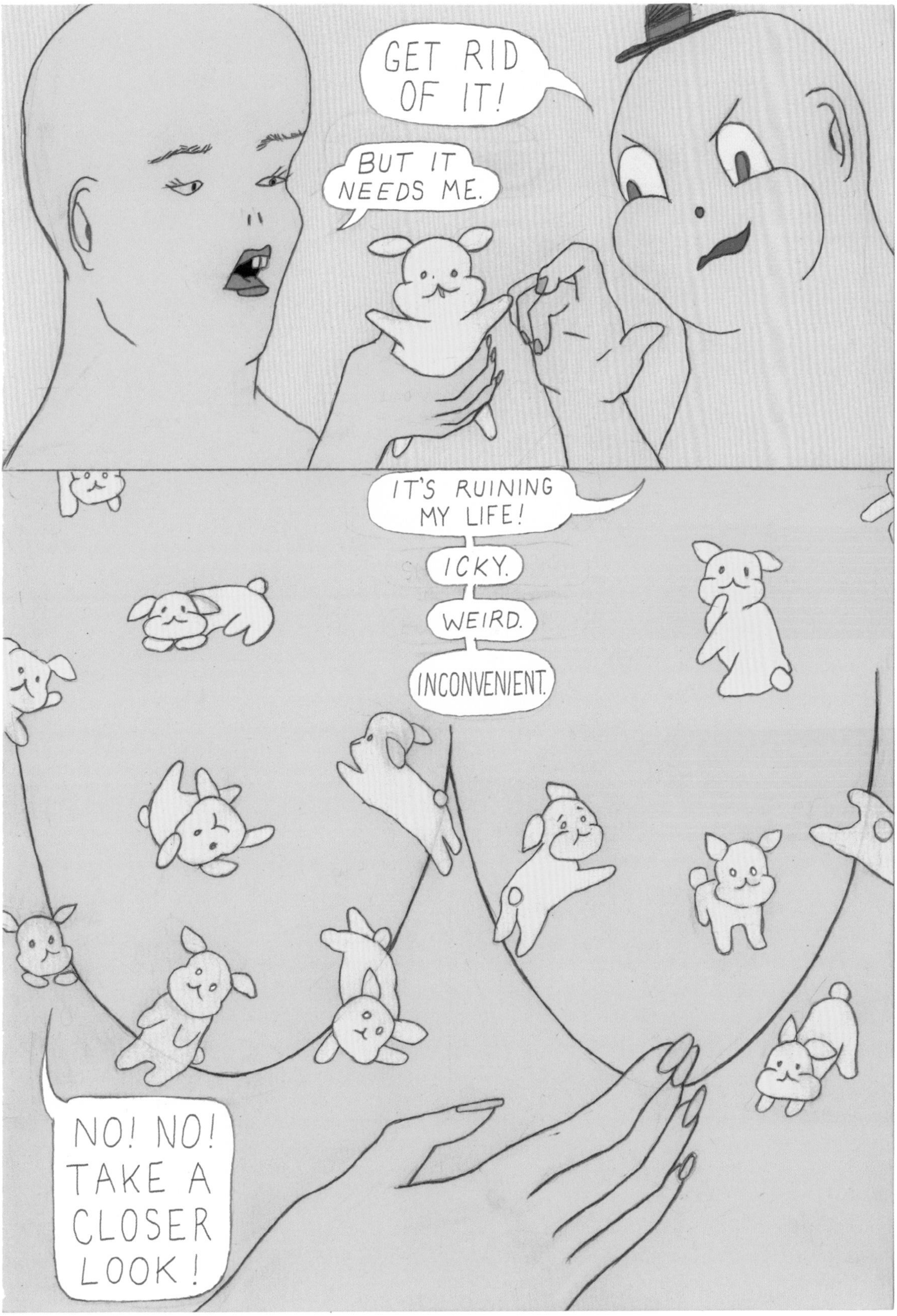
GET RID OF IT!
BUT IT NEEDS ME.
IT'S RUINING MY LIFE!
ICKY.
WEIRD.
INCONVENIENT.
NO! NO! TAKE A CLOSER LOOK!

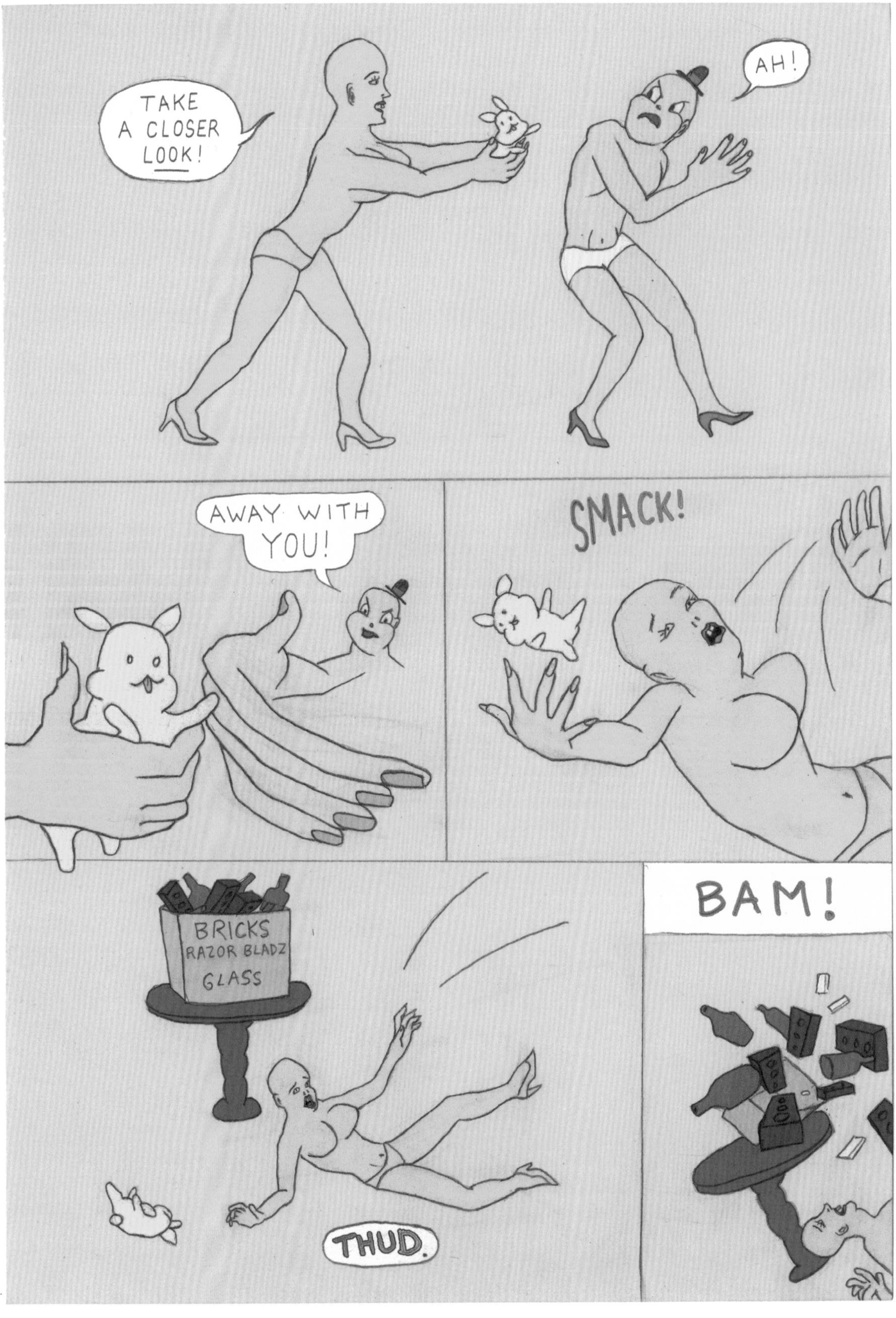
TAKE A CLOSER LOOK!
AH!
AWAY WITH YOU!
SMACK!
BRICKS
RAZOR BLADZ
GLASS
THUD.
BAM!

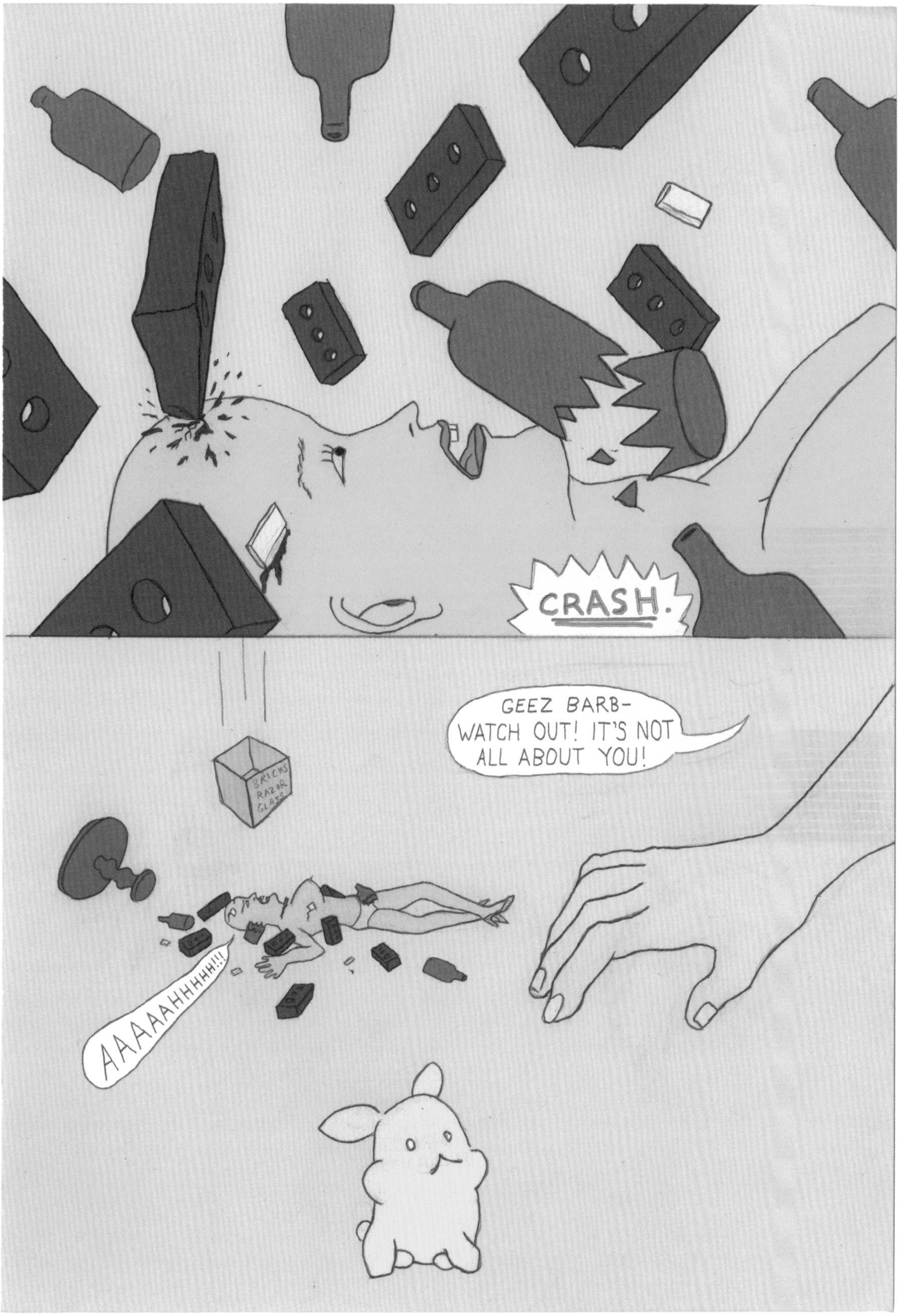
CRASH.
BRICKS RAZOR GLASS
GEEZ BARB- WATCH OUT! IT'S NOT ALL ABOUT YOU!
AAAAAHHHHHH!!!

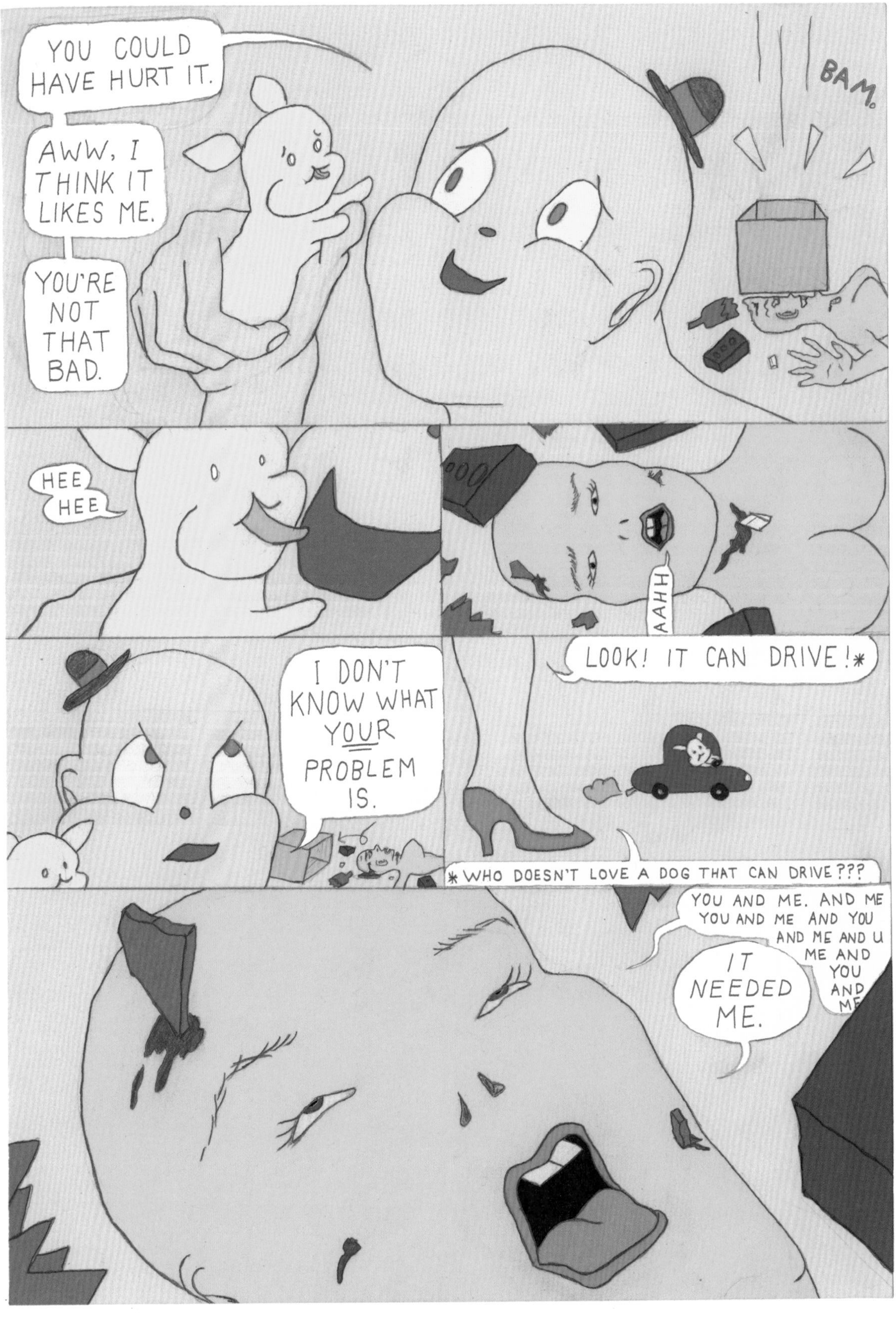
YOU COULD HAVE HURT IT.
AWW, I THINK IT LIKES ME.
YOU'RE NOT THAT BAD.
BAM.
HEE HEE
AAHH
I DON'T KNOW WHAT YOUR PROBLEM IS.
LOOK! IT CAN DRIVE!*
* WHO DOESN'T LOVE A DOG THAT CAN DRIVE???
YOU AND ME. AND ME YOU AND ME AND YOU AND ME AND U ME AND YOU AND
IT NEEDED ME.

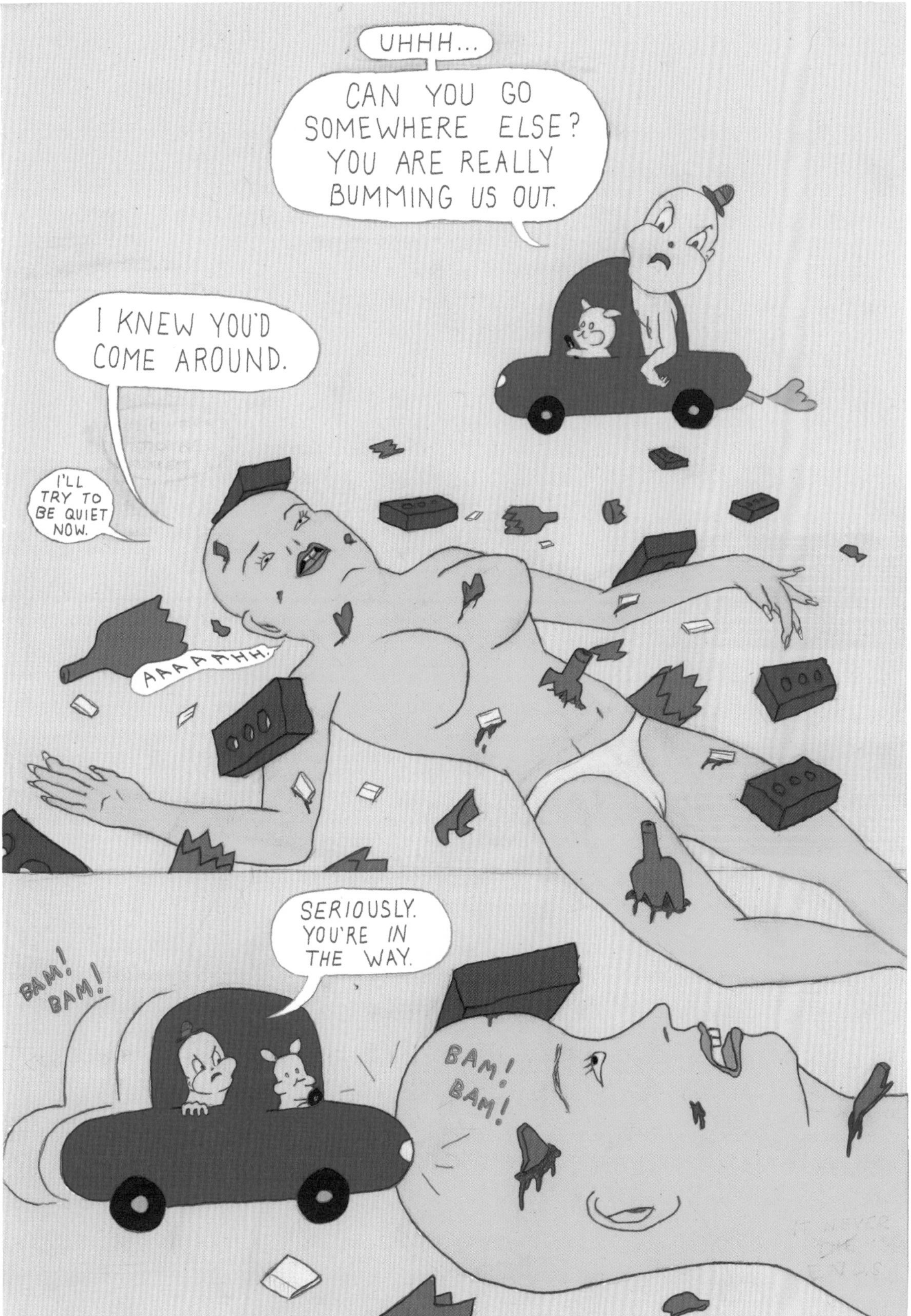
UHHH...
CAN YOU GO SOMEWHERE ELSE? YOU ARE REALLY BUMMING US OUT.
I KNEW YOU'D COME AROUND.
I'LL TRY TO BE QUIET NOW.
AAAAAHH.
BAM! BAM!
SERIOUSLY. YOU'RE IN THE WAY.
BAM! BAM!

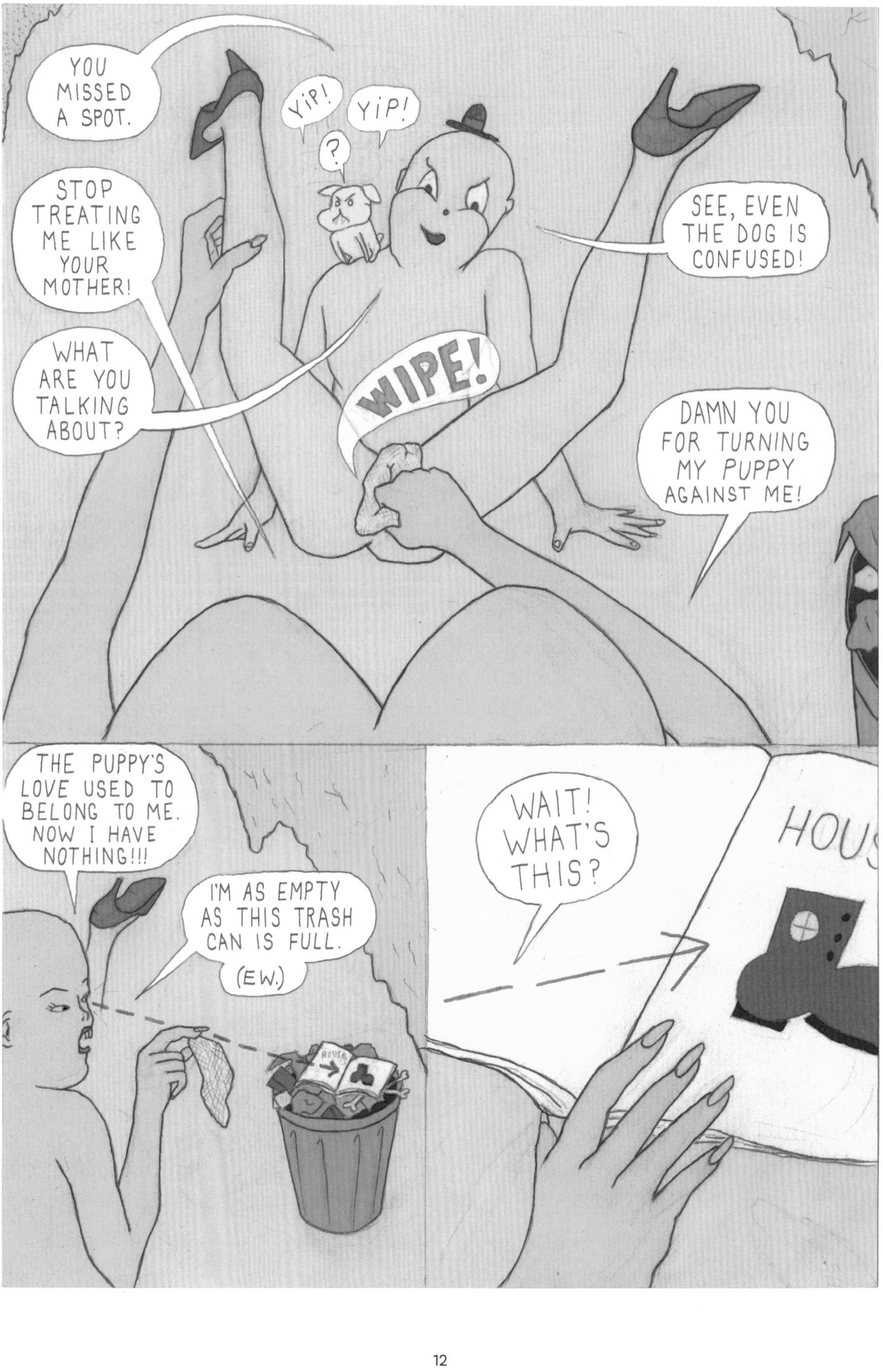
YOU MISSED A SPOT.
YIP!
YIP!
?
STOP TREATING ME LIKE YOUR MOTHER!
SEE, EVEN THE DOG IS CONFUSED!
WHAT ARE YOU TALKING ABOUT?
WIPE!
DAMN YOU FOR TURNING MY PUPPY AGAINST ME!
THE PUPPY'S LOVE USED TO BELONG TO ME. NOW I HAVE NOTHING!!!
I'M AS EMPTY AS THIS TRASH CAN IS FULL.
(EW.)
WAIT! WHAT'S THIS?
HOUS

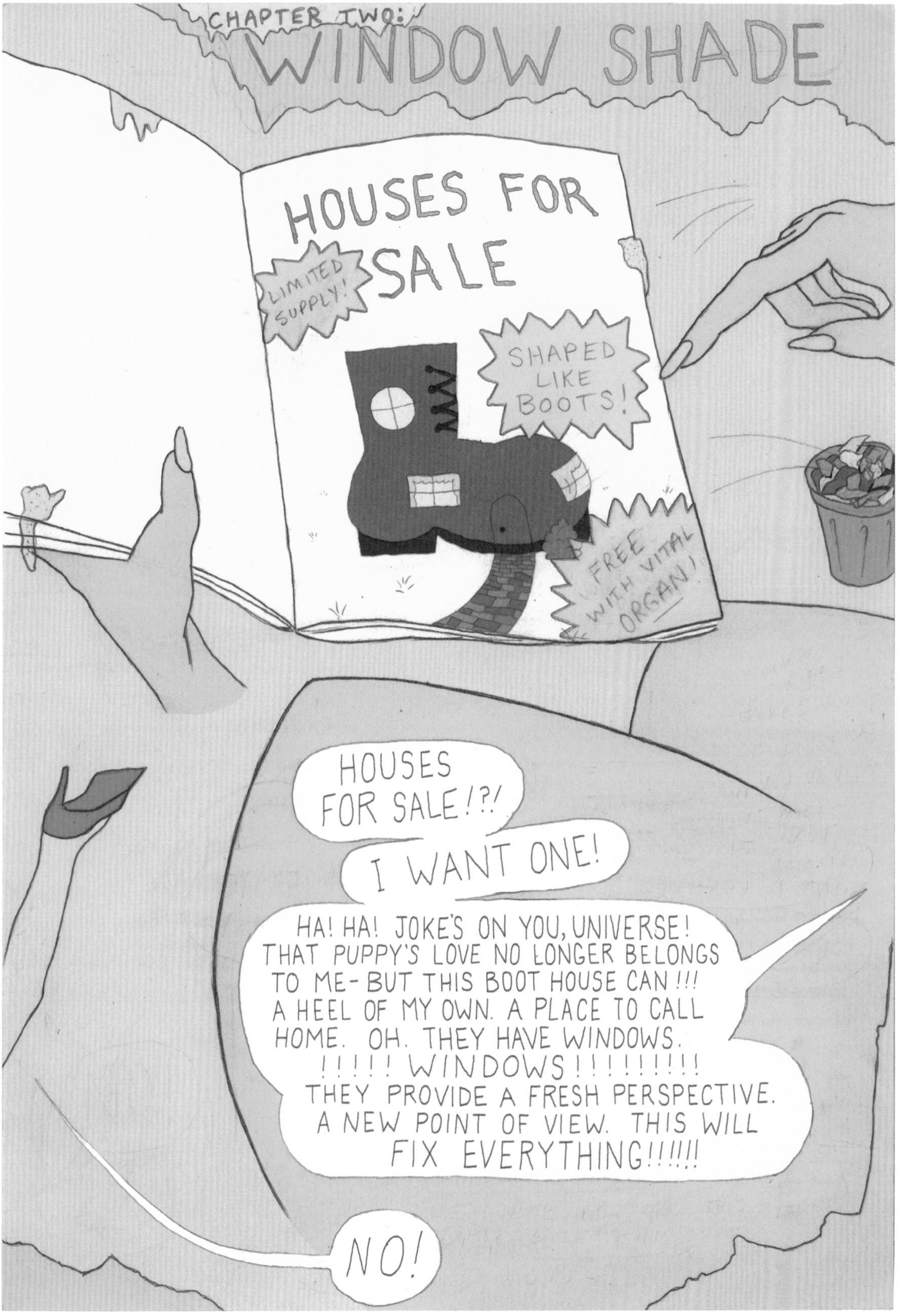
CHAPTER TWO:
WINDOW SHADE
HOUSES FOR SALE
LIMITED SUPPLY!
SHAPED LIKE BOOTS!
FREE WITH VITAL ORGAN!
HOUSES FOR SALE!?!
I WANT ONE!
HA! HA! JOKE'S ON YOU, UNIVERSE! THAT PUPPY'S LOVE NO LONGER BELONGS TO ME- BUT THIS BOOT HOUSE CAN!!! A HEEL OF MY OWN. A PLACE TO CALL HOME. OH. THEY HAVE WINDOWS. !!!!! WINDOWS!!!!!!!!! THEY PROVIDE A FRESH PERSPECTIVE. A NEW POINT OF VIEW. THIS WILL FIX EVERYTHING!!!!!!
NO!

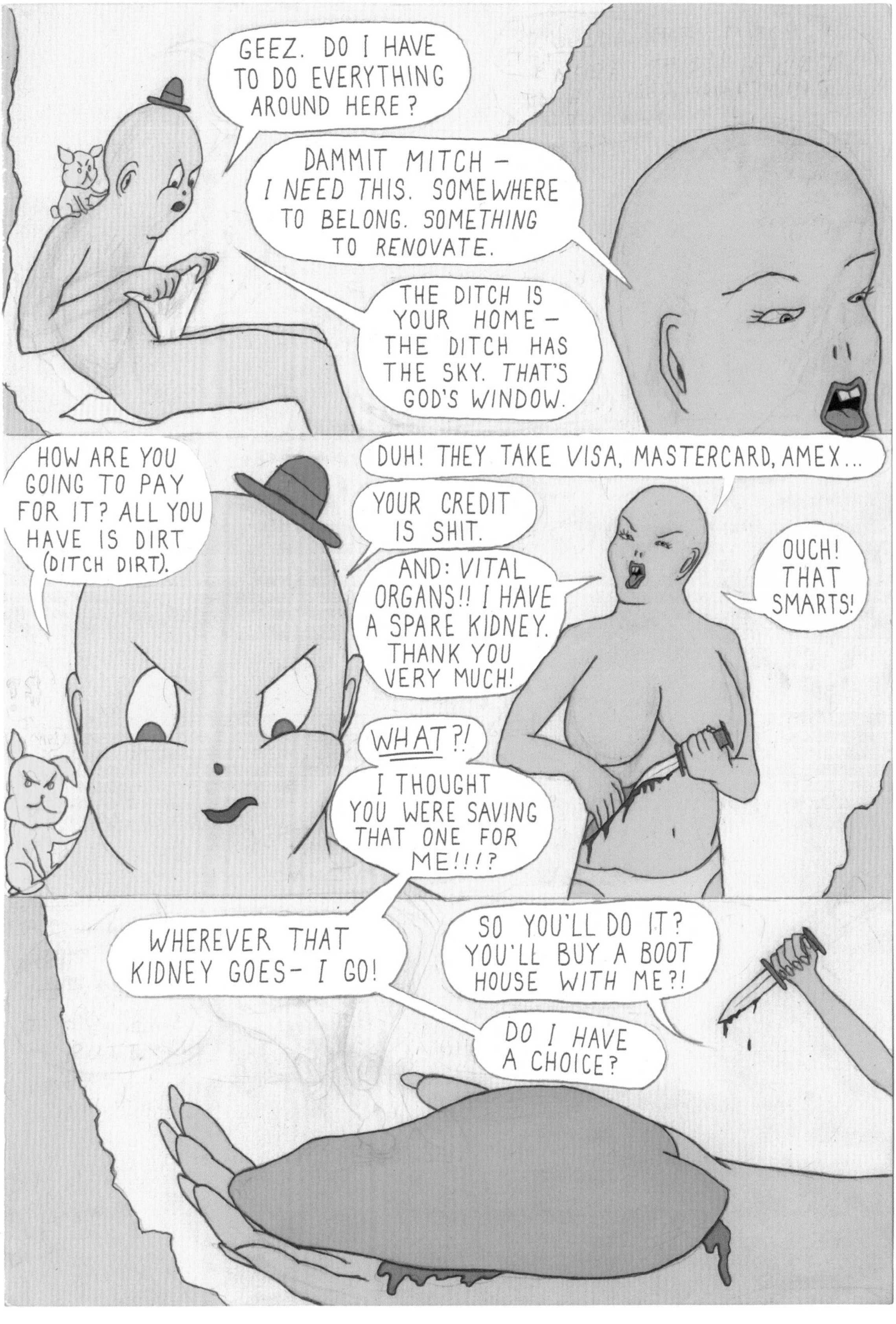
GEEZ. DO I HAVE TO DO EVERYTHING AROUND HERE?
DAMMIT MITCH – I NEED THIS. SOMEWHERE TO BELONG. SOMETHING TO RENOVATE.
THE DITCH IS YOUR HOME – THE DITCH HAS THE SKY. THAT'S GOD'S WINDOW.
HOW ARE YOU GOING TO PAY FOR IT? ALL YOU HAVE IS DIRT (DITCH DIRT).
DUH! THEY TAKE VISA, MASTERCARD, AMEX...
YOUR CREDIT IS SHIT.
AND: VITAL ORGANS!! I HAVE A SPARE KIDNEY. THANK YOU VERY MUCH!
OUCH! THAT SMARTS!
WHAT?!
I THOUGHT YOU WERE SAVING THAT ONE FOR ME!!!?
WHEREVER THAT KIDNEY GOES– I GO!
SO YOU'LL DO IT? YOU'LL BUY A BOOT HOUSE WITH ME?!
DO I HAVE A CHOICE?

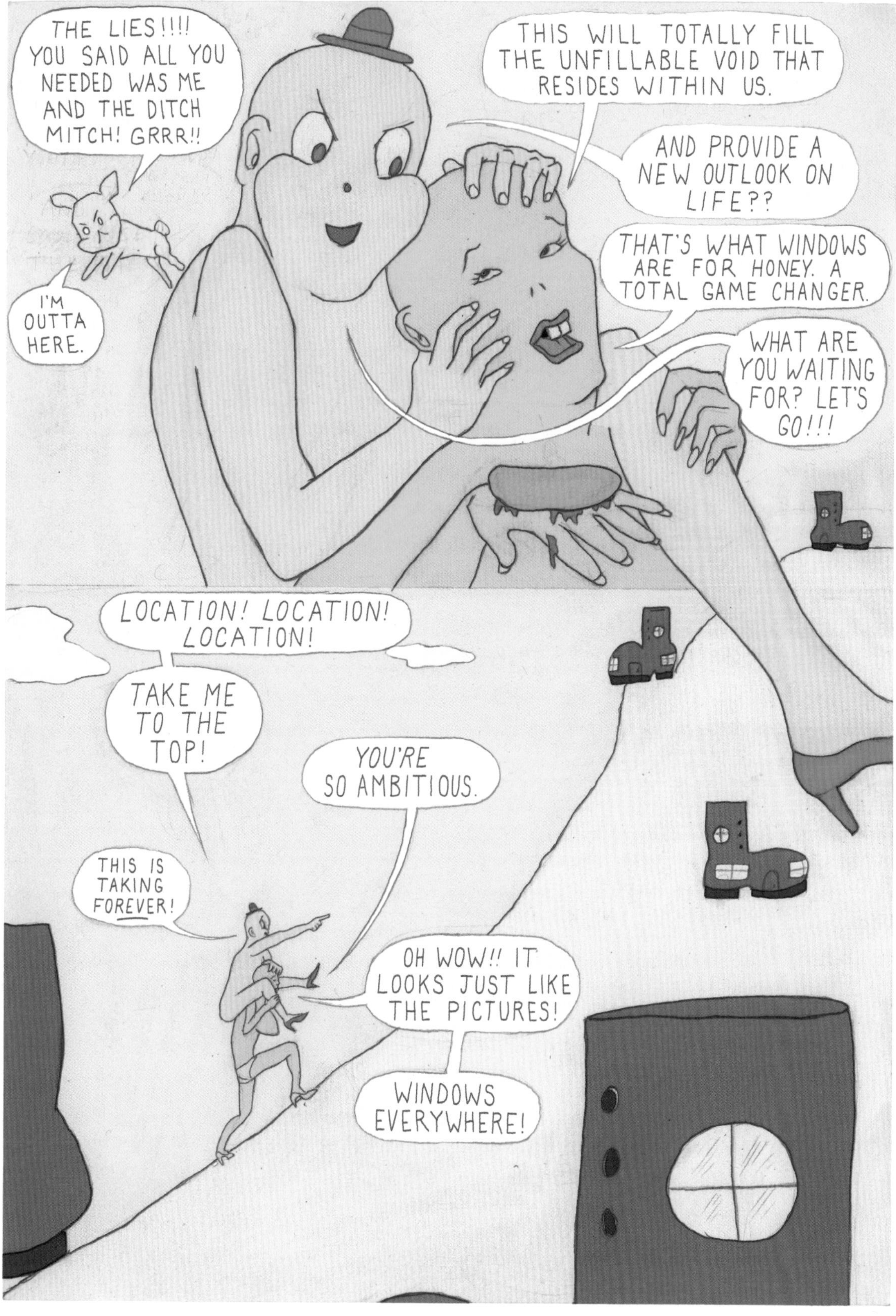
THE LIES!!!! YOU SAID ALL YOU NEEDED WAS ME AND THE DITCH MITCH! GRRR!!
I'M OUTTA HERE.
THIS WILL TOTALLY FILL THE UNFILLABLE VOID THAT RESIDES WITHIN US.
AND PROVIDE A NEW OUTLOOK ON LIFE??
THAT'S WHAT WINDOWS ARE FOR HONEY. A TOTAL GAME CHANGER.
WHAT ARE YOU WAITING FOR? LET'S GO!!!
LOCATION! LOCATION! LOCATION!
TAKE ME TO THE TOP!
YOU'RE SO AMBITIOUS.
THIS IS TAKING FOREVER!
OH WOW!! IT LOOKS JUST LIKE THE PICTURES!
WINDOWS EVERYWHERE!

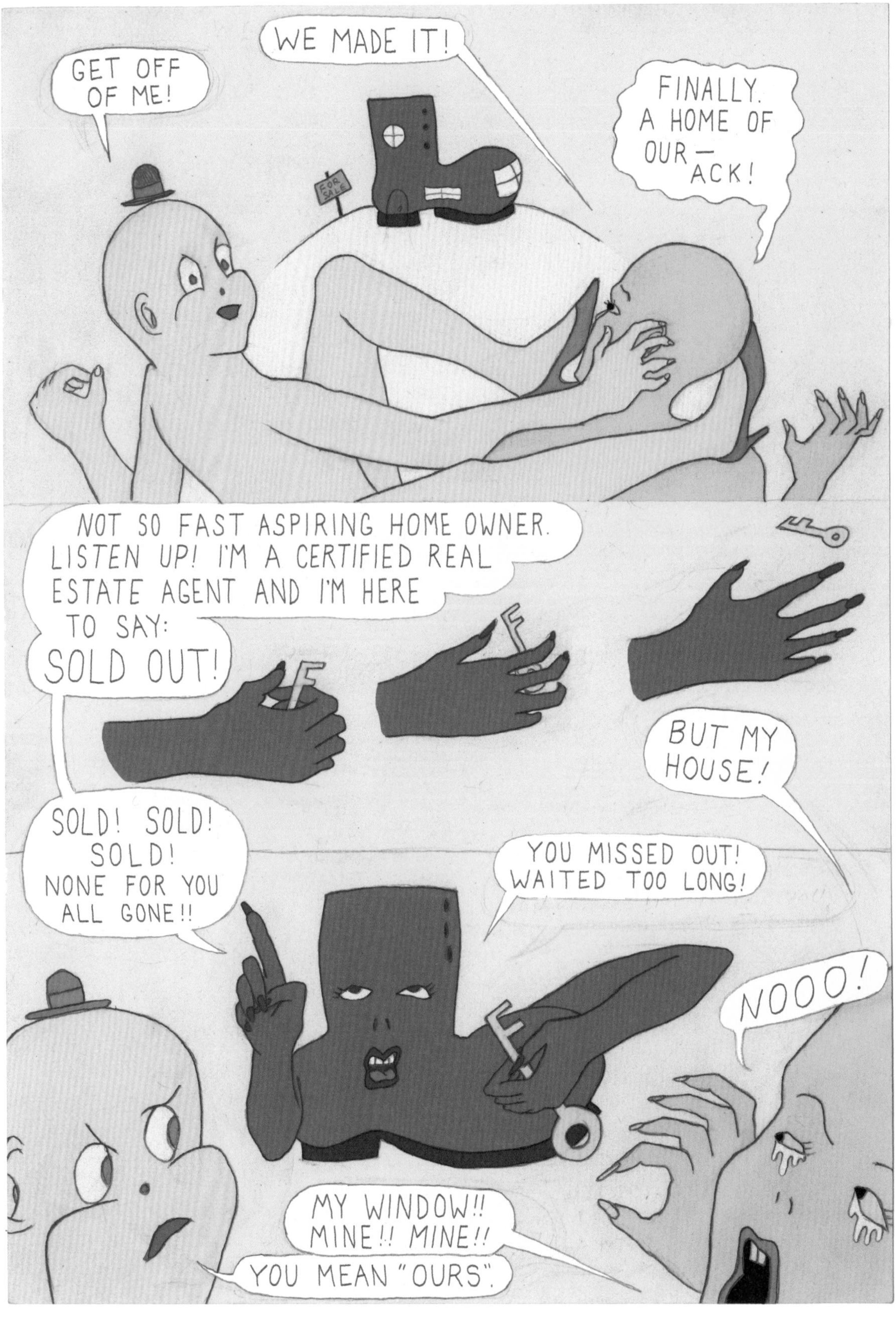
GET OFF OF ME!
WE MADE IT!
FINALLY. A HOME OF OUR — ACK!
FOR SALE
NOT SO FAST ASPIRING HOME OWNER. LISTEN UP! I'M A CERTIFIED REAL ESTATE AGENT AND I'M HERE TO SAY: SOLD OUT!
BUT MY HOUSE!
SOLD! SOLD! SOLD! NONE FOR YOU ALL GONE!!
YOU MISSED OUT! WAITED TOO LONG!
NOOO!
MY WINDOW!! MINE!! MINE!!
YOU MEAN "OURS".

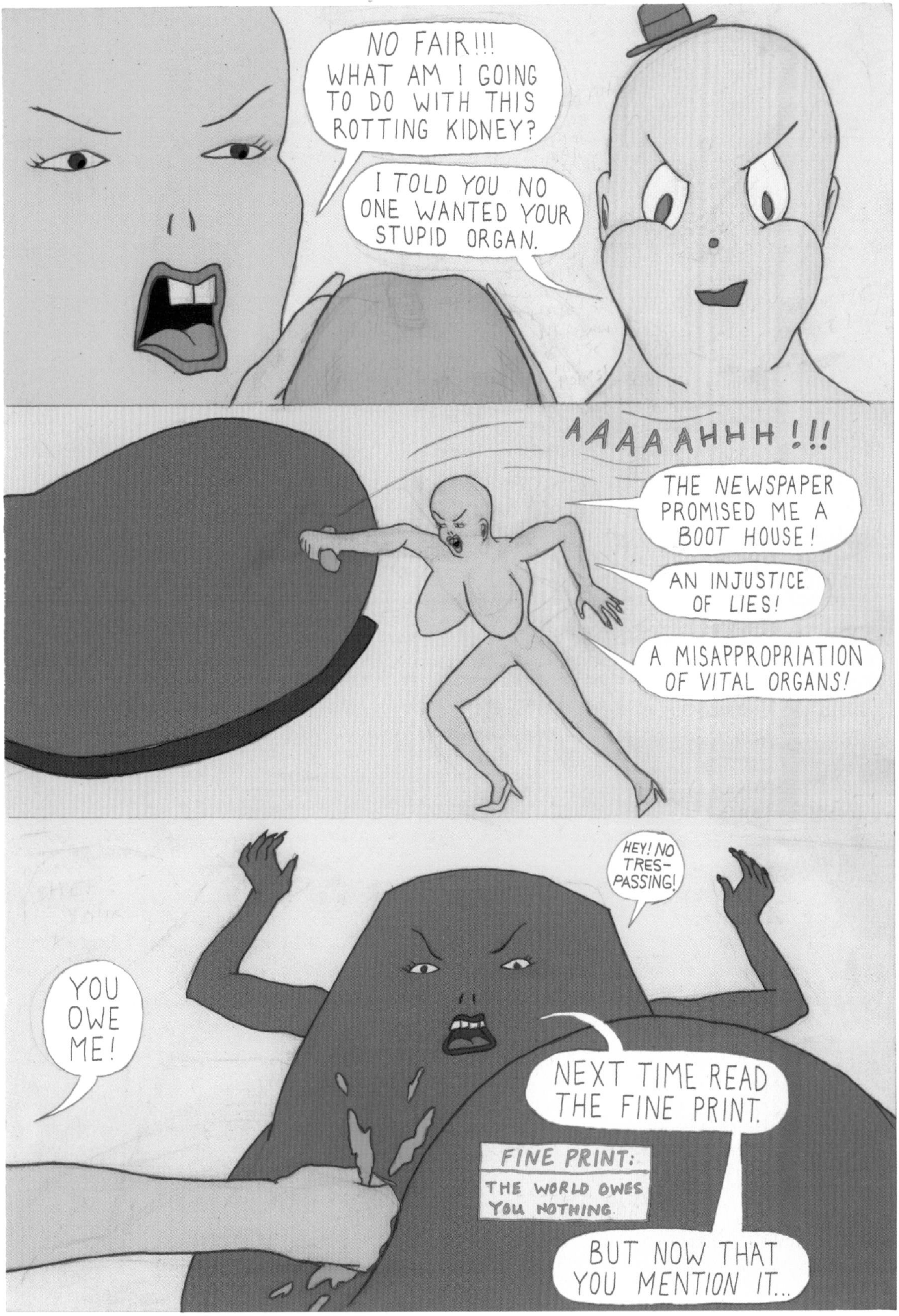
NO FAIR!!! WHAT AM I GOING TO DO WITH THIS ROTTING KIDNEY?
I TOLD YOU NO ONE WANTED YOUR STUPID ORGAN.
AAAAAHHH!!!
THE NEWSPAPER PROMISED ME A BOOT HOUSE!
AN INJUSTICE OF LIES!
A MISAPPROPRIATION OF VITAL ORGANS!
HEY! NO TRES-PASSING!
YOU OWE ME!
NEXT TIME READ THE FINE PRINT.
FINE PRINT:
THE WORLD OWES YOU NOTHING.
BUT NOW THAT YOU MENTION IT...

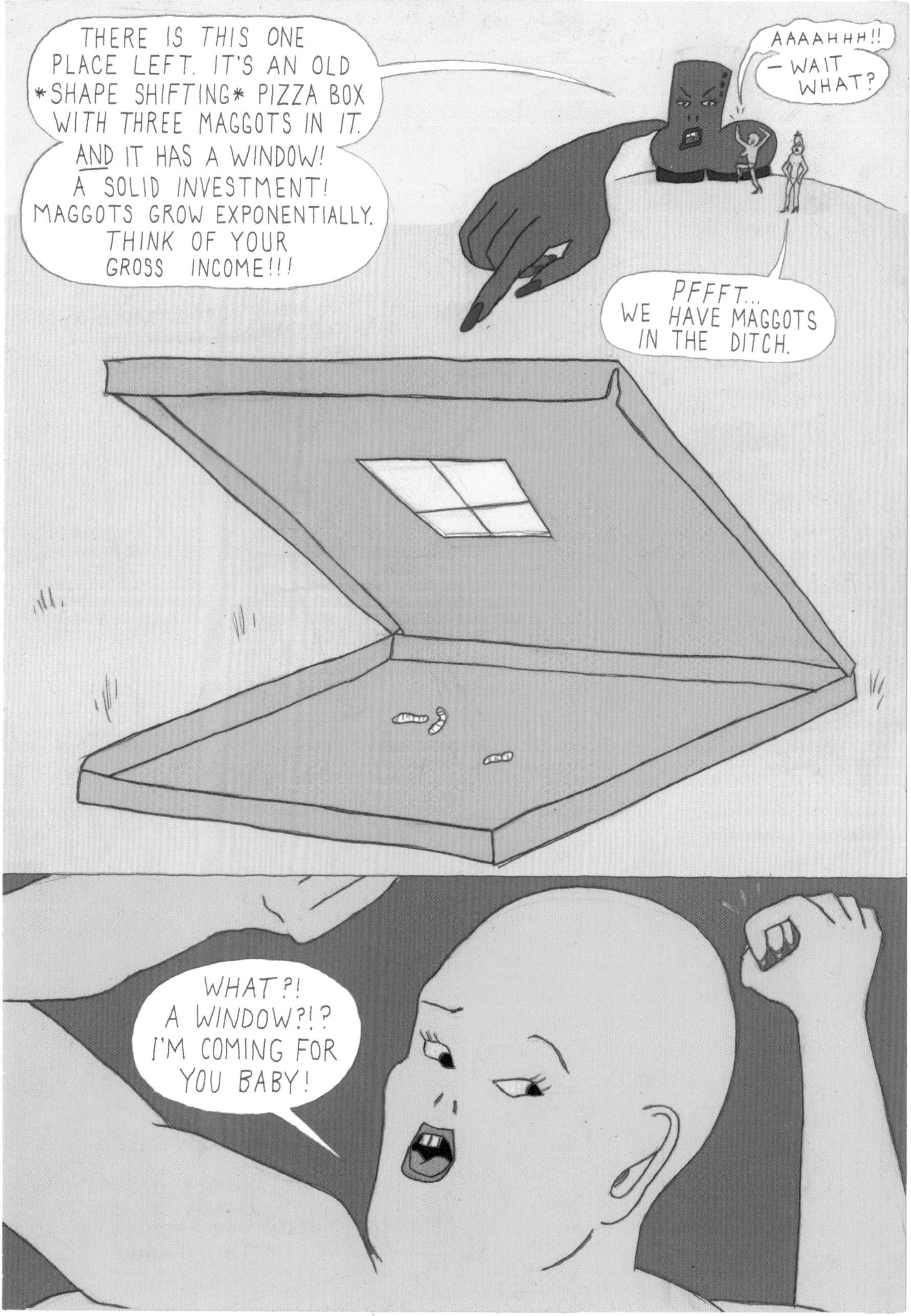
THERE IS THIS ONE PLACE LEFT. IT'S AN OLD *SHAPE SHIFTING* PIZZA BOX WITH THREE MAGGOTS IN IT.
AND IT HAS A WINDOW! A SOLID INVESTMENT! MAGGOTS GROW EXPONENTIALLY. THINK OF YOUR GROSS INCOME!!!
AAAAHHH!! —WAIT WHAT?
PFFFT... WE HAVE MAGGOTS IN THE DITCH.
WHAT?! A WINDOW?!? I'M COMING FOR YOU BABY!

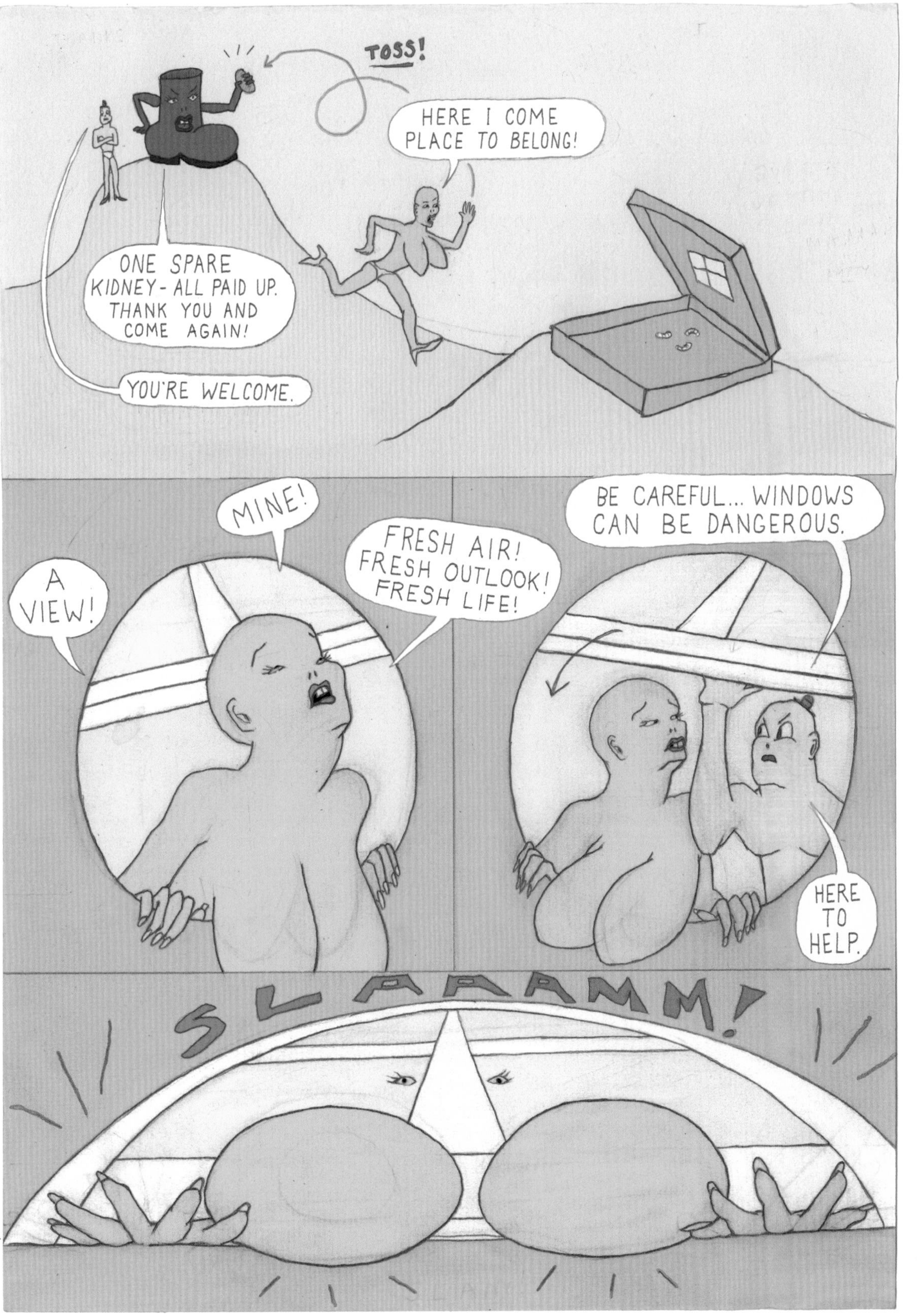
TOSS!
ONE SPARE KIDNEY - ALL PAID UP. THANK YOU AND COME AGAIN!
YOU'RE WELCOME.
HERE I COME PLACE TO BELONG!
A VIEW!
MINE!
FRESH AIR! FRESH OUTLOOK! FRESH LIFE!
BE CAREFUL... WINDOWS CAN BE DANGEROUS.
HERE TO HELP.
SLAAAMM!

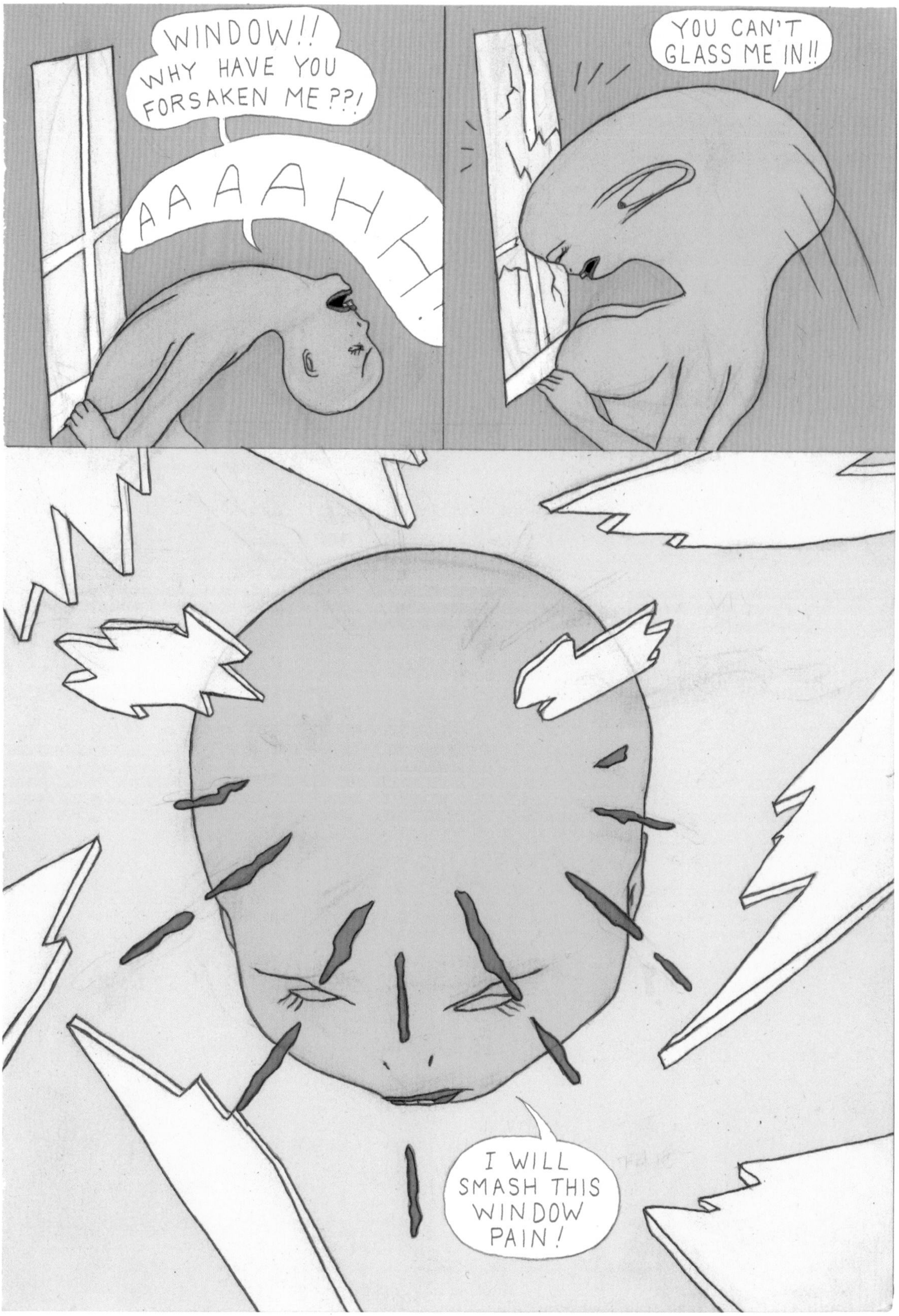
WINDOW!! WHY HAVE YOU FORSAKEN ME??!
AAAAHH!
YOU CAN'T GLASS ME IN!!
I WILL SMASH THIS WINDOW PAIN!

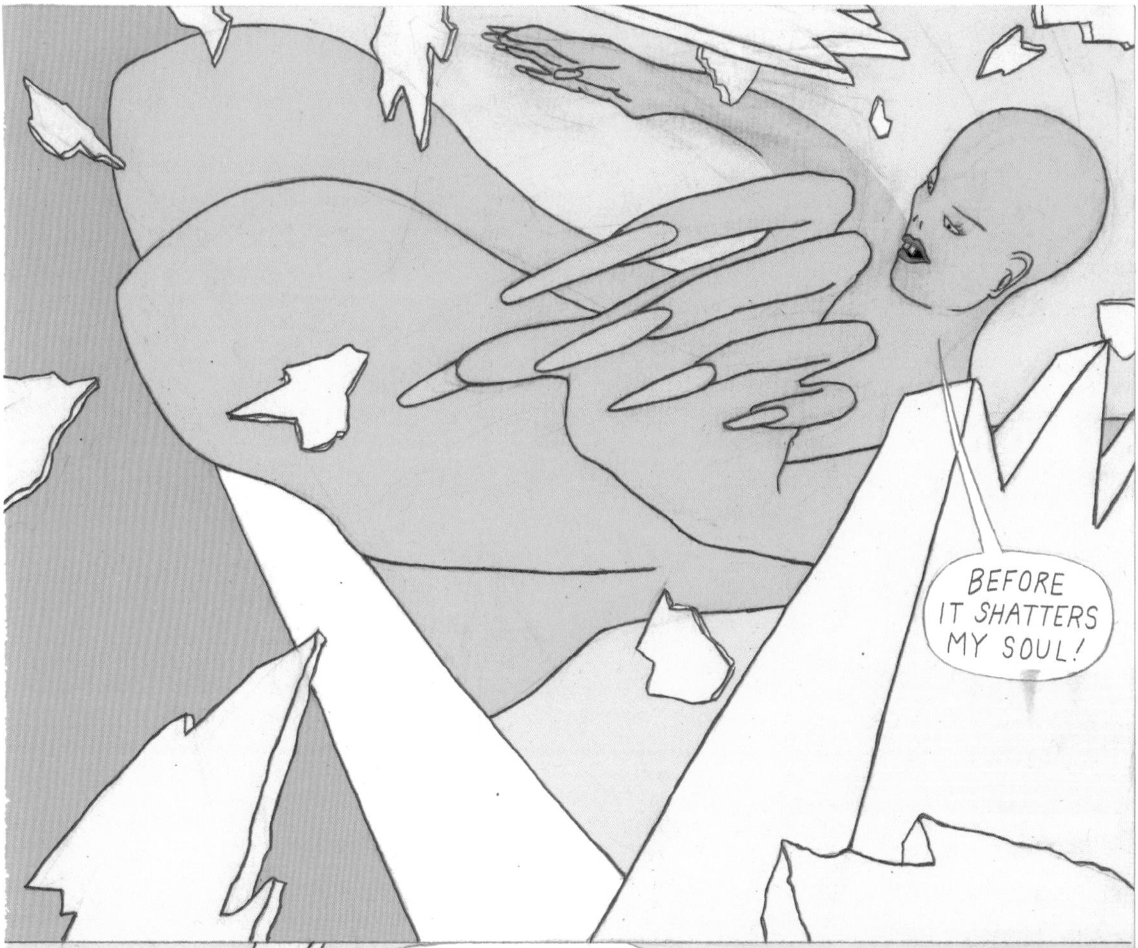
BEFORE IT SHATTERS MY SOUL!

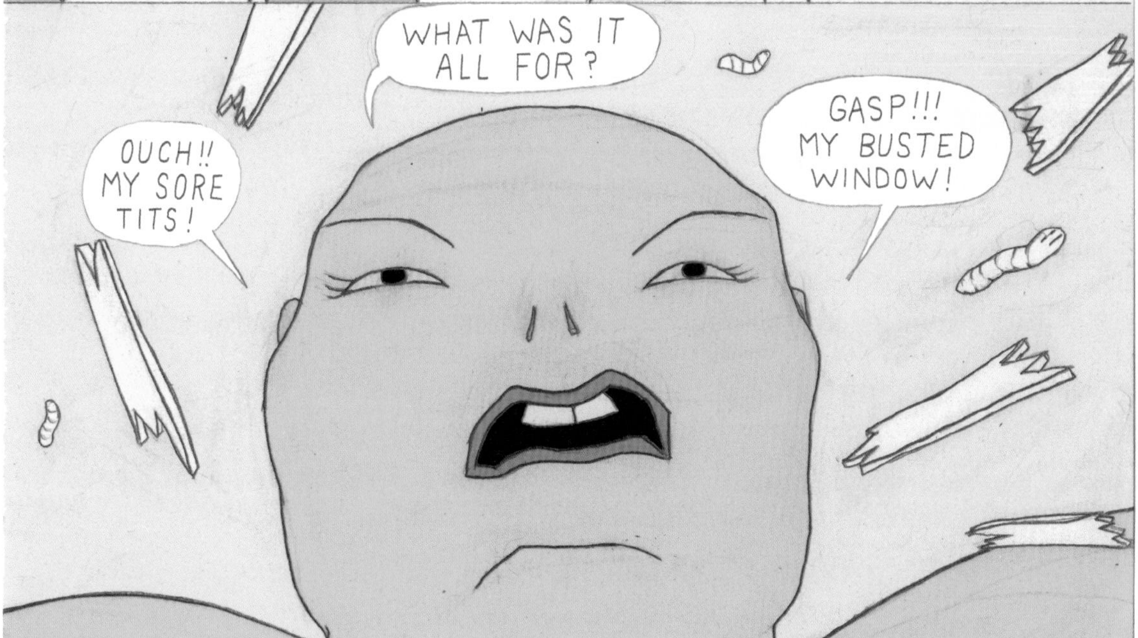
WHAT WAS IT ALL FOR?
OUCH!! MY SORE TITS!
GASP!!! MY BUSTED WINDOW!

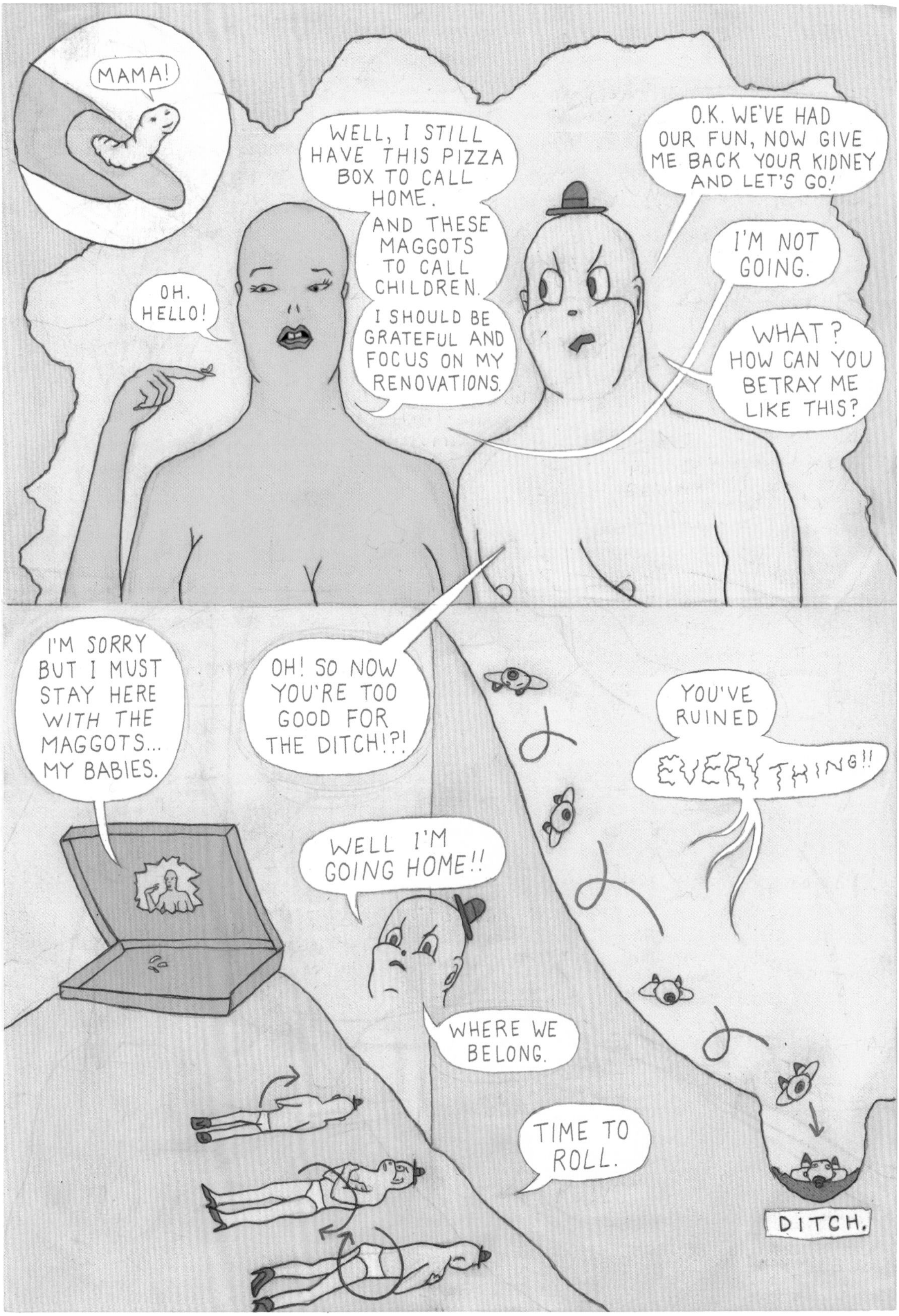
MAMA!
OH. HELLO!
WELL, I STILL HAVE THIS PIZZA BOX TO CALL HOME.
AND THESE MAGGOTS TO CALL CHILDREN.
I SHOULD BE GRATEFUL AND FOCUS ON MY RENOVATIONS.
O.K. WE'VE HAD OUR FUN, NOW GIVE ME BACK YOUR KIDNEY AND LET'S GO!
I'M NOT GOING.
WHAT? HOW CAN YOU BETRAY ME LIKE THIS?
I'M SORRY BUT I MUST STAY HERE WITH THE MAGGOTS... MY BABIES.
OH! SO NOW YOU'RE TOO GOOD FOR THE DITCH!?!
YOU'VE RUINED EVERYTHING!!
WELL I'M GOING HOME!!
WHERE WE BELONG.
TIME TO ROLL.
DITCH.

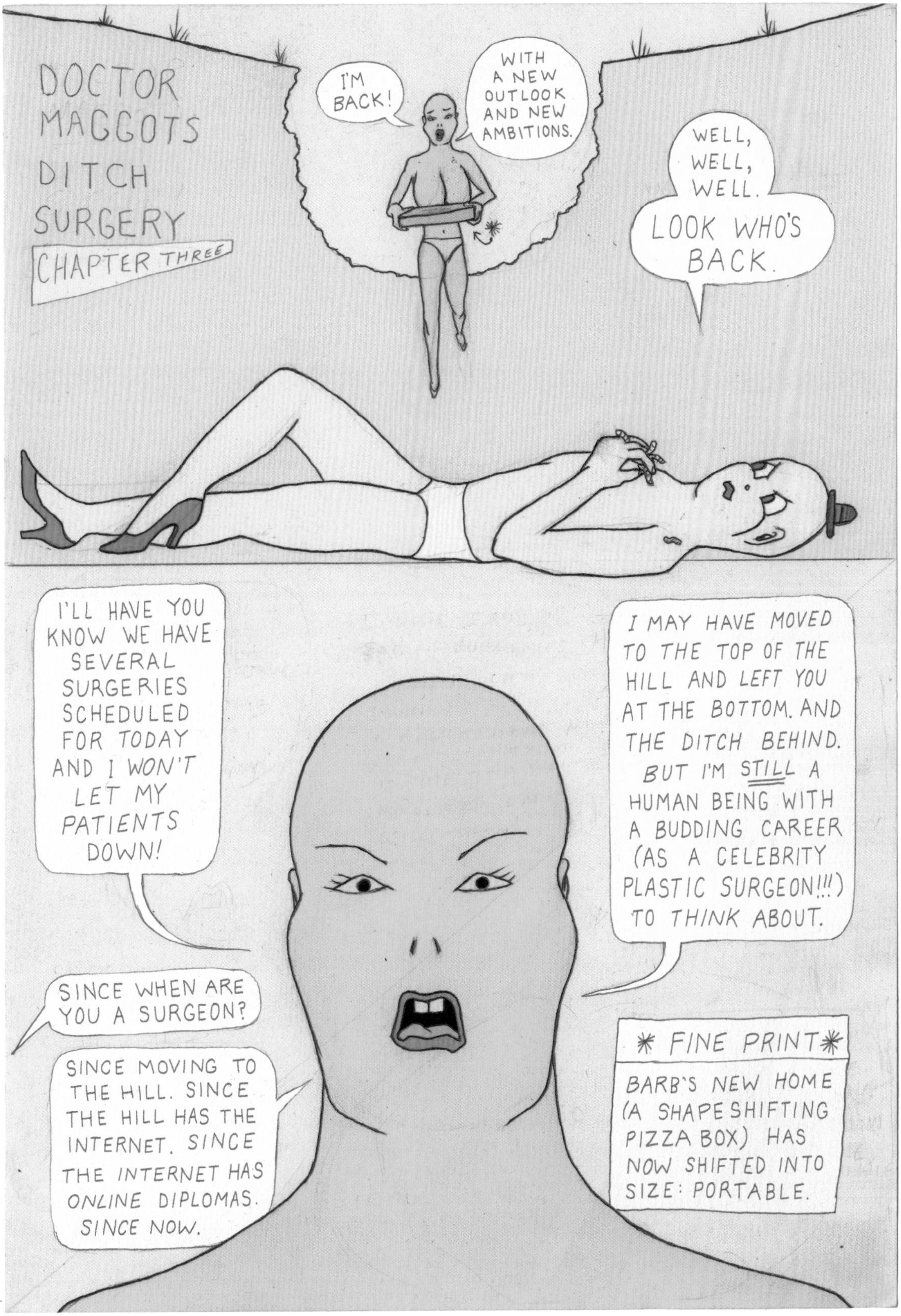
DOCTOR MAGGOTS DITCH SURGERY
CHAPTER THREE
I'M BACK!
WITH A NEW OUTLOOK AND NEW AMBITIONS.
WELL, WELL, WELL. LOOK WHO'S BACK.
I'LL HAVE YOU KNOW WE HAVE SEVERAL SURGERIES SCHEDULED FOR TODAY AND I WON'T LET MY PATIENTS DOWN!
I MAY HAVE MOVED TO THE TOP OF THE HILL AND LEFT YOU AT THE BOTTOM. AND THE DITCH BEHIND. BUT I'M STILL A HUMAN BEING WITH A BUDDING CAREER (AS A CELEBRITY PLASTIC SURGEON!!!) TO THINK ABOUT.
SINCE WHEN ARE YOU A SURGEON?
SINCE MOVING TO THE HILL. SINCE THE HILL HAS THE INTERNET. SINCE THE INTERNET HAS ONLINE DIPLOMAS. SINCE NOW.
* FINE PRINT *
BARB'S NEW HOME (A SHAPESHIFTING PIZZA BOX) HAS NOW SHIFTED INTO SIZE: PORTABLE.

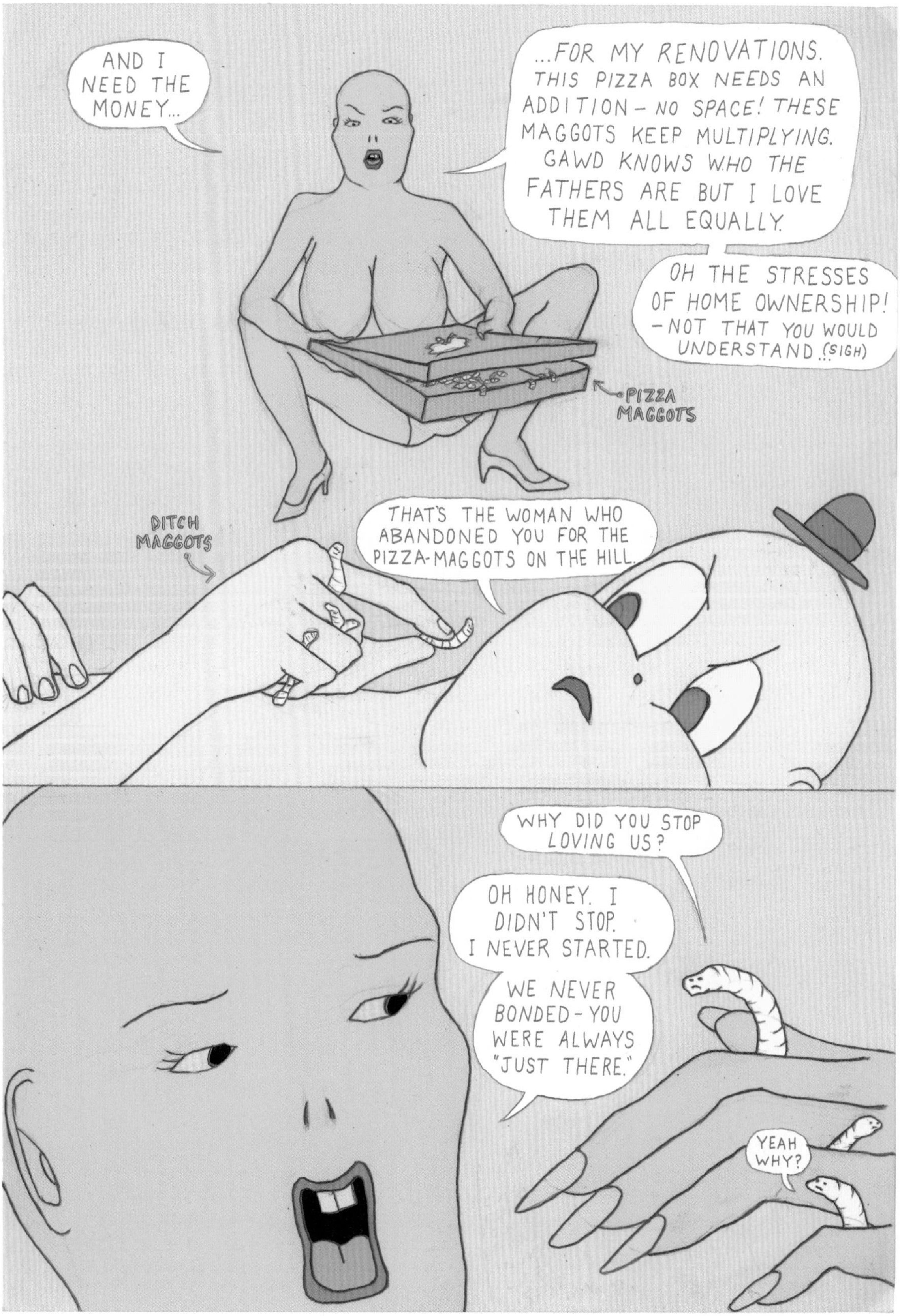
AND I NEED THE MONEY...
...FOR MY RENOVATIONS. THIS PIZZA BOX NEEDS AN ADDITION - NO SPACE! THESE MAGGOTS KEEP MULTIPLYING. GAWD KNOWS WHO THE FATHERS ARE BUT I LOVE THEM ALL EQUALLY.
OH THE STRESSES OF HOME OWNERSHIP! - NOT THAT YOU WOULD UNDERSTAND... (SIGH)
PIZZA MAGGOTS
DITCH MAGGOTS
THAT'S THE WOMAN WHO ABANDONED YOU FOR THE PIZZA-MAGGOTS ON THE HILL.
WHY DID YOU STOP LOVING US?
OH HONEY. I DIDN'T STOP. I NEVER STARTED.
WE NEVER BONDED - YOU WERE ALWAYS "JUST THERE."
YEAH WHY?

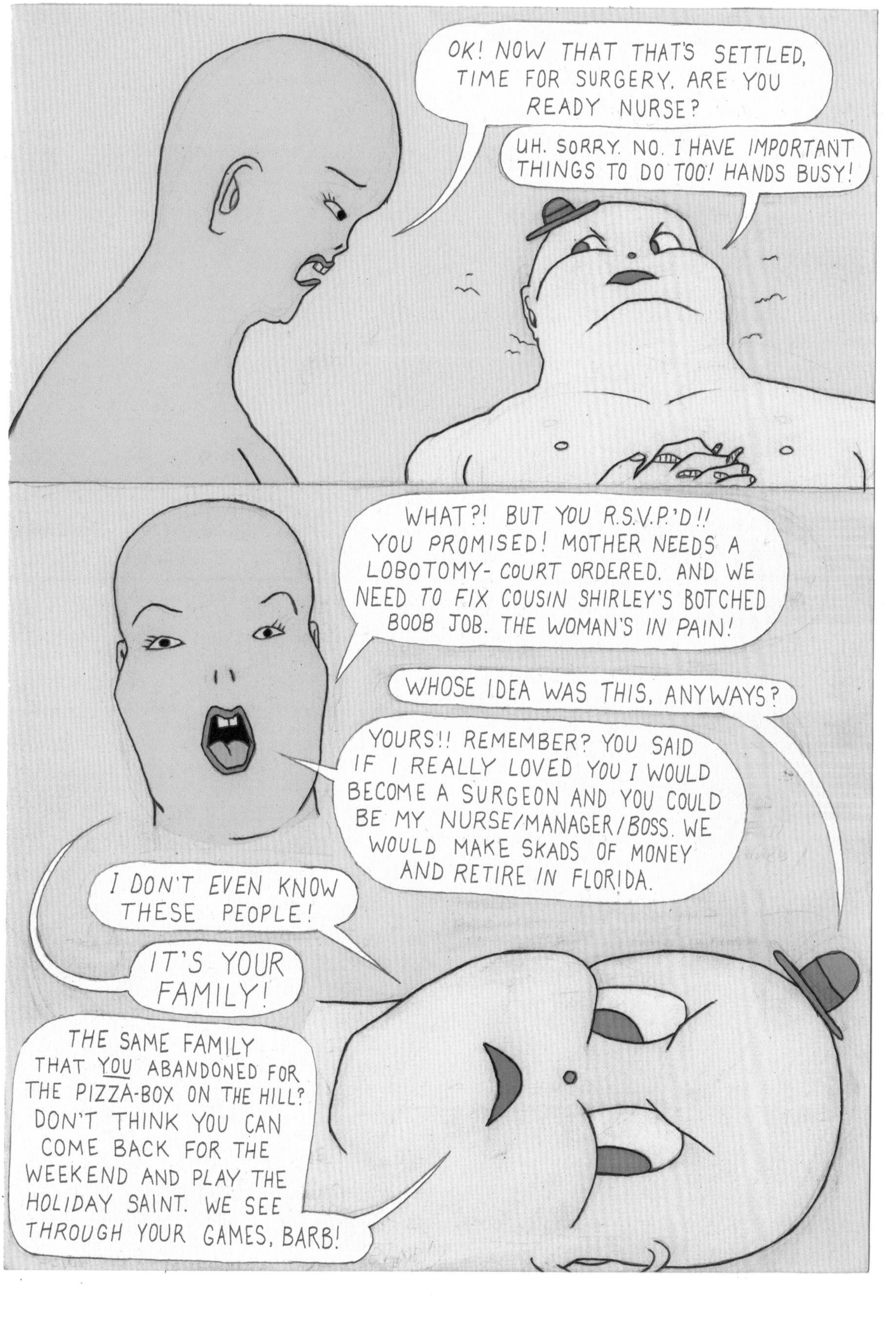
OK! NOW THAT THAT'S SETTLED, TIME FOR SURGERY. ARE YOU READY NURSE?
UH. SORRY. NO. I HAVE IMPORTANT THINGS TO DO TOO! HANDS BUSY!
WHAT?! BUT YOU R.S.V.P.'D!! YOU PROMISED! MOTHER NEEDS A LOBOTOMY- COURT ORDERED. AND WE NEED TO FIX COUSIN SHIRLEY'S BOTCHED BOOB JOB. THE WOMAN'S IN PAIN!
WHOSE IDEA WAS THIS, ANYWAYS?
YOURS!! REMEMBER? YOU SAID IF I REALLY LOVED YOU I WOULD BECOME A SURGEON AND YOU COULD BE MY NURSE/MANAGER/BOSS. WE WOULD MAKE SKADS OF MONEY AND RETIRE IN FLORIDA.
I DON'T EVEN KNOW THESE PEOPLE!
IT'S YOUR FAMILY!
THE SAME FAMILY THAT YOU ABANDONED FOR THE PIZZA-BOX ON THE HILL? DON'T THINK YOU CAN COME BACK FOR THE WEEKEND AND PLAY THE HOLIDAY SAINT. WE SEE THROUGH YOUR GAMES, BARB!

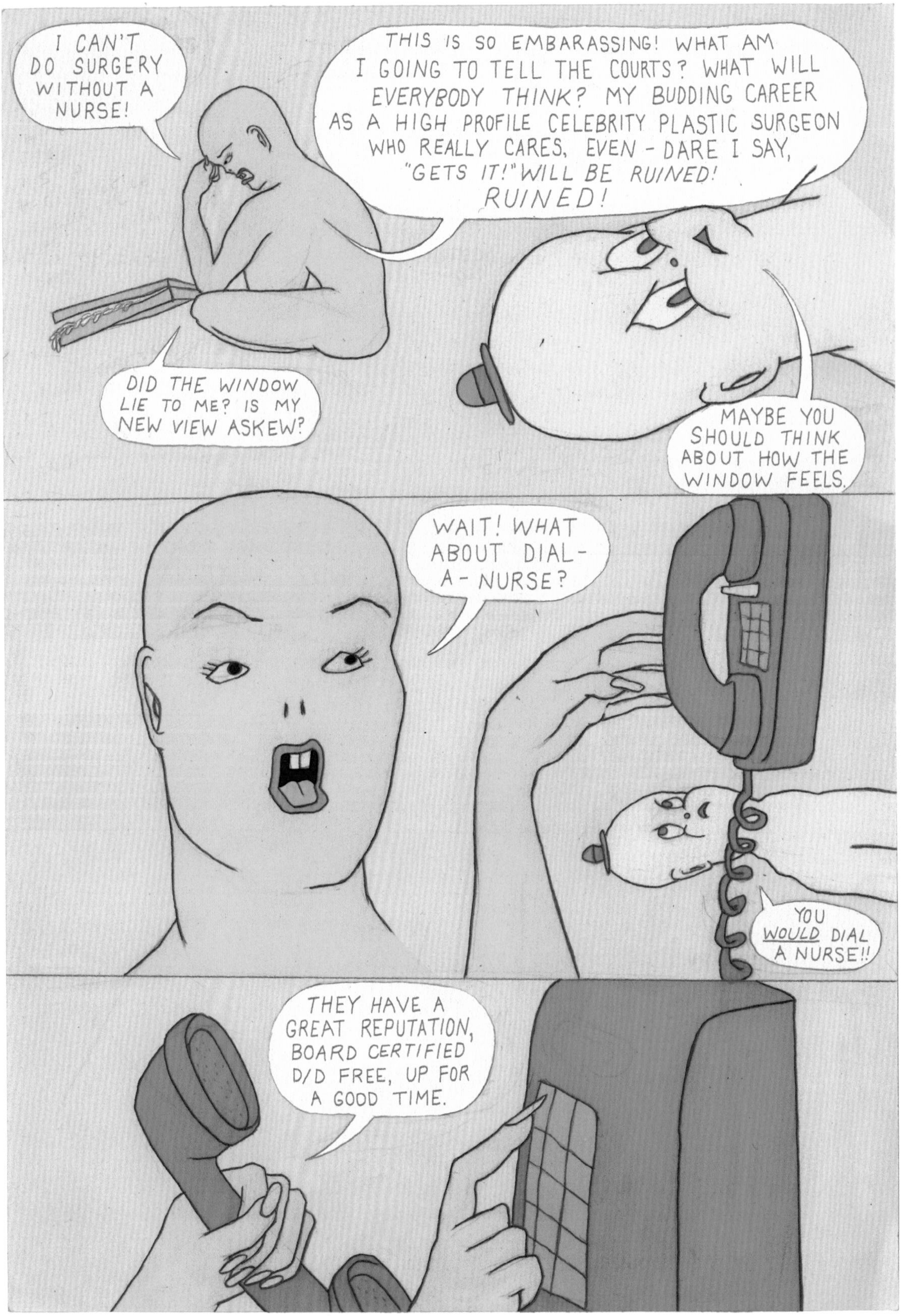
I CAN'T DO SURGERY WITHOUT A NURSE!
THIS IS SO EMBARASSING! WHAT AM I GOING TO TELL THE COURTS? WHAT WILL EVERYBODY THINK? MY BUDDING CAREER AS A HIGH PROFILE CELEBRITY PLASTIC SURGEON WHO REALLY CARES, EVEN - DARE I SAY, "GETS IT!" WILL BE RUINED! RUINED!
DID THE WINDOW LIE TO ME? IS MY NEW VIEW ASKEW?
MAYBE YOU SHOULD THINK ABOUT HOW THE WINDOW FEELS.
WAIT! WHAT ABOUT DIAL-A-NURSE?
YOU WOULD DIAL A NURSE!!
THEY HAVE A GREAT REPUTATION, BOARD CERTIFIED D/D FREE, UP FOR A GOOD TIME.

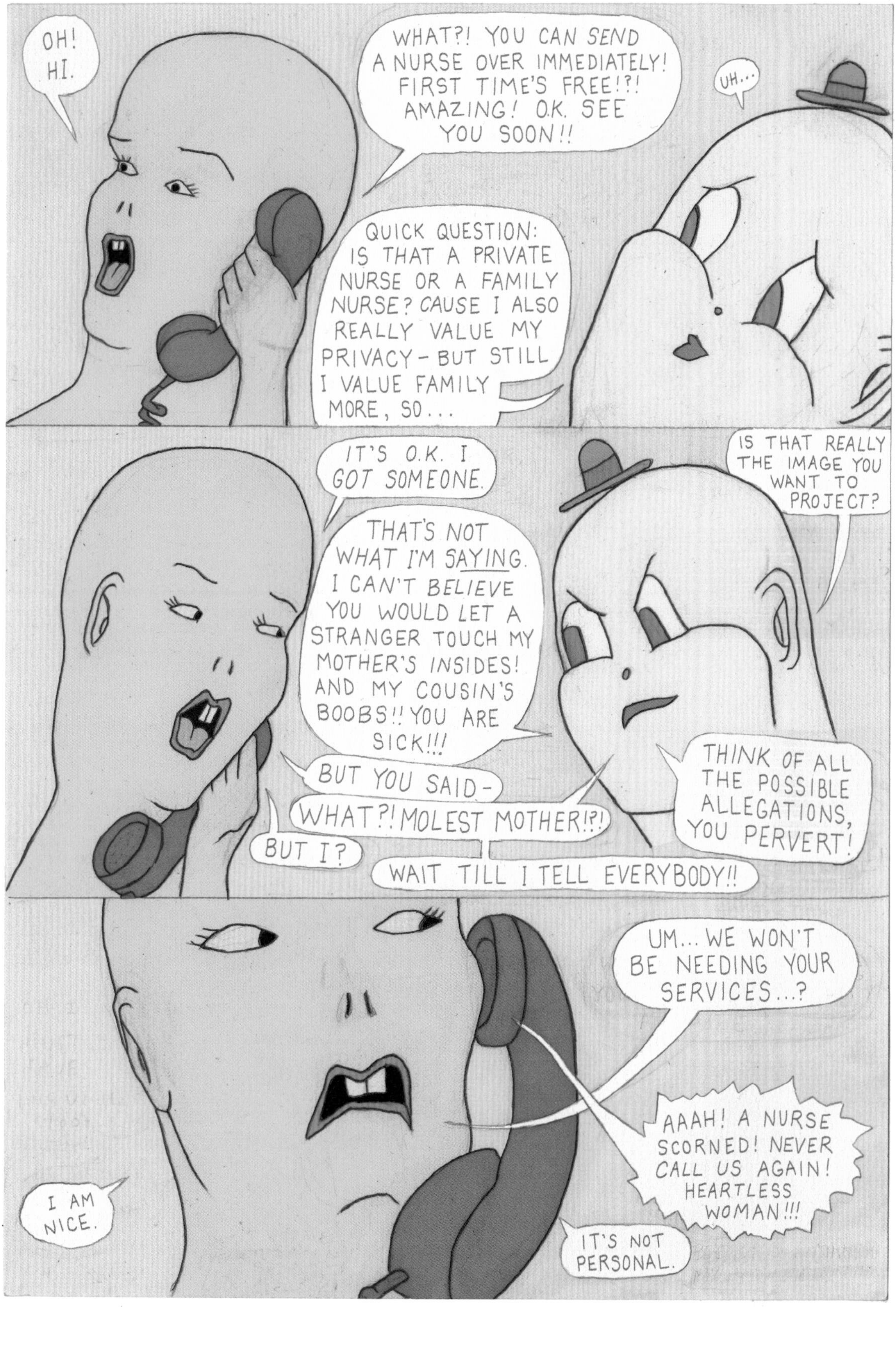
OH! HI.
WHAT?! YOU CAN SEND A NURSE OVER IMMEDIATELY! FIRST TIME'S FREE!?! AMAZING! O.K. SEE YOU SOON!!
UH...
QUICK QUESTION: IS THAT A PRIVATE NURSE OR A FAMILY NURSE? CAUSE I ALSO REALLY VALUE MY PRIVACY - BUT STILL I VALUE FAMILY MORE, SO...
IT'S O.K. I GOT SOMEONE.
IS THAT REALLY THE IMAGE YOU WANT TO PROJECT?
THAT'S NOT WHAT I'M SAYING. I CAN'T BELIEVE YOU WOULD LET A STRANGER TOUCH MY MOTHER'S INSIDES! AND MY COUSIN'S BOOBS!! YOU ARE SICK!!!
BUT YOU SAID-
THINK OF ALL THE POSSIBLE ALLEGATIONS, YOU PERVERT!
WHAT?! MOLEST MOTHER!?!
BUT I?
WAIT TILL I TELL EVERYBODY!!
UM... WE WON'T BE NEEDING YOUR SERVICES...?
AAAH! A NURSE SCORNED! NEVER CALL US AGAIN! HEARTLESS WOMAN!!!
I AM NICE.
IT'S NOT PERSONAL.

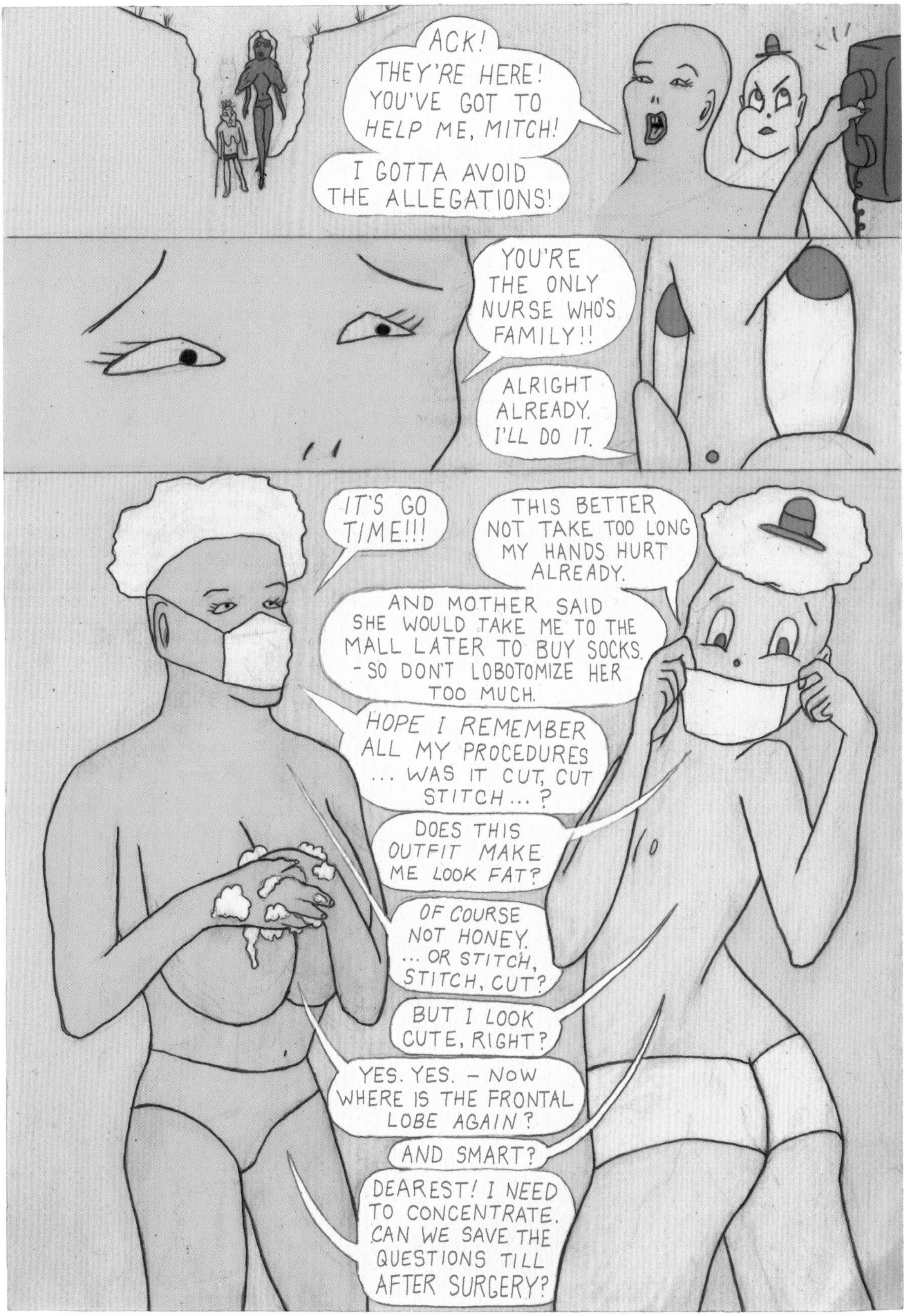
ACK! THEY'RE HERE! YOU'VE GOT TO HELP ME, MITCH!
I GOTTA AVOID THE ALLEGATIONS!
YOU'RE THE ONLY NURSE WHO'S FAMILY!!
ALRIGHT ALREADY. I'LL DO IT.
IT'S GO TIME!!!
THIS BETTER NOT TAKE TOO LONG MY HANDS HURT ALREADY.
AND MOTHER SAID SHE WOULD TAKE ME TO THE MALL LATER TO BUY SOCKS. - SO DON'T LOBOTOMIZE HER TOO MUCH.
HOPE I REMEMBER ALL MY PROCEDURES ... WAS IT CUT, CUT STITCH ... ?
DOES THIS OUTFIT MAKE ME LOOK FAT?
OF COURSE NOT HONEY. ... OR STITCH, STITCH, CUT?
BUT I LOOK CUTE, RIGHT?
YES. YES. - NOW WHERE IS THE FRONTAL LOBE AGAIN?
AND SMART?
DEAREST! I NEED TO CONCENTRATE. CAN WE SAVE THE QUESTIONS TILL AFTER SURGERY?

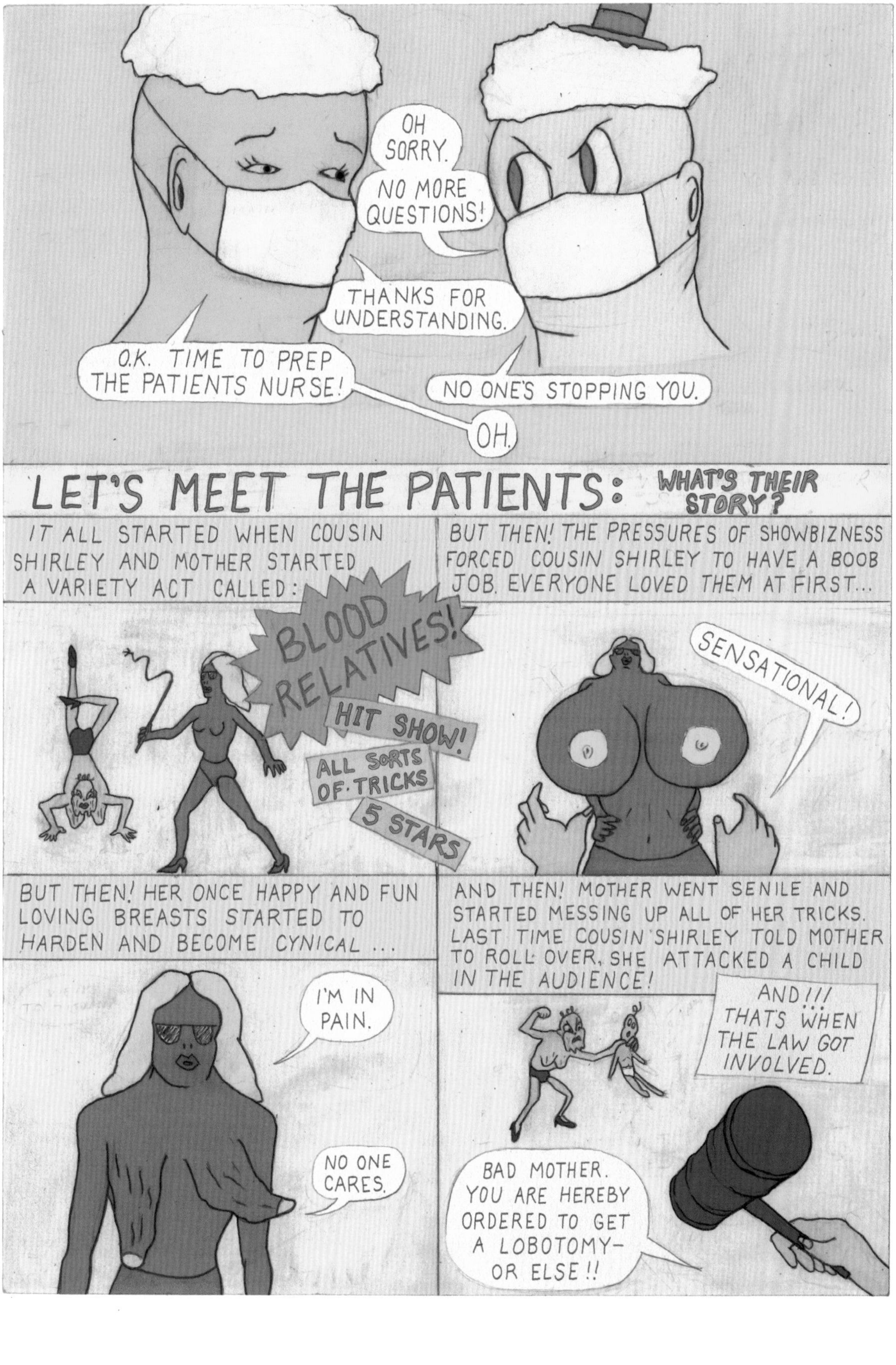

OH SORRY.
NO MORE QUESTIONS!
THANKS FOR UNDERSTANDING.
O.K. TIME TO PREP THE PATIENTS NURSE!
NO ONE'S STOPPING YOU.
OH.
LET'S MEET THE PATIENTS: WHAT'S THEIR STORY?
IT ALL STARTED WHEN COUSIN SHIRLEY AND MOTHER STARTED A VARIETY ACT CALLED:
BLOOD RELATIVES!
HIT SHOW!
ALL SORTS OF·TRICKS
5 STARS
BUT THEN! THE PRESSURES OF SHOWBIZNESS FORCED COUSIN SHIRLEY TO HAVE A BOOB JOB. EVERYONE LOVED THEM AT FIRST...
SENSATIONAL!
BUT THEN! HER ONCE HAPPY AND FUN LOVING BREASTS STARTED TO HARDEN AND BECOME CYNICAL ...
I'M IN PAIN.
NO ONE CARES.
AND THEN! MOTHER WENT SENILE AND STARTED MESSING UP ALL OF HER TRICKS. LAST TIME COUSIN SHIRLEY TOLD MOTHER TO ROLL OVER, SHE ATTACKED A CHILD IN THE AUDIENCE!
AND!!! THAT'S WHEN THE LAW GOT INVOLVED.
BAD MOTHER. YOU ARE HEREBY ORDERED TO GET A LOBOTOMY- OR ELSE!!

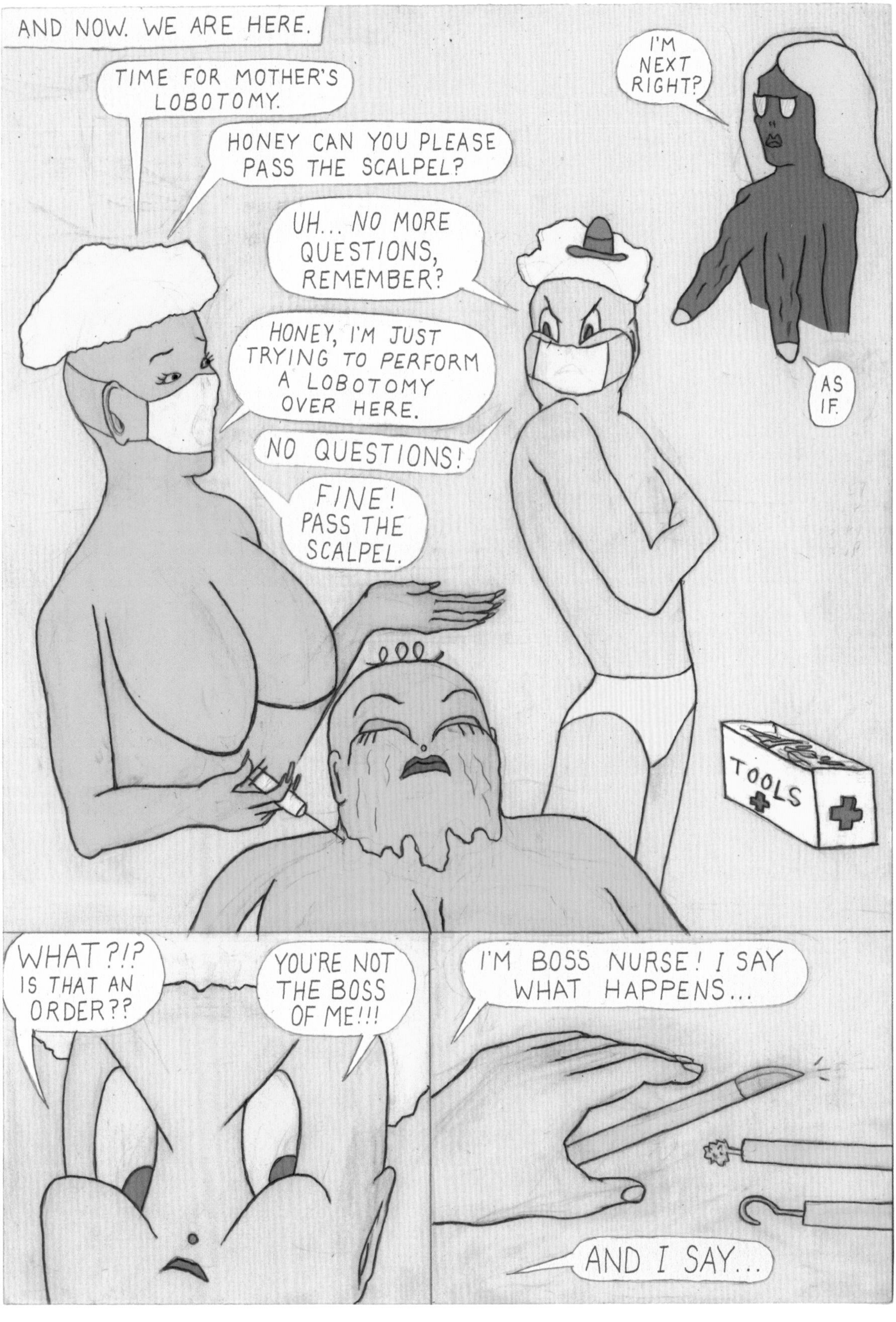
AND NOW. WE ARE HERE.
TIME FOR MOTHER'S LOBOTOMY.
HONEY CAN YOU PLEASE PASS THE SCALPEL?
I'M NEXT RIGHT?
UH... NO MORE QUESTIONS, REMEMBER?
HONEY, I'M JUST TRYING TO PERFORM A LOBOTOMY OVER HERE.
AS IF.
NO QUESTIONS!
FINE! PASS THE SCALPEL.
TOOLS
WHAT?!? IS THAT AN ORDER??
YOU'RE NOT THE BOSS OF ME!!!
I'M BOSS NURSE! I SAY WHAT HAPPENS...
AND I SAY...

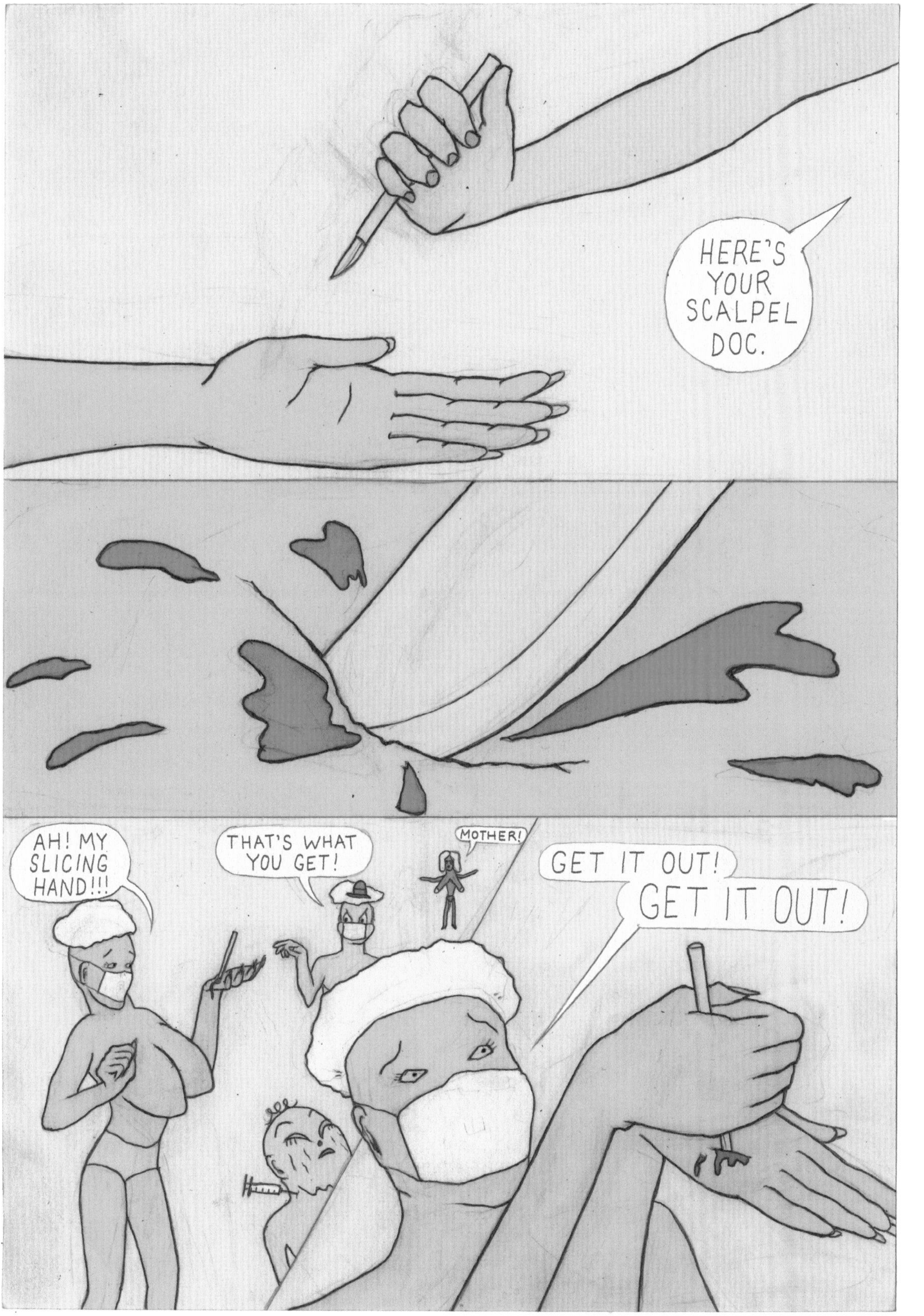
HERE'S YOUR SCALPEL DOC.
AH! MY SLICING HAND!!!
THAT'S WHAT YOU GET!
MOTHER!
GET IT OUT!
GET IT OUT!

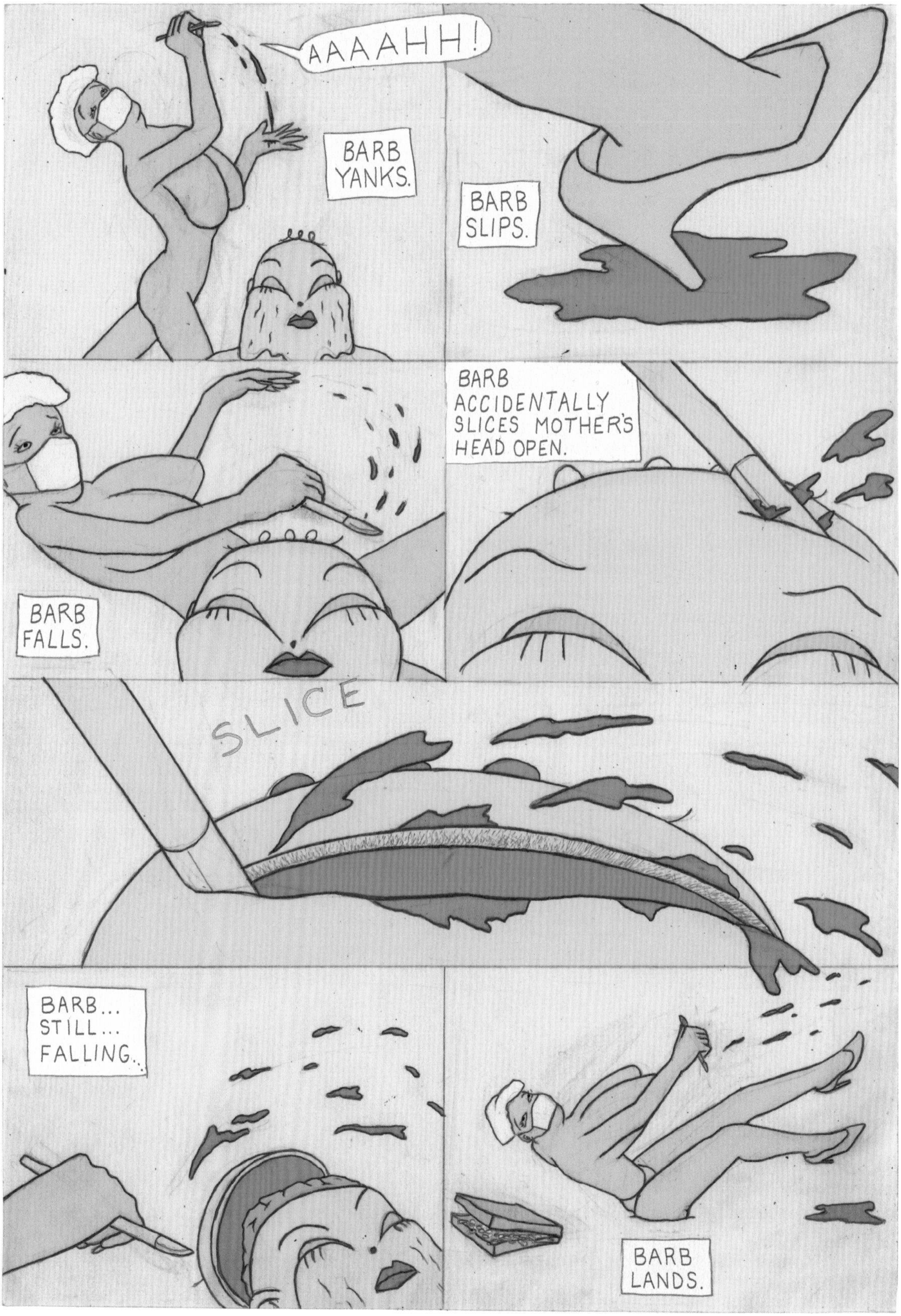
AAAAHH!
BARB YANKS.
BARB SLIPS.
BARB FALLS.
BARB ACCIDENTALLY SLICES MOTHER'S HEAD OPEN.
SLICE
BARB... STILL... FALLING...
BARB LANDS.

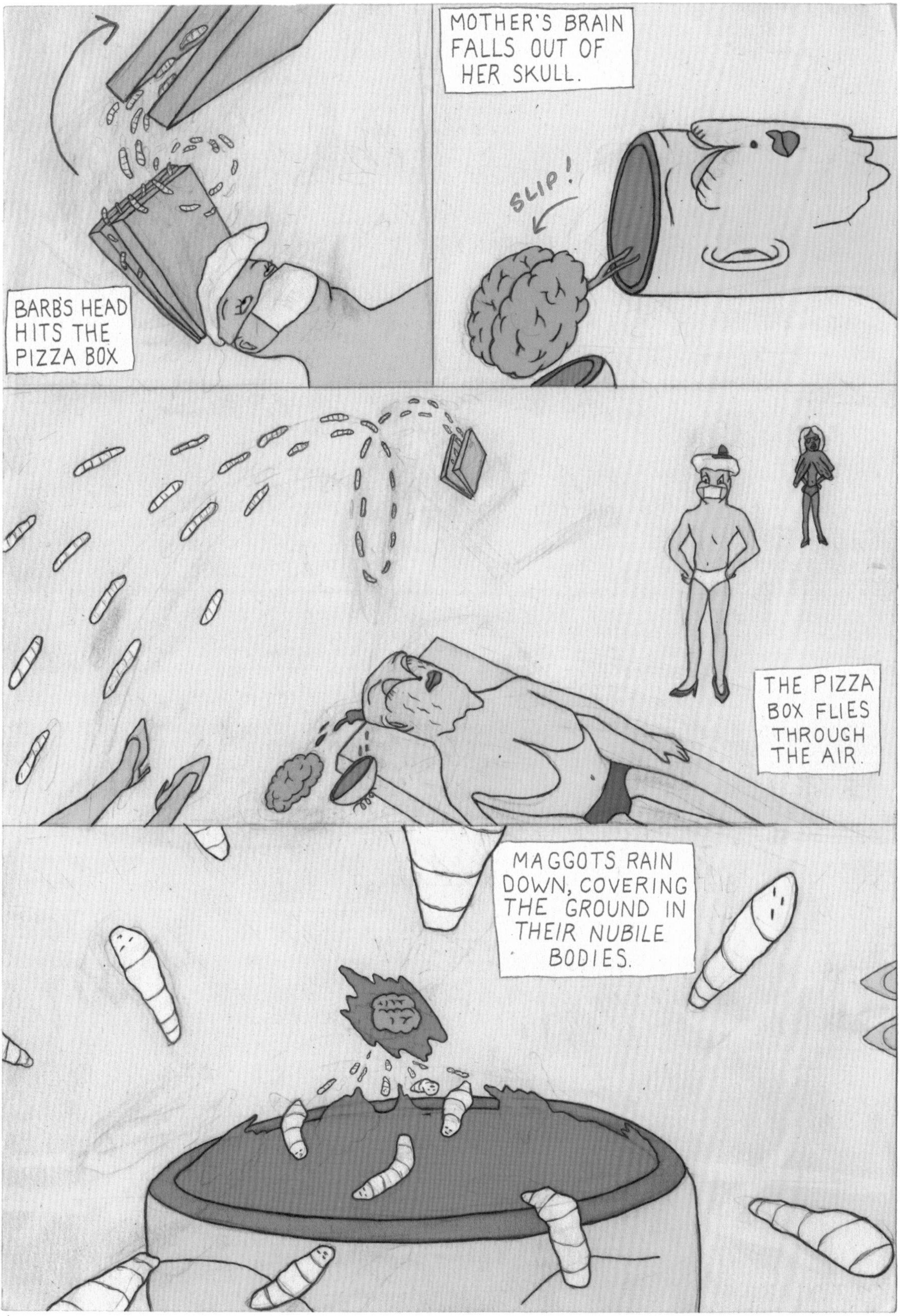
BARB'S HEAD HITS THE PIZZA BOX
MOTHER'S BRAIN FALLS OUT OF HER SKULL.
SLIP!
THE PIZZA BOX FLIES THROUGH THE AIR.
MAGGOTS RAIN DOWN, COVERING THE GROUND IN THEIR NUBILE BODIES.

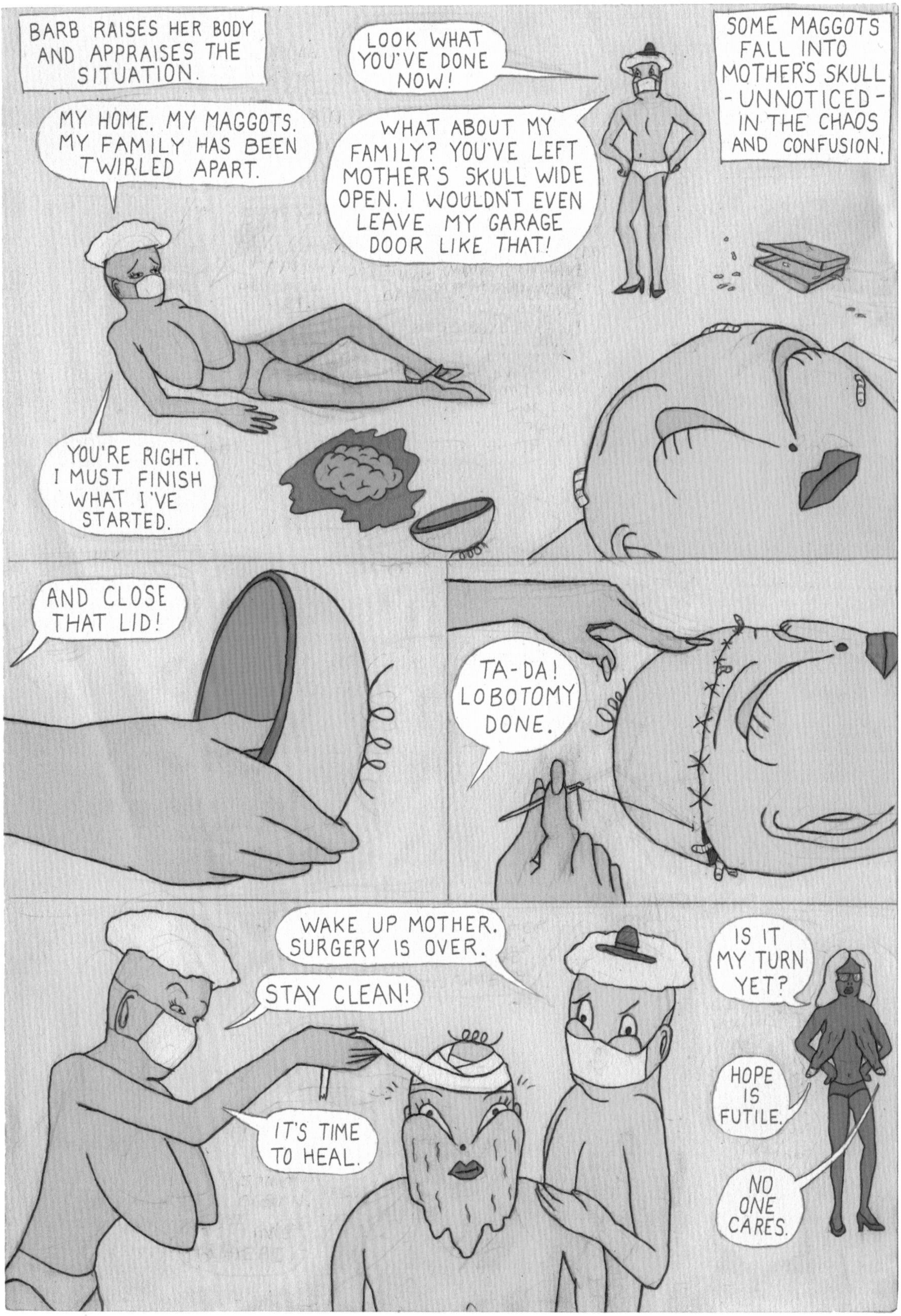
BARB RAISES HER BODY AND APPRAISES THE SITUATION.
MY HOME. MY MAGGOTS. MY FAMILY HAS BEEN TWIRLED APART.
LOOK WHAT YOU'VE DONE NOW!
WHAT ABOUT MY FAMILY? YOU'VE LEFT MOTHER'S SKULL WIDE OPEN. I WOULDN'T EVEN LEAVE MY GARAGE DOOR LIKE THAT!
SOME MAGGOTS FALL INTO MOTHER'S SKULL -UNNOTICED- IN THE CHAOS AND CONFUSION.
YOU'RE RIGHT. I MUST FINISH WHAT I'VE STARTED.
AND CLOSE THAT LID!
TA-DA! LOBOTOMY DONE.
WAKE UP MOTHER. SURGERY IS OVER.
STAY CLEAN!
IT'S TIME TO HEAL.
IS IT MY TURN YET?
HOPE IS FUTILE.
NO ONE CARES.

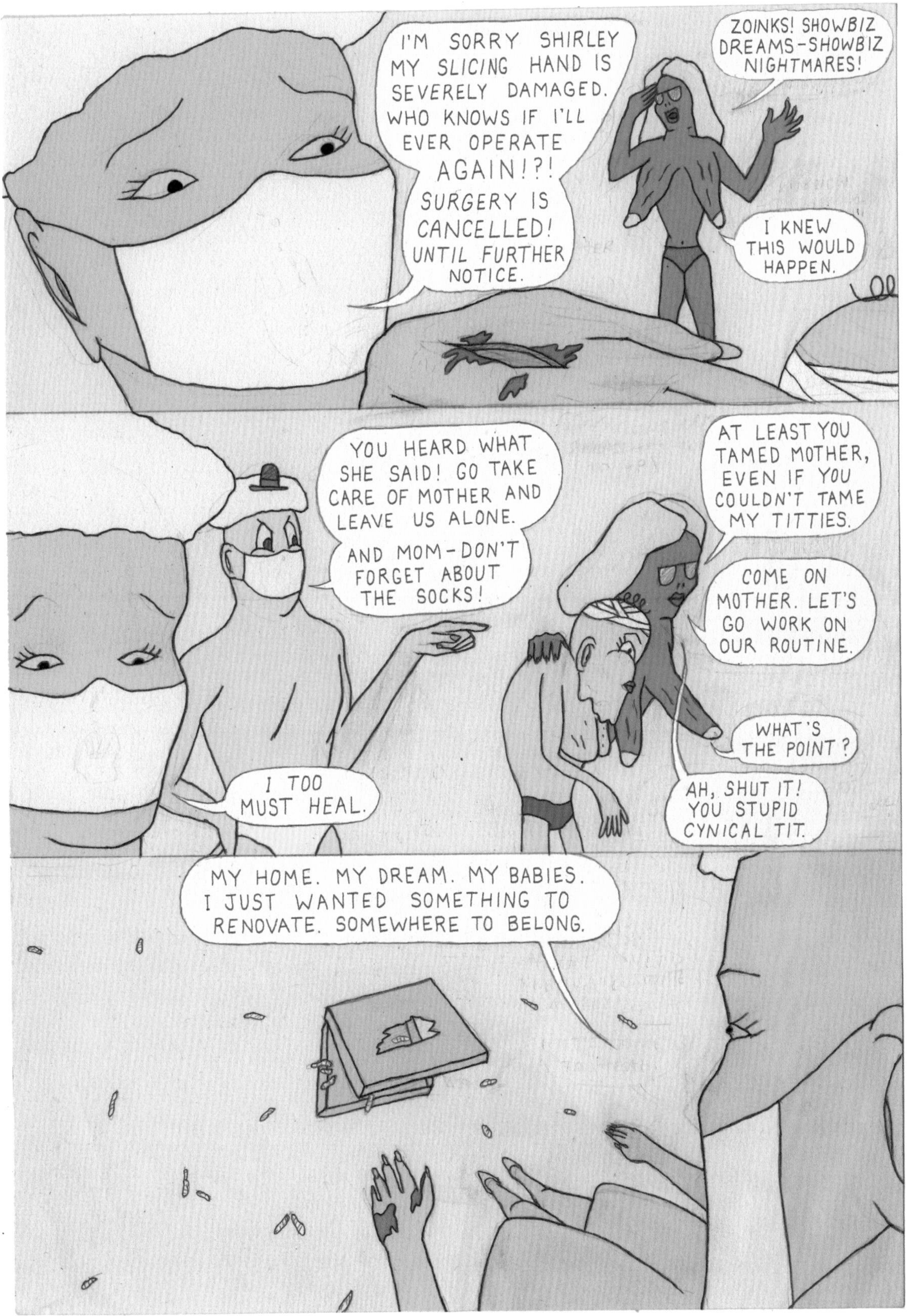
I'M SORRY SHIRLEY MY SLICING HAND IS SEVERELY DAMAGED. WHO KNOWS IF I'LL EVER OPERATE AGAIN!?! SURGERY IS CANCELLED! UNTIL FURTHER NOTICE.
ZOINKS! SHOWBIZ DREAMS-SHOWBIZ NIGHTMARES!
I KNEW THIS WOULD HAPPEN.
YOU HEARD WHAT SHE SAID! GO TAKE CARE OF MOTHER AND LEAVE US ALONE.
AND MOM-DON'T FORGET ABOUT THE SOCKS!
I TOO MUST HEAL.
AT LEAST YOU TAMED MOTHER, EVEN IF YOU COULDN'T TAME MY TITTIES.
COME ON MOTHER. LET'S GO WORK ON OUR ROUTINE.
WHAT'S THE POINT?
AH, SHUT IT! YOU STUPID CYNICAL TIT.
MY HOME. MY DREAM. MY BABIES. I JUST WANTED SOMETHING TO RENOVATE. SOMEWHERE TO BELONG.

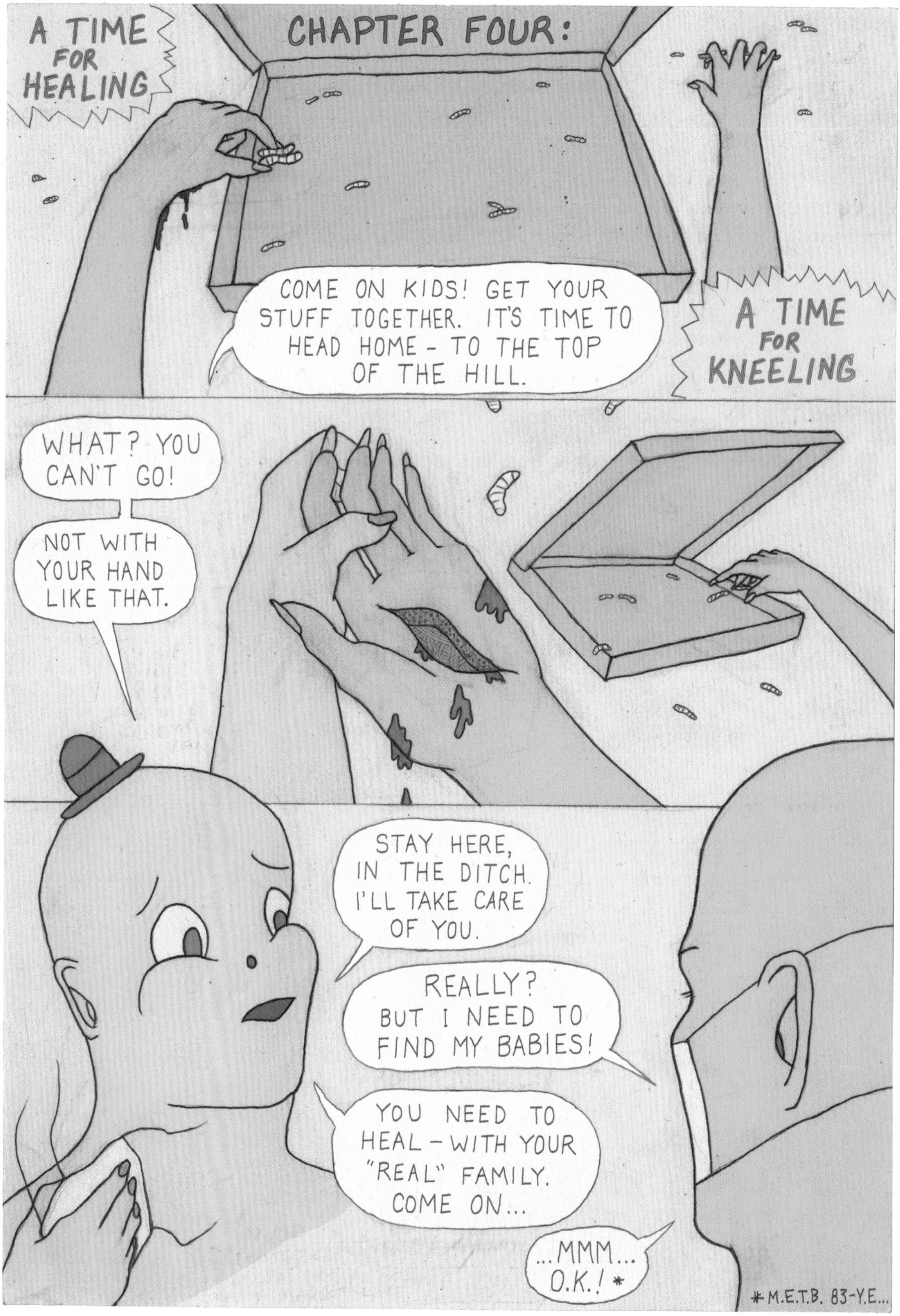
A TIME FOR HEALING
CHAPTER FOUR:
COME ON KIDS! GET YOUR STUFF TOGETHER. IT'S TIME TO HEAD HOME - TO THE TOP OF THE HILL.
A TIME FOR KNEELING
WHAT? YOU CAN'T GO!
NOT WITH YOUR HAND LIKE THAT.
STAY HERE, IN THE DITCH. I'LL TAKE CARE OF YOU.
REALLY? BUT I NEED TO FIND MY BABIES!
YOU NEED TO HEAL - WITH YOUR "REAL" FAMILY. COME ON...
...MMM... O.K.! *
* M.E.T.B. 83-Y.E...

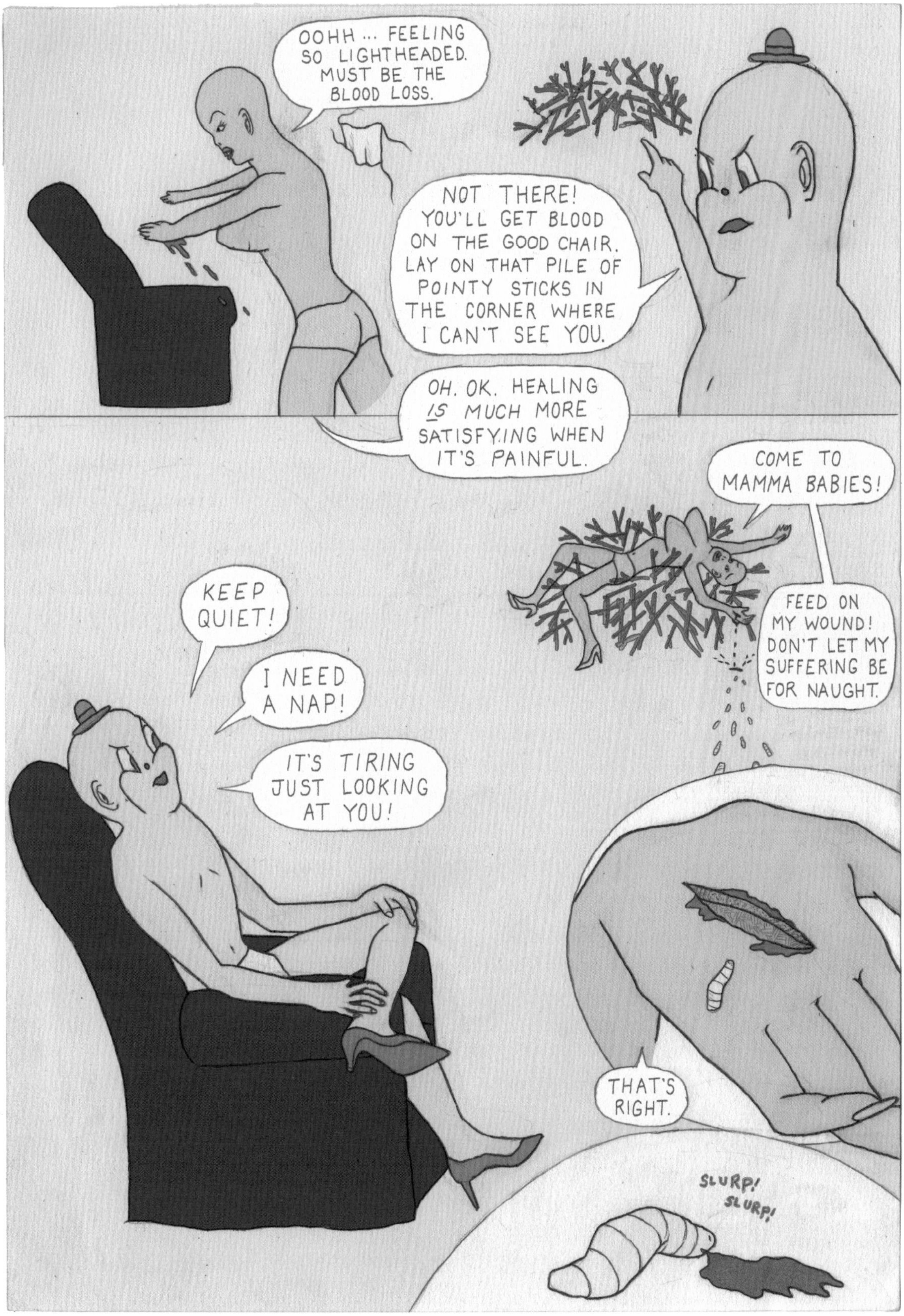
OOHH ... FEELING SO LIGHTHEADED. MUST BE THE BLOOD LOSS.
NOT THERE! YOU'LL GET BLOOD ON THE GOOD CHAIR. LAY ON THAT PILE OF POINTY STICKS IN THE CORNER WHERE I CAN'T SEE YOU.
OH. OK. HEALING *IS* MUCH MORE SATISFYING WHEN IT'S PAINFUL.
COME TO MAMMA BABIES!
FEED ON MY WOUND! DON'T LET MY SUFFERING BE FOR NAUGHT.
KEEP QUIET!
I NEED A NAP!
IT'S TIRING JUST LOOKING AT YOU!
THAT'S RIGHT.
SLURP! SLURP!

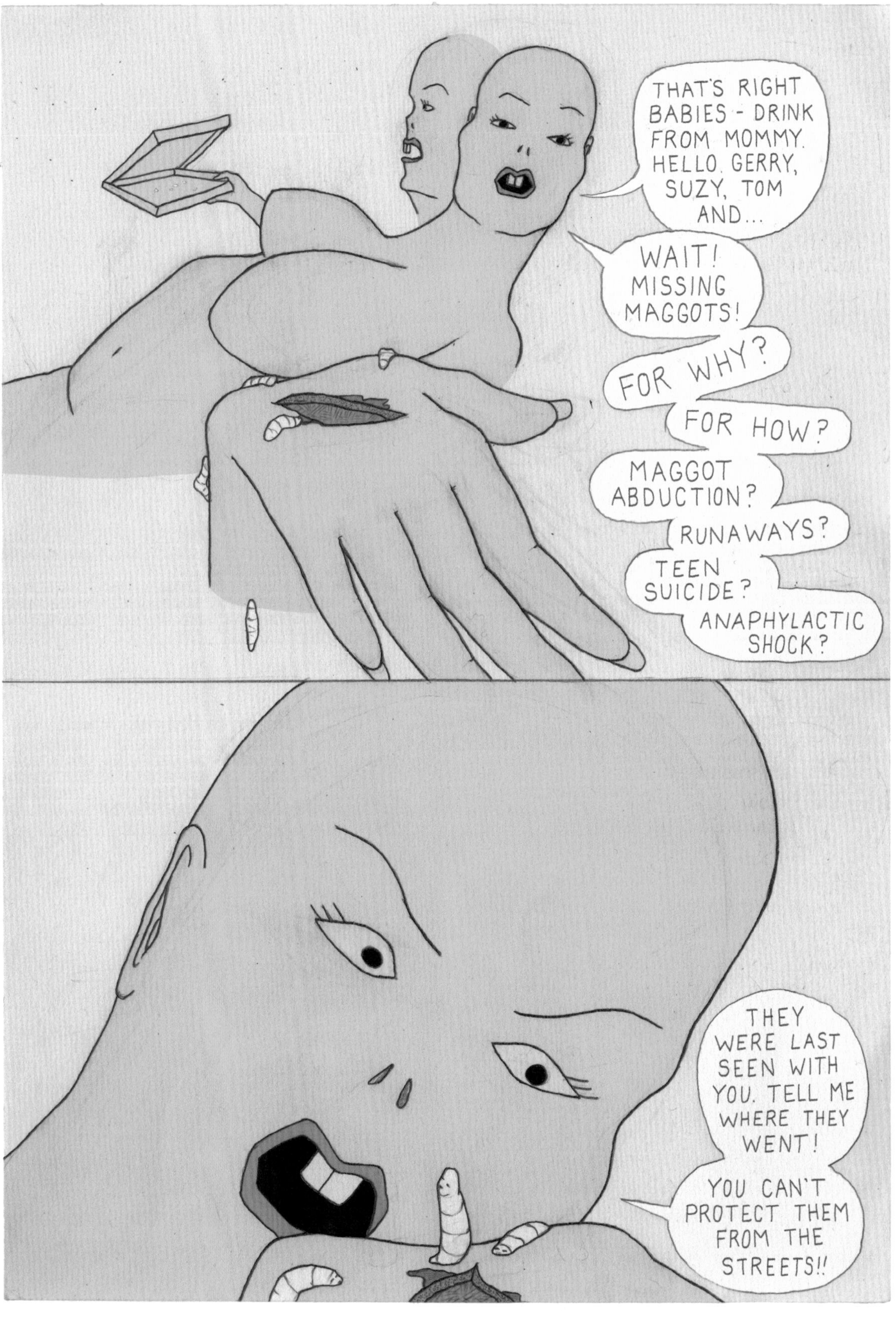
THAT'S RIGHT BABIES - DRINK FROM MOMMY. HELLO. GERRY, SUZY, TOM AND...
WAIT! MISSING MAGGOTS!
FOR WHY?
FOR HOW?
MAGGOT ABDUCTION?
RUNAWAYS?
TEEN SUICIDE?
ANAPHYLACTIC SHOCK?
THEY WERE LAST SEEN WITH YOU. TELL ME WHERE THEY WENT!
YOU CAN'T PROTECT THEM FROM THE STREETS!!

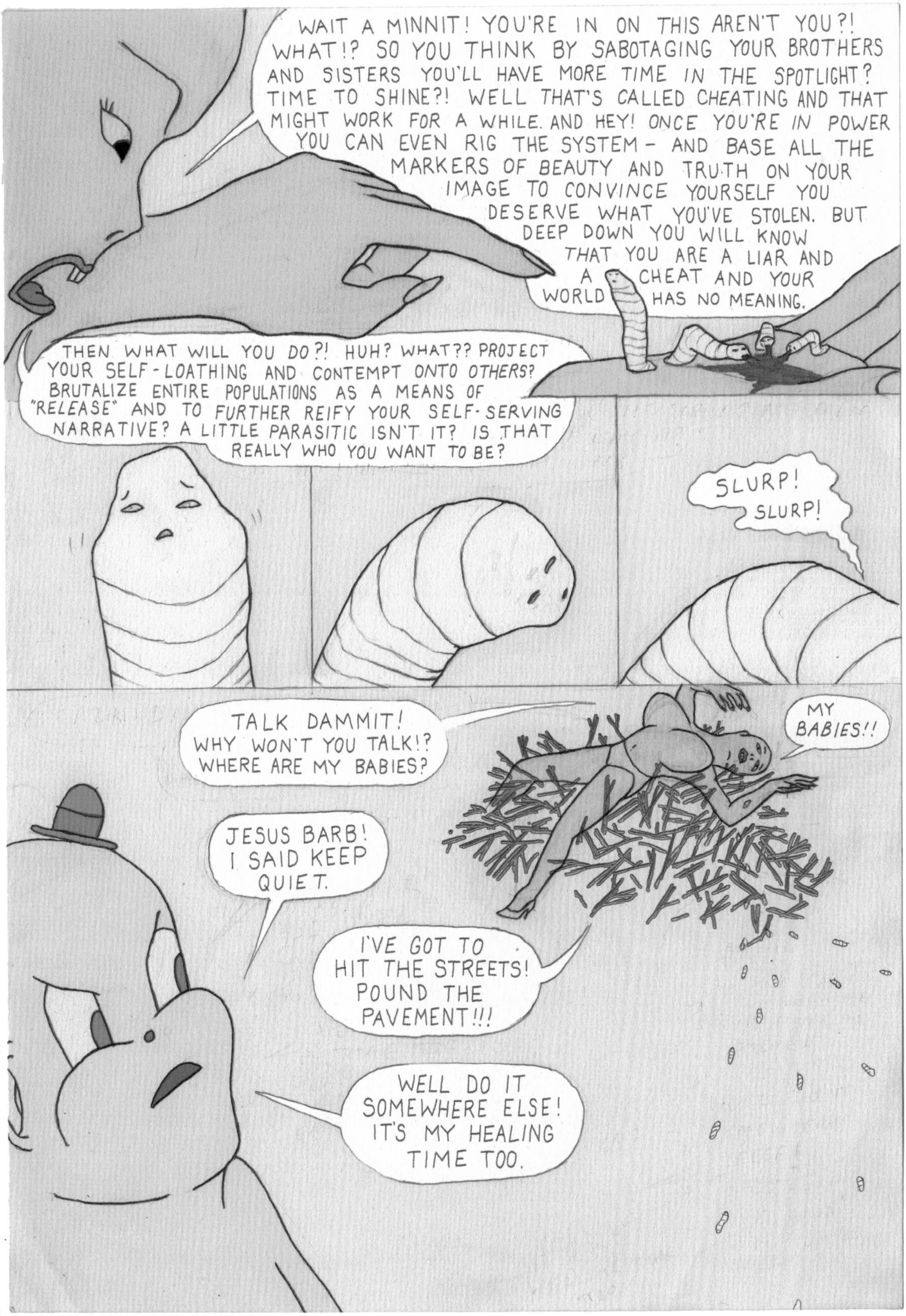
WAIT A MINNIT! YOU'RE IN ON THIS AREN'T YOU?! WHAT!? SO YOU THINK BY SABOTAGING YOUR BROTHERS AND SISTERS YOU'LL HAVE MORE TIME IN THE SPOTLIGHT? TIME TO SHINE?! WELL THAT'S CALLED CHEATING AND THAT MIGHT WORK FOR A WHILE. AND HEY! ONCE YOU'RE IN POWER YOU CAN EVEN RIG THE SYSTEM - AND BASE ALL THE MARKERS OF BEAUTY AND TRUTH ON YOUR IMAGE TO CONVINCE YOURSELF YOU DESERVE WHAT YOU'VE STOLEN. BUT DEEP DOWN YOU WILL KNOW THAT YOU ARE A LIAR AND A CHEAT AND YOUR WORLD HAS NO MEANING.
THEN WHAT WILL YOU DO?! HUH? WHAT?? PROJECT YOUR SELF-LOATHING AND CONTEMPT ONTO OTHERS? BRUTALIZE ENTIRE POPULATIONS AS A MEANS OF "RELEASE" AND TO FURTHER REIFY YOUR SELF-SERVING NARRATIVE? A LITTLE PARASITIC ISN'T IT? IS THAT REALLY WHO YOU WANT TO BE?
SLURP! SLURP!
TALK DAMMIT! WHY WON'T YOU TALK!? WHERE ARE MY BABIES?
MY BABIES!!
JESUS BARB! I SAID KEEP QUIET.
I'VE GOT TO HIT THE STREETS! POUND THE PAVEMENT!!!
WELL DO IT SOMEWHERE ELSE! IT'S MY HEALING TIME TOO.

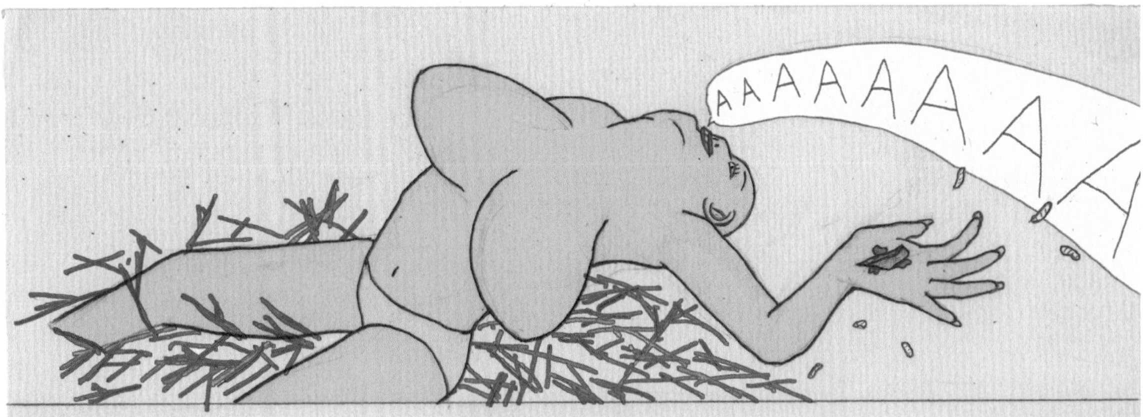
AAAAAAAA

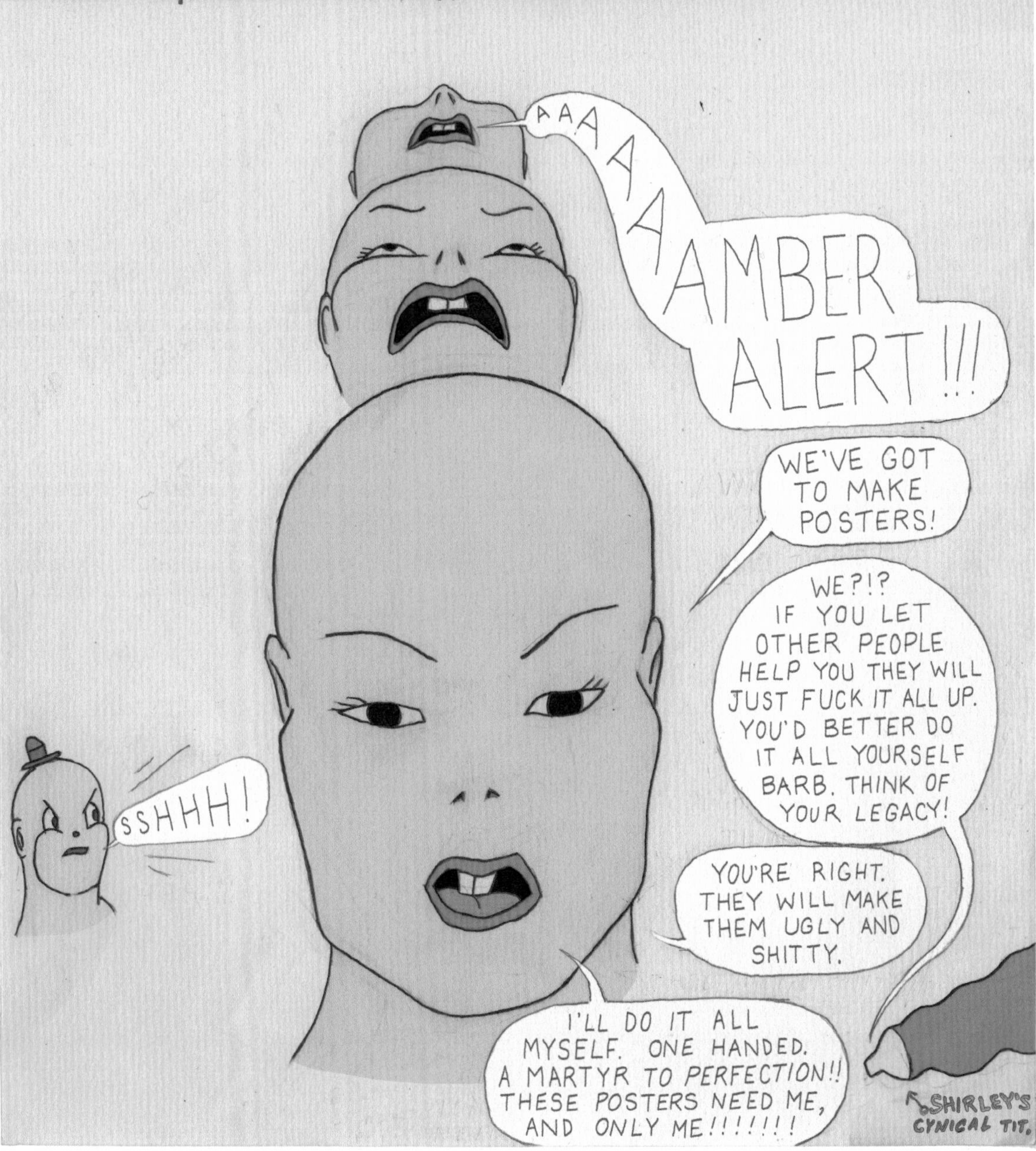
AAAAAAAMBER ALERT!!!
WE'VE GOT TO MAKE POSTERS!
WE?!? IF YOU LET OTHER PEOPLE HELP YOU THEY WILL JUST FUCK IT ALL UP. YOU'D BETTER DO IT ALL YOURSELF BARB. THINK OF YOUR LEGACY!
SSHHH!
YOU'RE RIGHT. THEY WILL MAKE THEM UGLY AND SHITTY.
I'LL DO IT ALL MYSELF. ONE HANDED. A MARTYR TO *PERFECTION*!! THESE POSTERS NEED ME, AND ONLY ME!!!!!!!
SHIRLEY'S CYNICAL TIT.

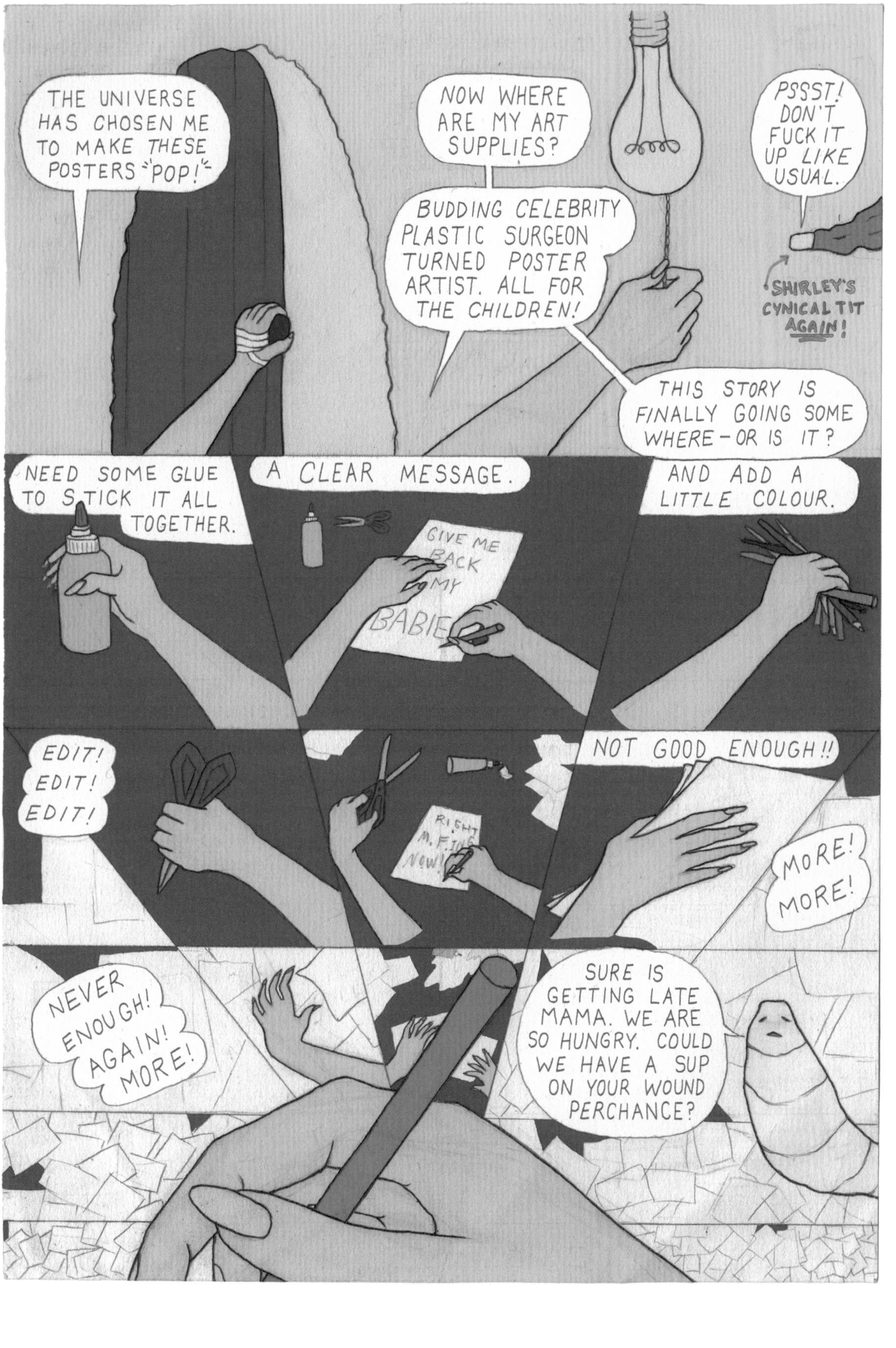
THE UNIVERSE HAS CHOSEN ME TO MAKE THESE POSTERS POP!
NOW WHERE ARE MY ART SUPPLIES?
BUDDING CELEBRITY PLASTIC SURGEON TURNED POSTER ARTIST. ALL FOR THE CHILDREN!
PSSST! DON'T FUCK IT UP LIKE USUAL.
SHIRLEY'S CYNICAL TIT AGAIN!
THIS STORY IS FINALLY GOING SOME WHERE - OR IS IT?
NEED SOME GLUE TO STICK IT ALL TOGETHER.
A CLEAR MESSAGE.
GIVE ME BACK MY BABIE
AND ADD A LITTLE COLOUR.
EDIT! EDIT! EDIT!
RIGHT M.F.ING NOW!
NOT GOOD ENOUGH!!
MORE! MORE!
NEVER ENOUGH! AGAIN! MORE!
SURE IS GETTING LATE MAMA. WE ARE SO HUNGRY. COULD WE HAVE A SUP ON YOUR WOUND PERCHANCE?

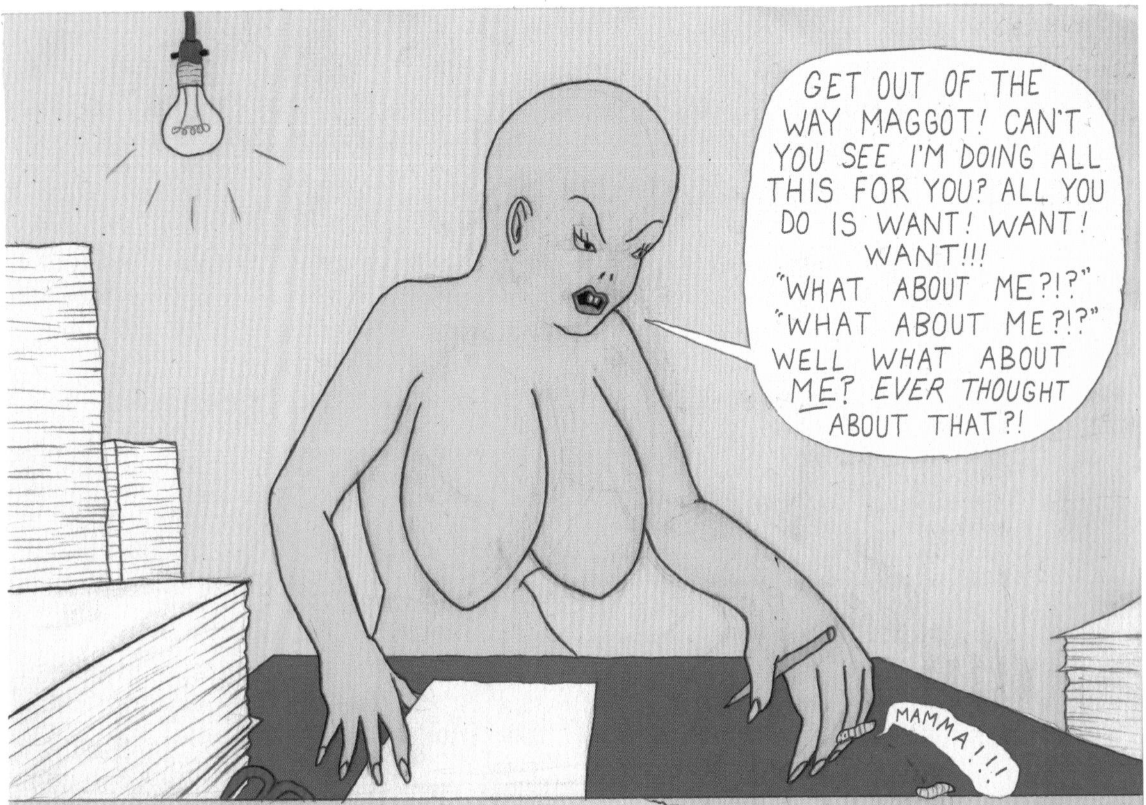
GET OUT OF THE WAY MAGGOT! CAN'T YOU SEE I'M DOING ALL THIS FOR YOU? ALL YOU DO IS WANT! WANT! WANT!!! "WHAT ABOUT ME?!?" "WHAT ABOUT ME?!?" WELL WHAT ABOUT ME? EVER THOUGHT ABOUT THAT?!
MAMMA!!!

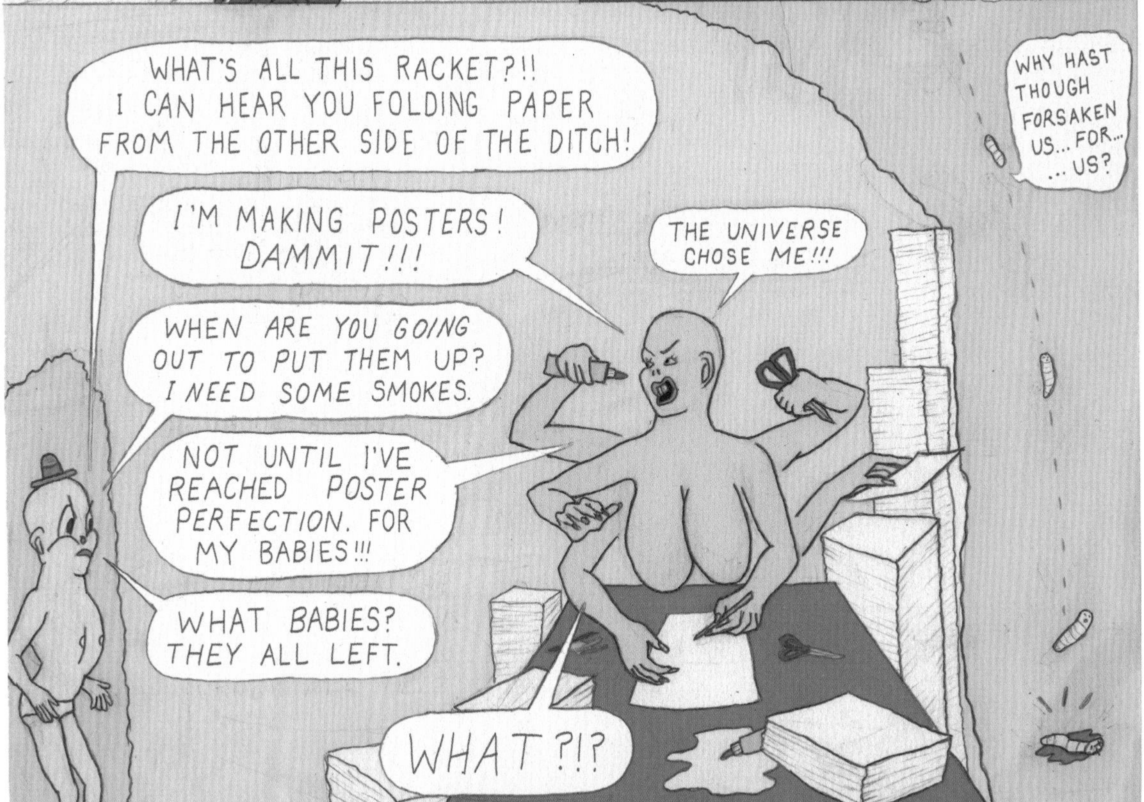
WHAT'S ALL THIS RACKET?!! I CAN HEAR YOU FOLDING PAPER FROM THE OTHER SIDE OF THE DITCH!
WHY HAST THOUGH FORSAKEN US... FOR... ...US?
I'M MAKING POSTERS! DAMMIT!!!
THE UNIVERSE CHOSE ME!!!
WHEN ARE YOU GOING OUT TO PUT THEM UP? I NEED SOME SMOKES.
NOT UNTIL I'VE REACHED POSTER PERFECTION. FOR MY BABIES!!!
WHAT BABIES? THEY ALL LEFT.
WHAT?!?

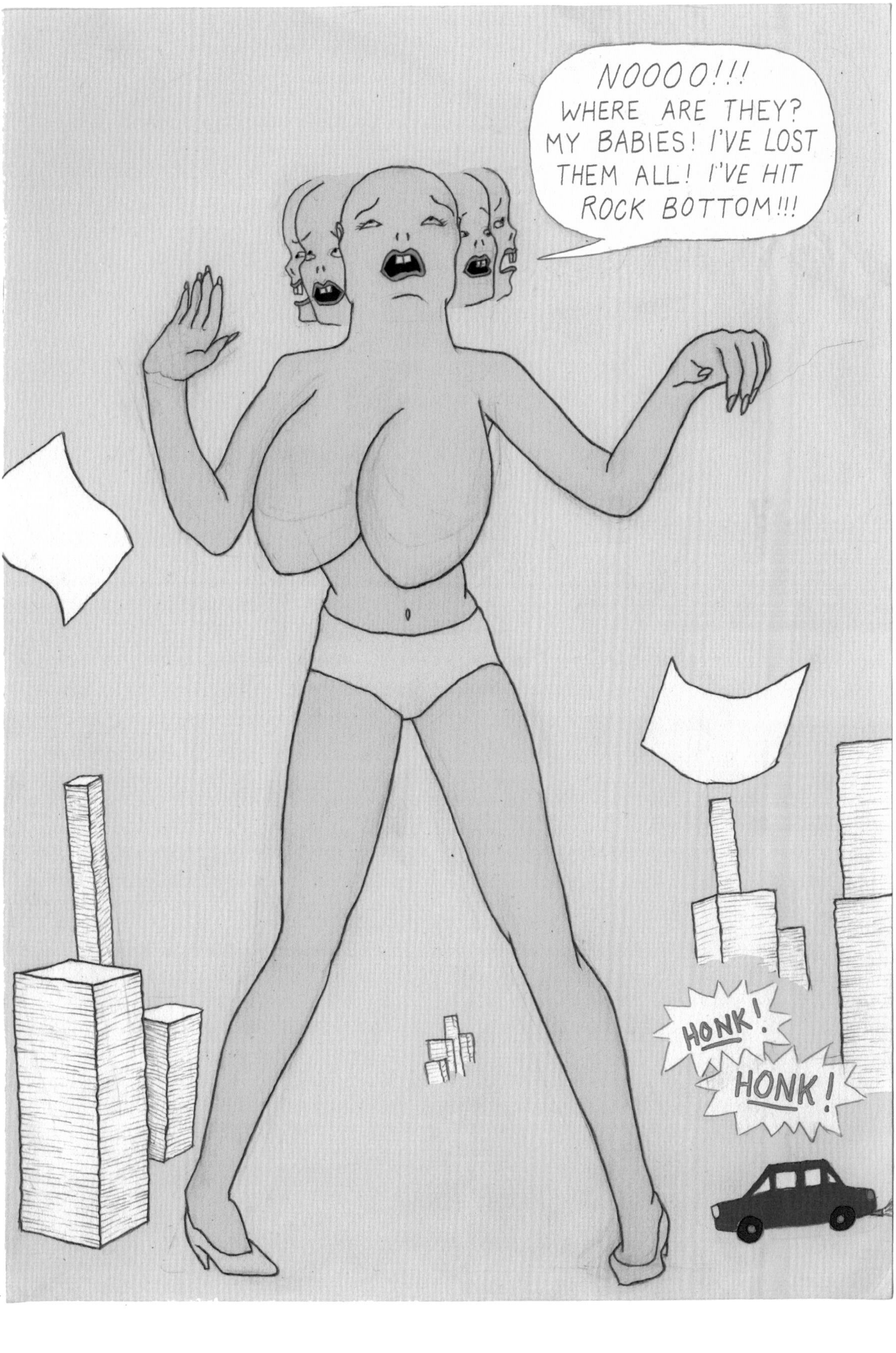
NOOOO!!! WHERE ARE THEY? MY BABIES! I'VE LOST THEM ALL! I'VE HIT ROCK BOTTOM!!!
HONK!
HONK!

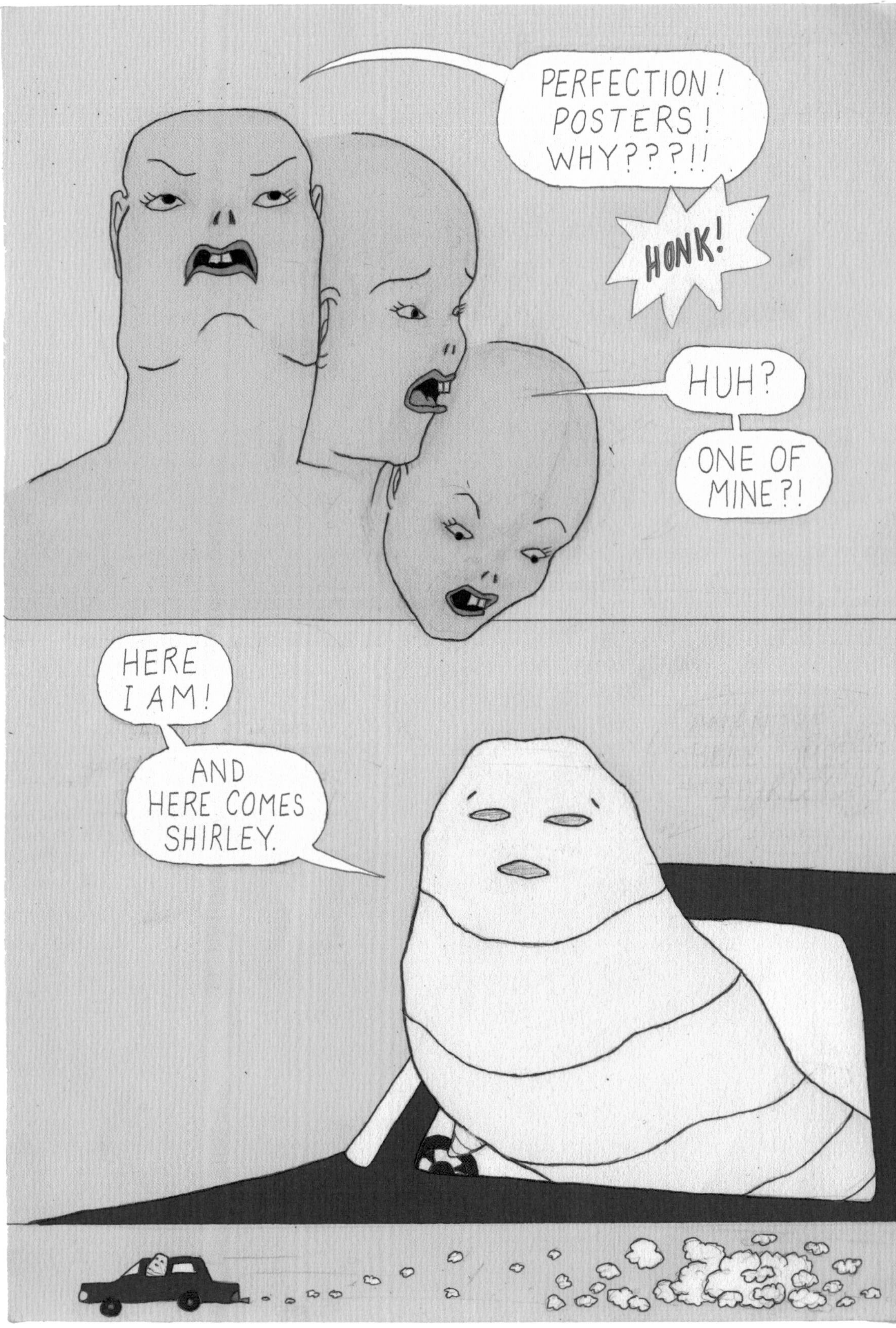
PERFECTION! POSTERS! WHY???!!
HONK!
HUH?
ONE OF MINE?!
HERE I AM!
AND HERE COMES SHIRLEY.

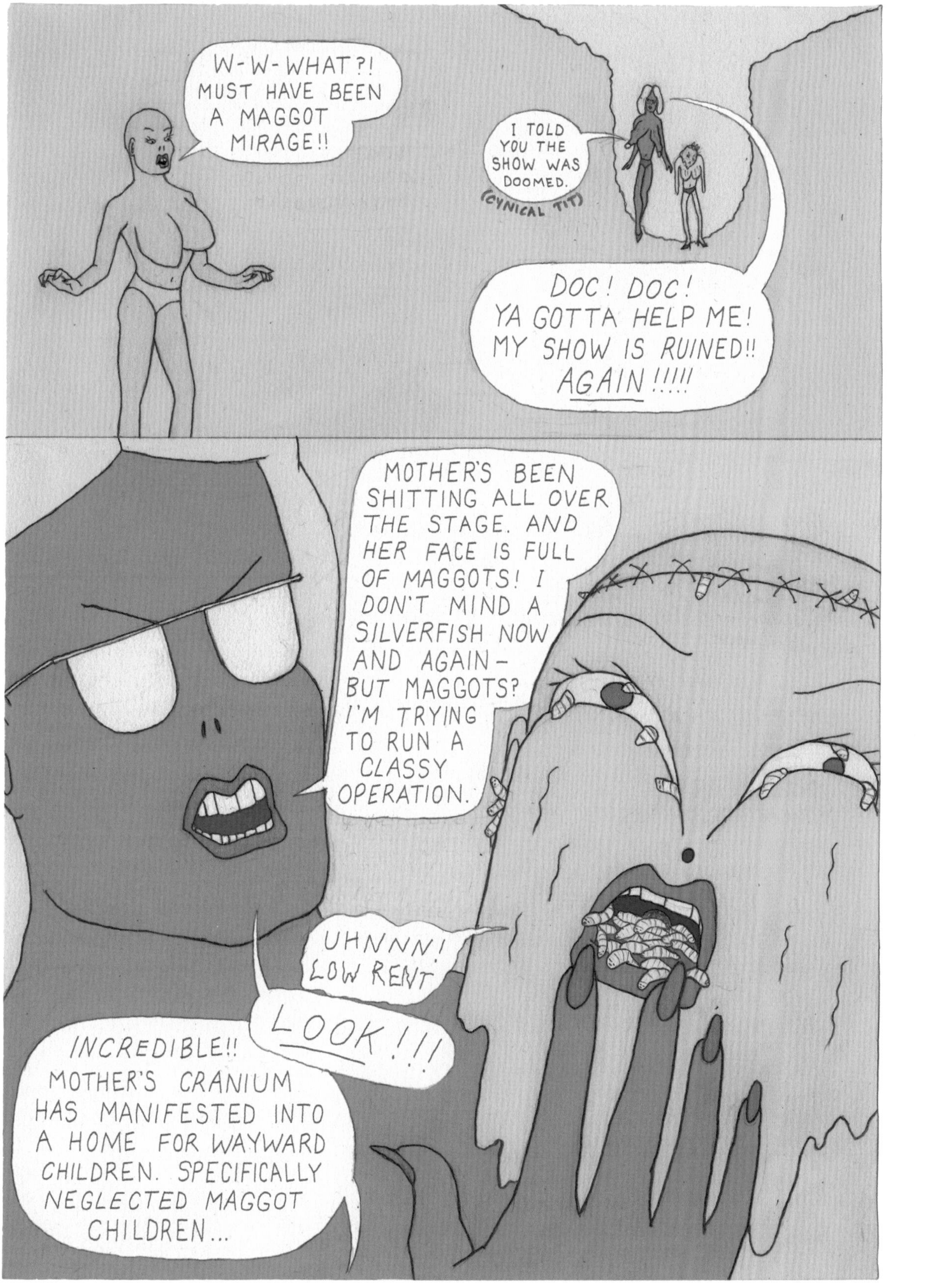
W-W-WHAT?! MUST HAVE BEEN A MAGGOT MIRAGE!!
I TOLD YOU THE SHOW WAS DOOMED.
(CYNICAL TIT)
DOC! DOC! YA GOTTA HELP ME! MY SHOW IS RUINED!! AGAIN!!!!!
MOTHER'S BEEN SHITTING ALL OVER THE STAGE. AND HER FACE IS FULL OF MAGGOTS! I DON'T MIND A SILVERFISH NOW AND AGAIN - BUT MAGGOTS? I'M TRYING TO RUN A CLASSY OPERATION.
UHNNN! LOW RENT
LOOK!!!
INCREDIBLE!! MOTHER'S CRANIUM HAS MANIFESTED INTO A HOME FOR WAYWARD CHILDREN. SPECIFICALLY NEGLECTED MAGGOT CHILDREN...

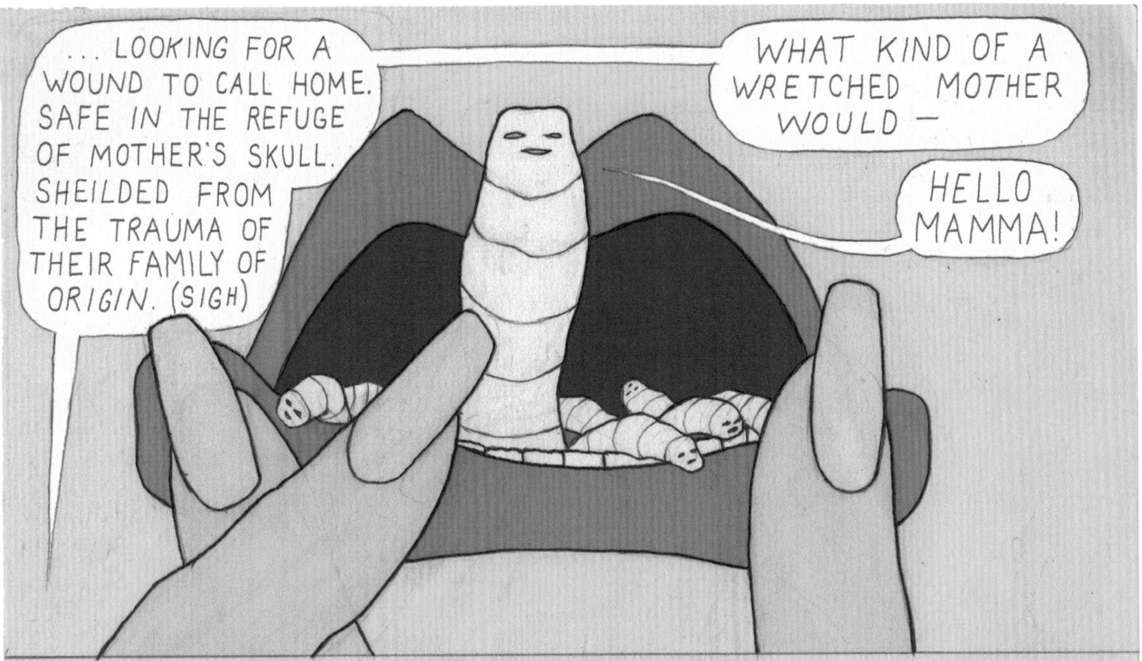
...LOOKING FOR A WOUND TO CALL HOME. SAFE IN THE REFUGE OF MOTHER'S SKULL. SHEILDED FROM THE TRAUMA OF THEIR FAMILY OF ORIGIN. (SIGH)
WHAT KIND OF A WRETCHED MOTHER WOULD —
HELLO MAMMA!

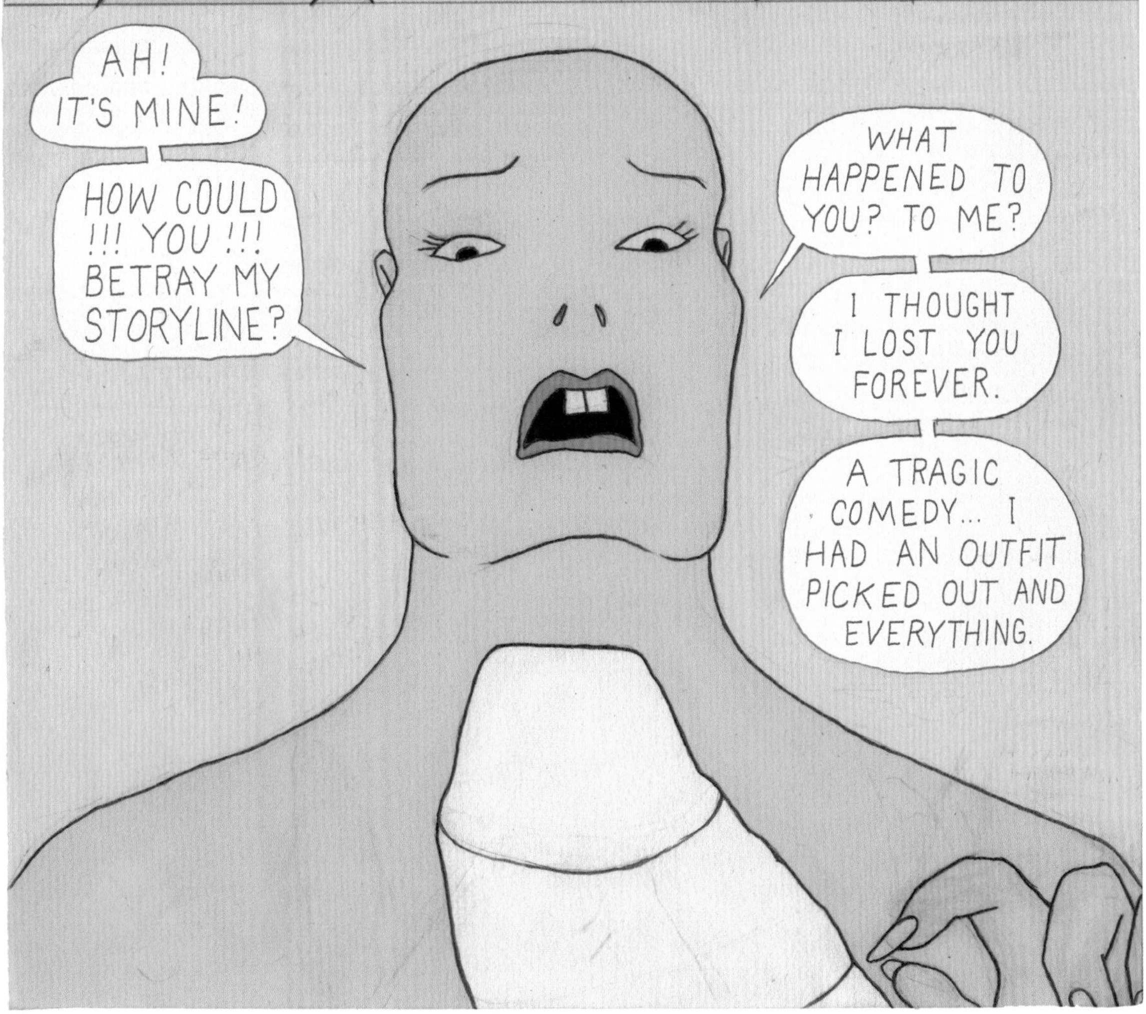
AH! IT'S MINE!
HOW COULD !!! YOU !!! BETRAY MY STORYLINE?
WHAT HAPPENED TO YOU? TO ME?
I THOUGHT I LOST YOU FOREVER.
A TRAGIC COMEDY... I HAD AN OUTFIT PICKED OUT AND EVERYTHING.

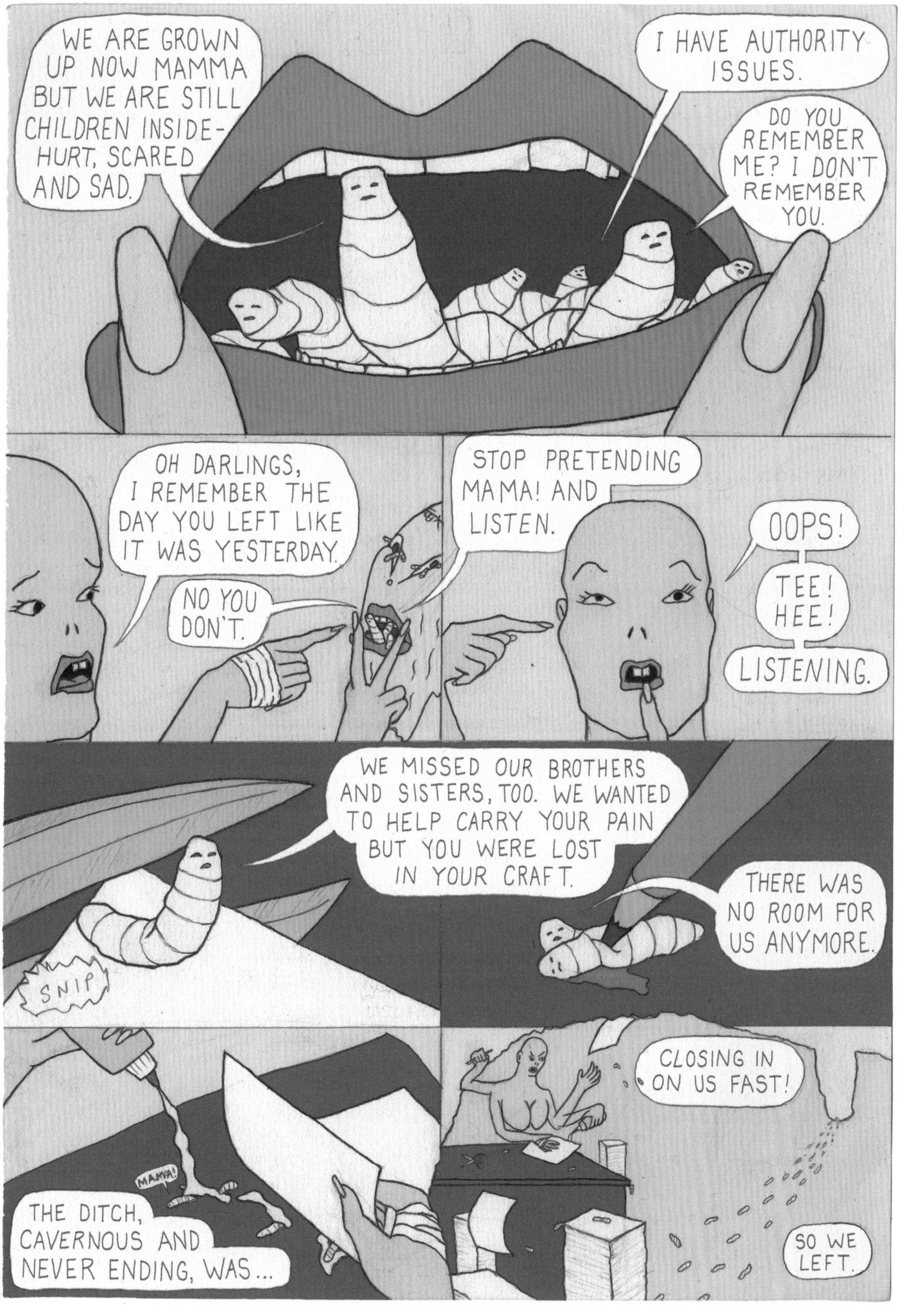
WE ARE GROWN UP NOW MAMMA BUT WE ARE STILL CHILDREN INSIDE- HURT, SCARED AND SAD.
I HAVE AUTHORITY ISSUES.
DO YOU REMEMBER ME? I DON'T REMEMBER YOU.
OH DARLINGS, I REMEMBER THE DAY YOU LEFT LIKE IT WAS YESTERDAY.
NO YOU DON'T.
STOP PRETENDING MAMA! AND LISTEN.
OOPS!
TEE! HEE!
LISTENING.
WE MISSED OUR BROTHERS AND SISTERS, TOO. WE WANTED TO HELP CARRY YOUR PAIN BUT YOU WERE LOST IN YOUR CRAFT.
SNIP
THERE WAS NO ROOM FOR US ANYMORE.
THE DITCH, CAVERNOUS AND NEVER ENDING, WAS...
CLOSING IN ON US FAST!
SO WE LEFT.

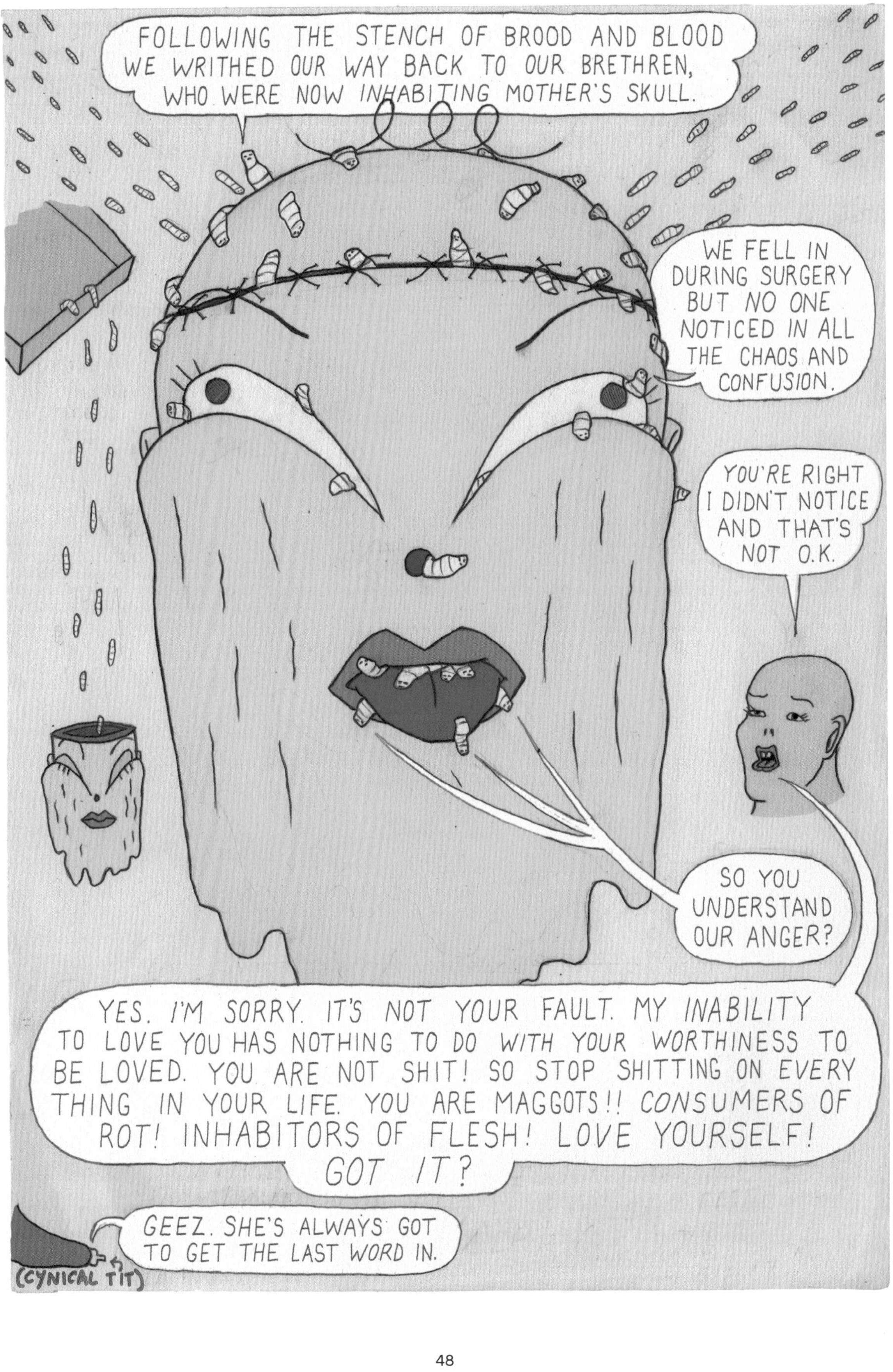
FOLLOWING THE STENCH OF BROOD AND BLOOD WE WRITHED OUR WAY BACK TO OUR BRETHREN, WHO WERE NOW INHABITING MOTHER'S SKULL.
WE FELL IN DURING SURGERY BUT NO ONE NOTICED IN ALL THE CHAOS AND CONFUSION.
YOU'RE RIGHT I DIDN'T NOTICE AND THAT'S NOT O.K.
SO YOU UNDERSTAND OUR ANGER?
YES. I'M SORRY. IT'S NOT YOUR FAULT. MY INABILITY TO LOVE YOU HAS NOTHING TO DO WITH YOUR WORTHINESS TO BE LOVED. YOU ARE NOT SHIT! SO STOP SHITTING ON EVERY THING IN YOUR LIFE. YOU ARE MAGGOTS!! CONSUMERS OF ROT! INHABITORS OF FLESH! LOVE YOURSELF! GOT IT?
GEEZ. SHE'S ALWAYS GOT TO GET THE LAST WORD IN.
(CYNICAL TIT)

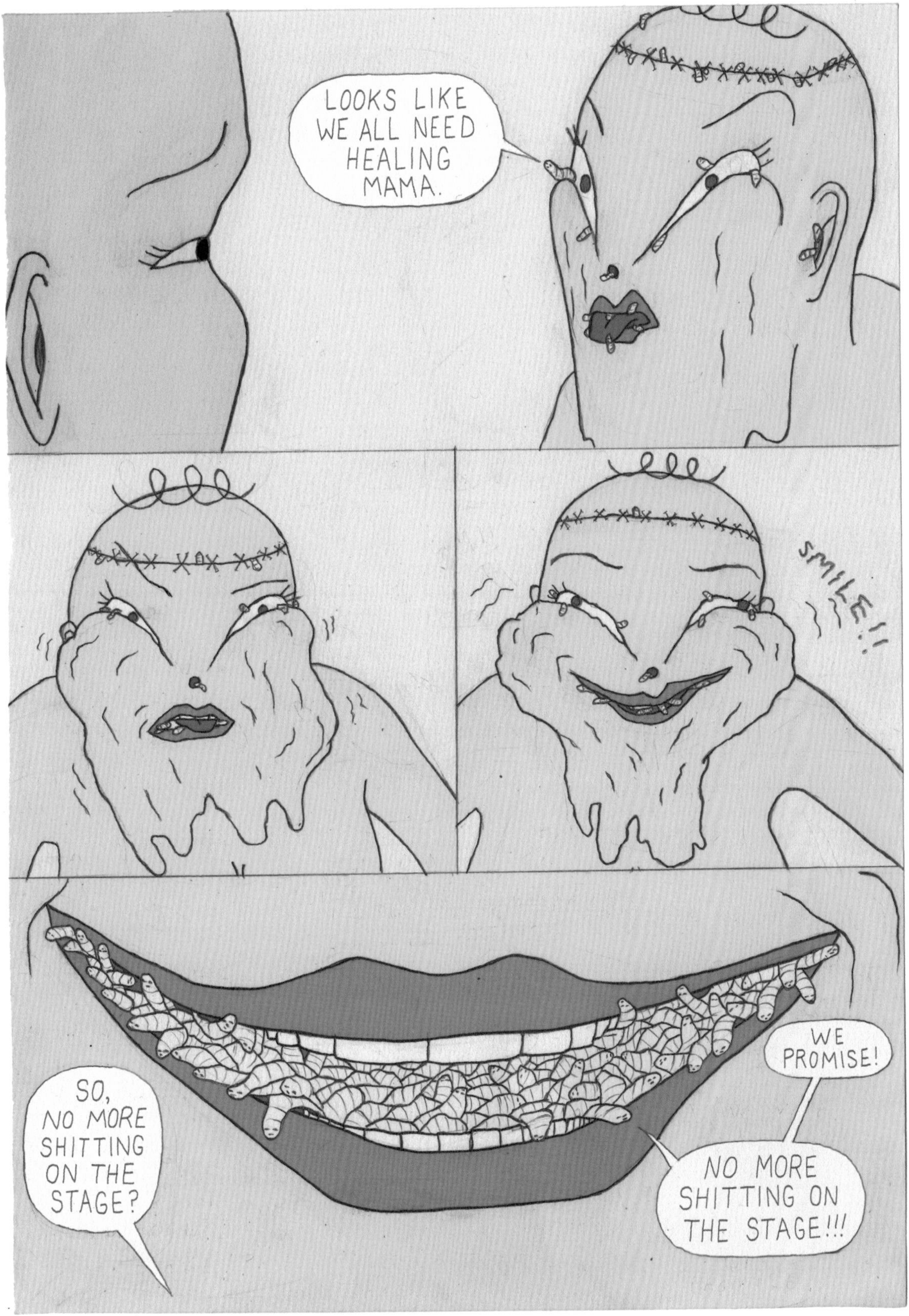
LOOKS LIKE WE ALL NEED HEALING MAMA.
SMILE!!
SO, NO MORE SHITTING ON THE STAGE?
WE PROMISE!
NO MORE SHITTING ON THE STAGE!!!

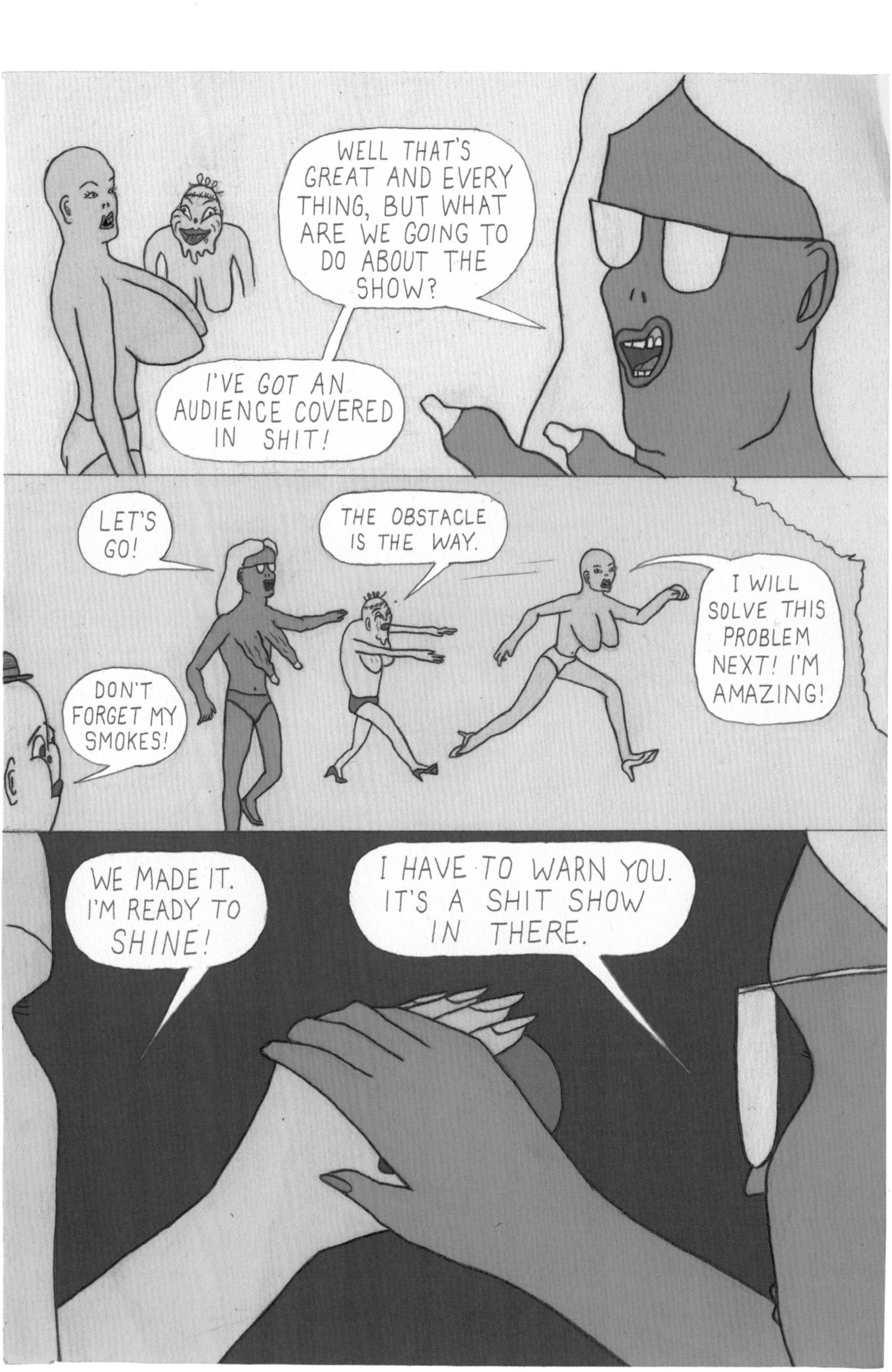
WELL THAT'S GREAT AND EVERY THING, BUT WHAT ARE WE GOING TO DO ABOUT THE SHOW?
I'VE GOT AN AUDIENCE COVERED IN SHIT!
LET'S GO!
THE OBSTACLE IS THE WAY.
I WILL SOLVE THIS PROBLEM NEXT! I'M AMAZING!
DON'T FORGET MY SMOKES!
WE MADE IT. I'M READY TO SHINE!
I HAVE TO WARN YOU. IT'S A SHIT SHOW IN THERE.

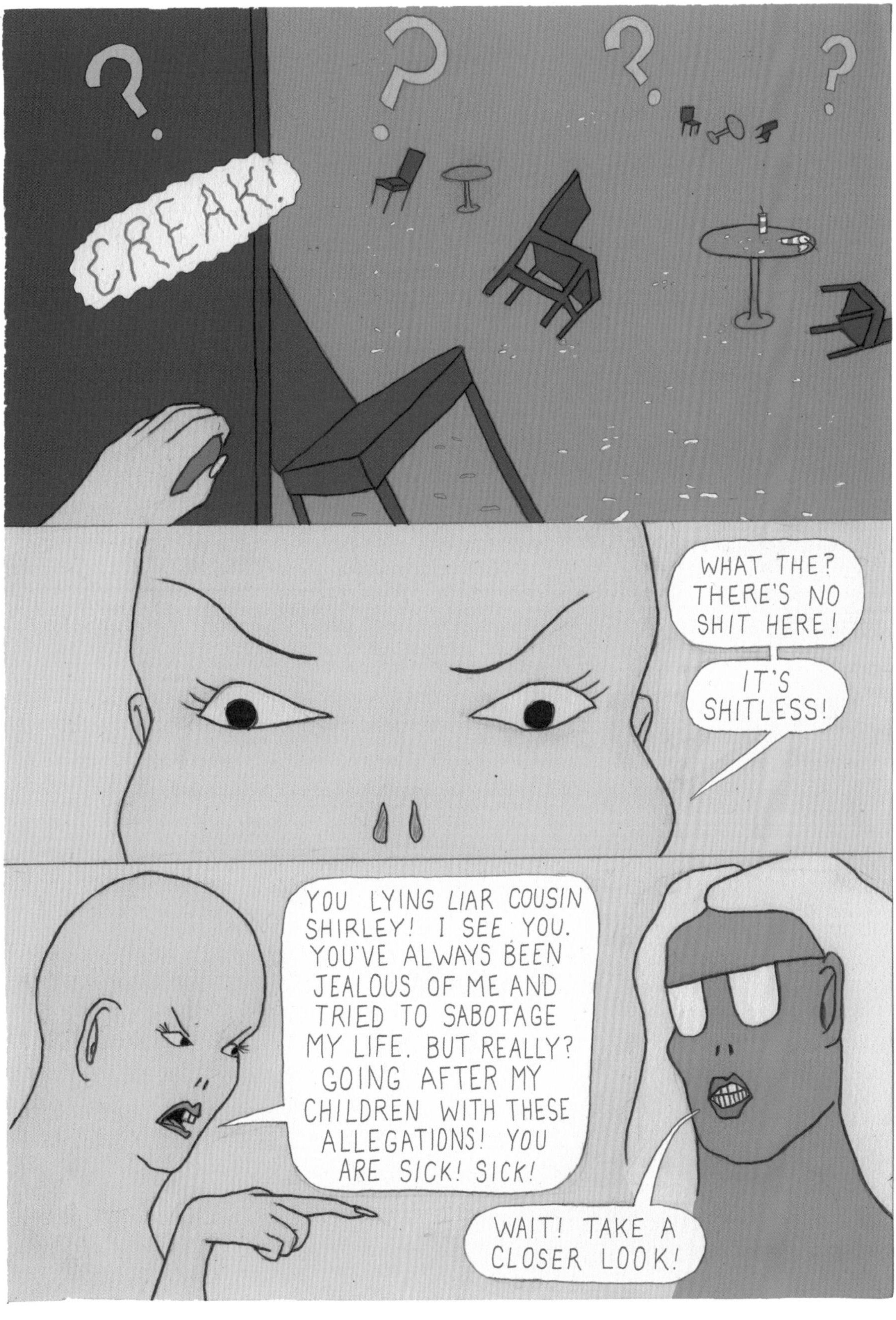
CREAK!
WHAT THE? THERE'S NO SHIT HERE!
IT'S SHITLESS!
YOU LYING *LIAR* COUSIN SHIRLEY! I SEE YOU. YOU'VE ALWAYS BEEN JEALOUS OF ME AND TRIED TO SABOTAGE MY LIFE. BUT REALLY? GOING AFTER MY CHILDREN WITH THESE ALLEGATIONS! YOU ARE SICK! SICK!
WAIT! TAKE A CLOSER LOOK!

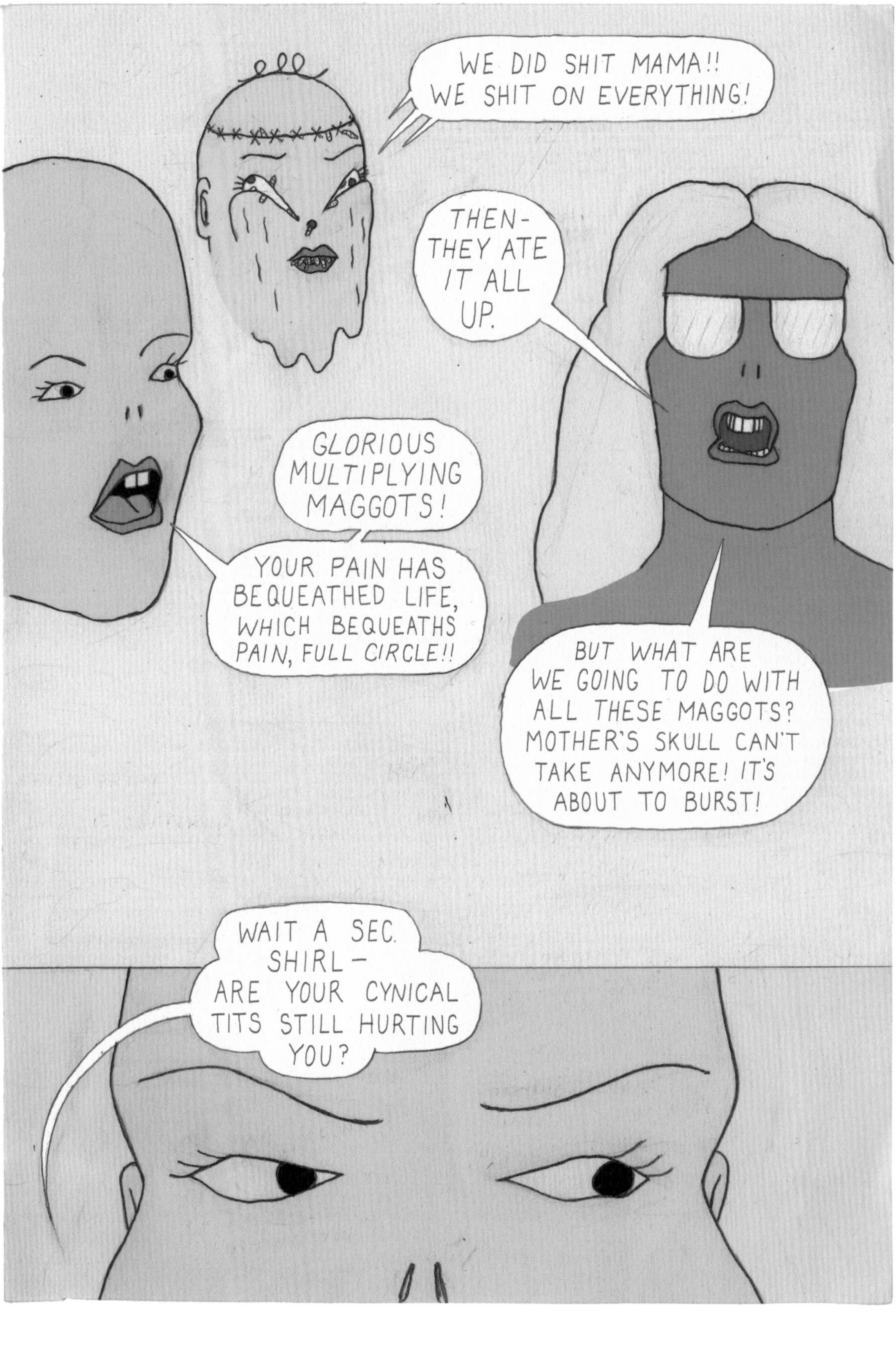
WE DID SHIT MAMA!! WE SHIT ON EVERYTHING!
THEN- THEY ATE IT ALL UP.
GLORIOUS MULTIPLYING MAGGOTS!
YOUR PAIN HAS BEQUEATHED LIFE, WHICH BEQUEATHS PAIN, FULL CIRCLE!!
BUT WHAT ARE WE GOING TO DO WITH ALL THESE MAGGOTS? MOTHER'S SKULL CAN'T TAKE ANYMORE! IT'S ABOUT TO BURST!
WAIT A SEC. SHIRL- ARE YOUR CYNICAL TITS STILL HURTING YOU?

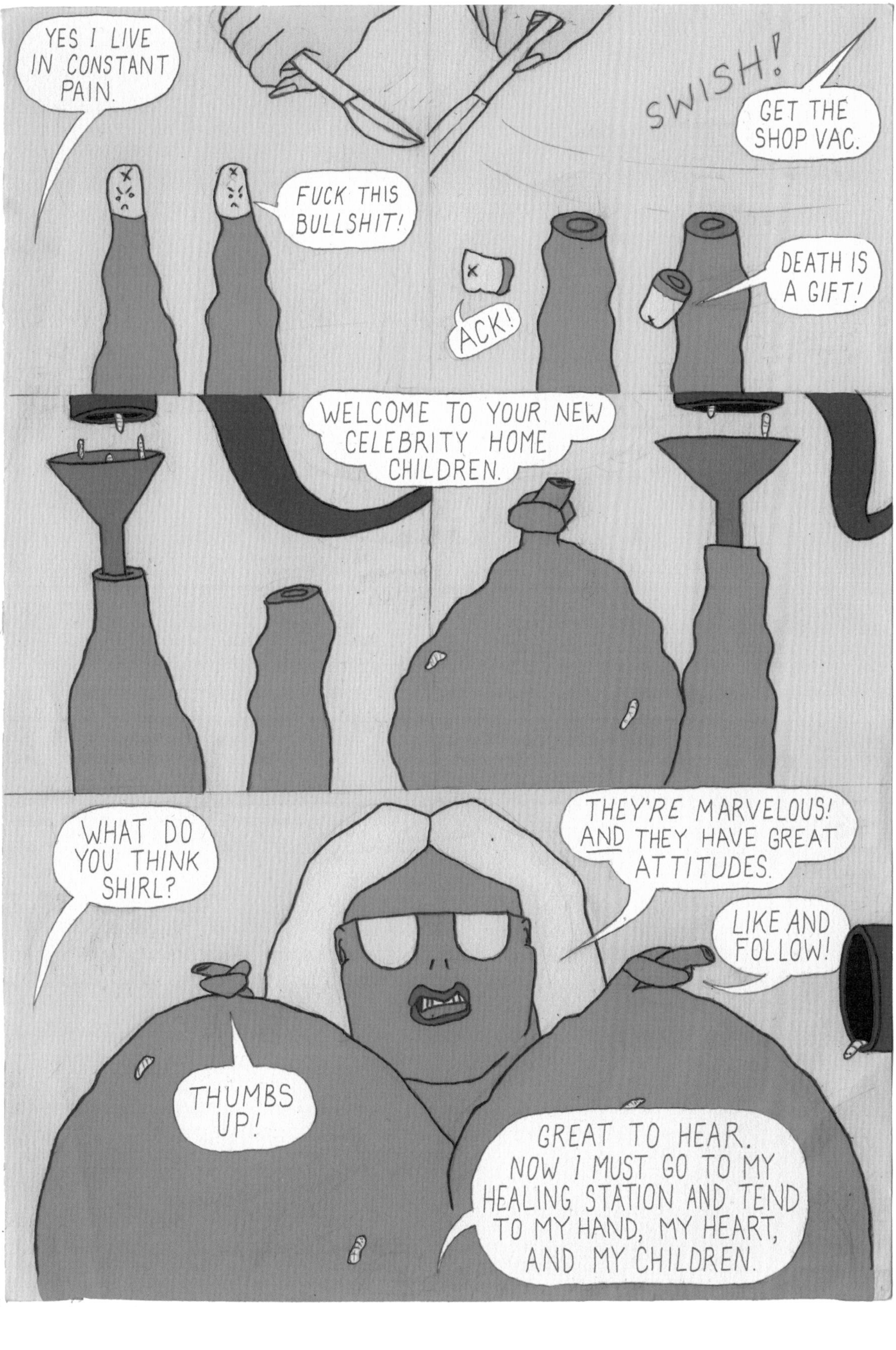
YES I LIVE IN CONSTANT PAIN.
FUCK THIS BULLSHIT!
SWISH!
GET THE SHOP VAC.
ACK!
DEATH IS A GIFT!
WELCOME TO YOUR NEW CELEBRITY HOME CHILDREN.
WHAT DO YOU THINK SHIRL?
THEY'RE MARVELOUS! AND THEY HAVE GREAT ATTITUDES.
LIKE AND FOLLOW!
THUMBS UP!
GREAT TO HEAR. NOW I MUST GO TO MY HEALING STATION AND TEND TO MY HAND, MY HEART, AND MY CHILDREN.

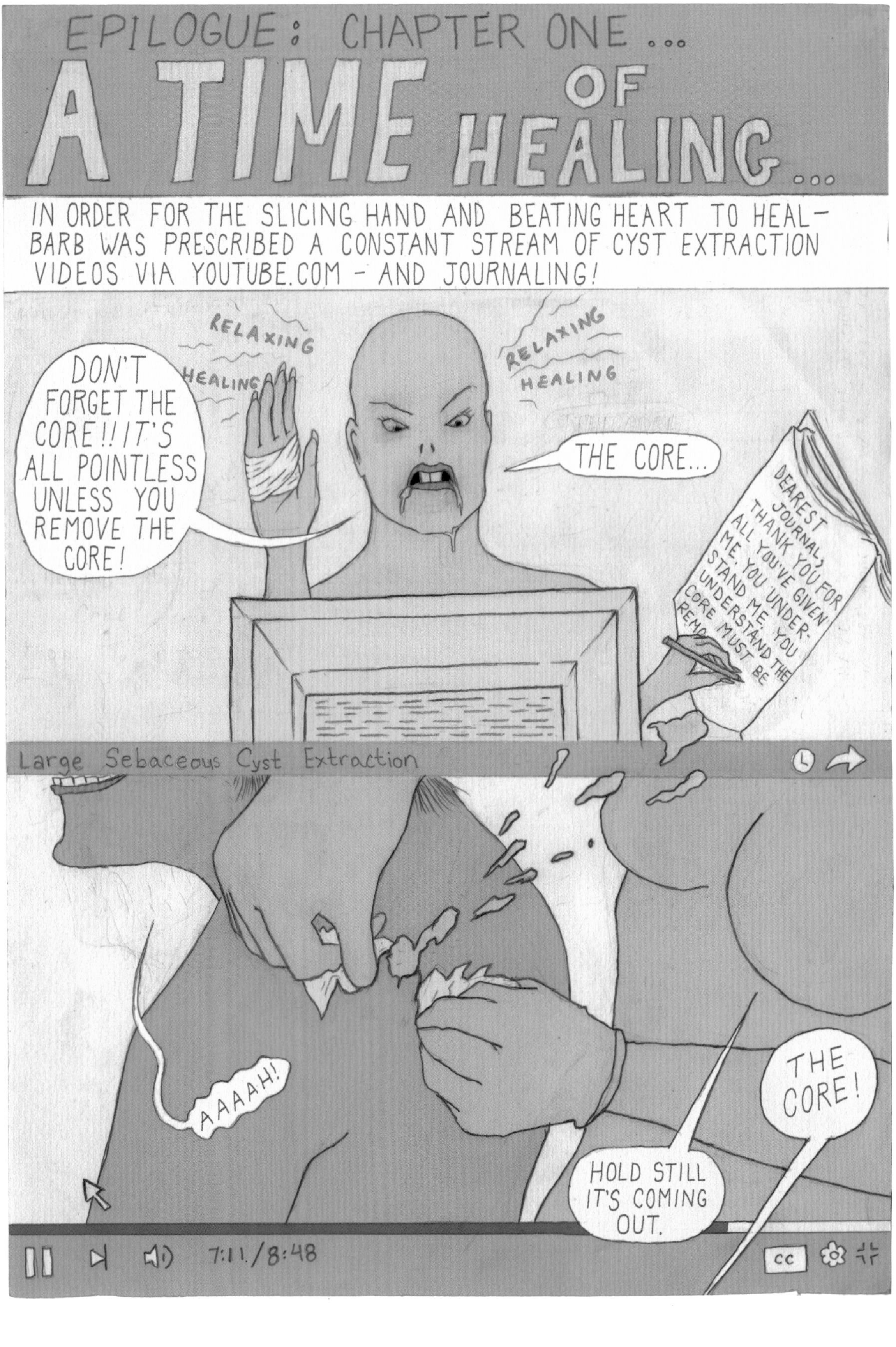
EPILOGUE: CHAPTER ONE...
A TIME OF HEALING...
IN ORDER FOR THE SLICING HAND AND BEATING HEART TO HEAL- BARB WAS PRESCRIBED A CONSTANT STREAM OF CYST EXTRACTION VIDEOS VIA YOUTUBE.COM - AND JOURNALING!
RELAXING
HEALING
RELAXING
HEALING
DON'T FORGET THE CORE!! IT'S ALL POINTLESS UNLESS YOU REMOVE THE CORE!
THE CORE...
DEAREST JOURNAL, THANK YOU FOR ALL YOU'VE GIVEN ME. YOU UNDER- STAND ME. YOU UNDERSTAND THE CORE MUST BE REMO
Large Sebaceous Cyst Extraction
AAAAH!
THE CORE!
HOLD STILL IT'S COMING OUT.
7:11/8:48
cc

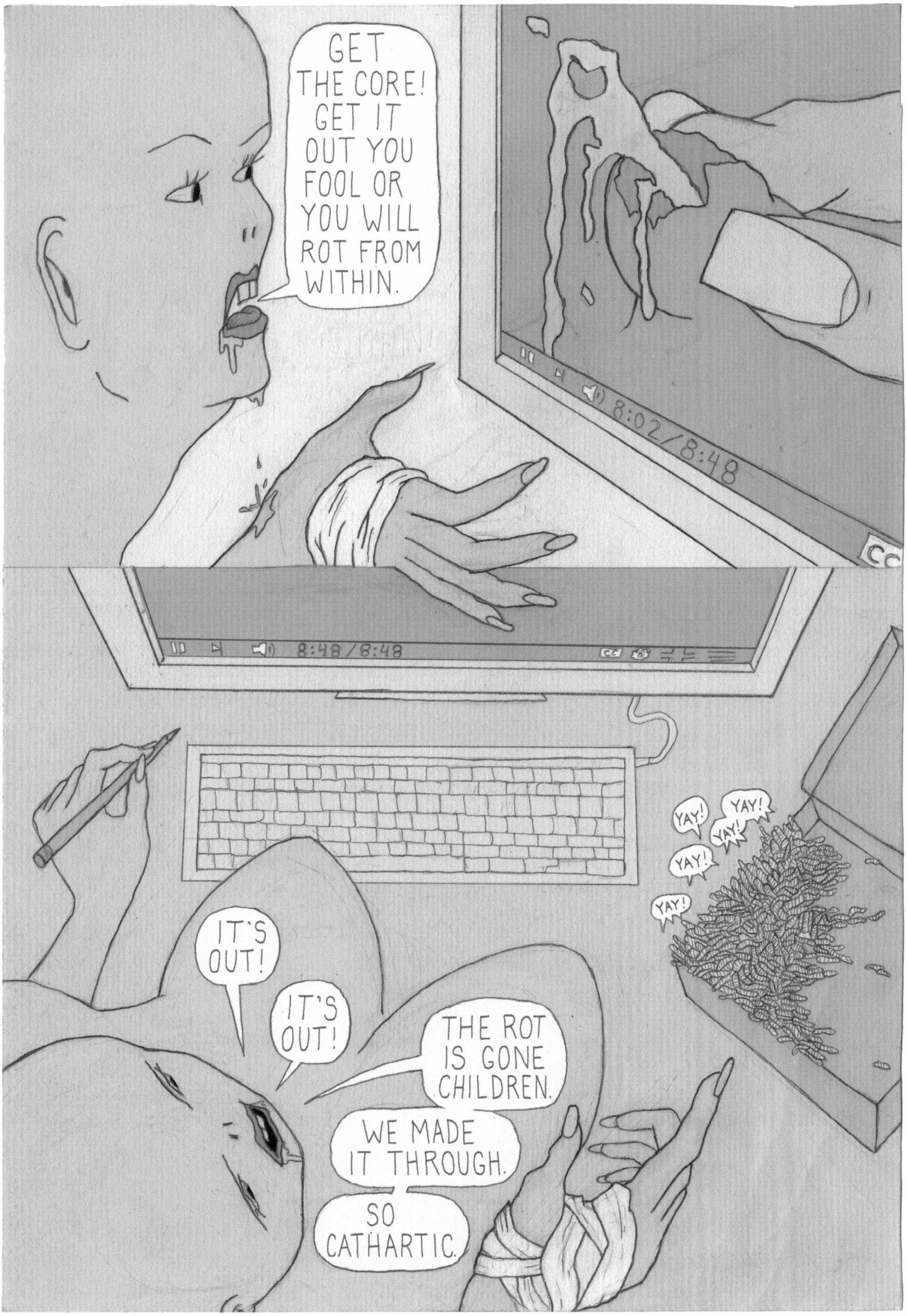
GET THE CORE! GET IT OUT YOU FOOL OR YOU WILL ROT FROM WITHIN.
8:02/8:48
8:48/8:48
YAY!
YAY!
YAY!
YAY!
YAY!
IT'S OUT!
IT'S OUT!
THE ROT IS GONE CHILDREN.
WE MADE IT THROUGH.
SO CATHARTIC.

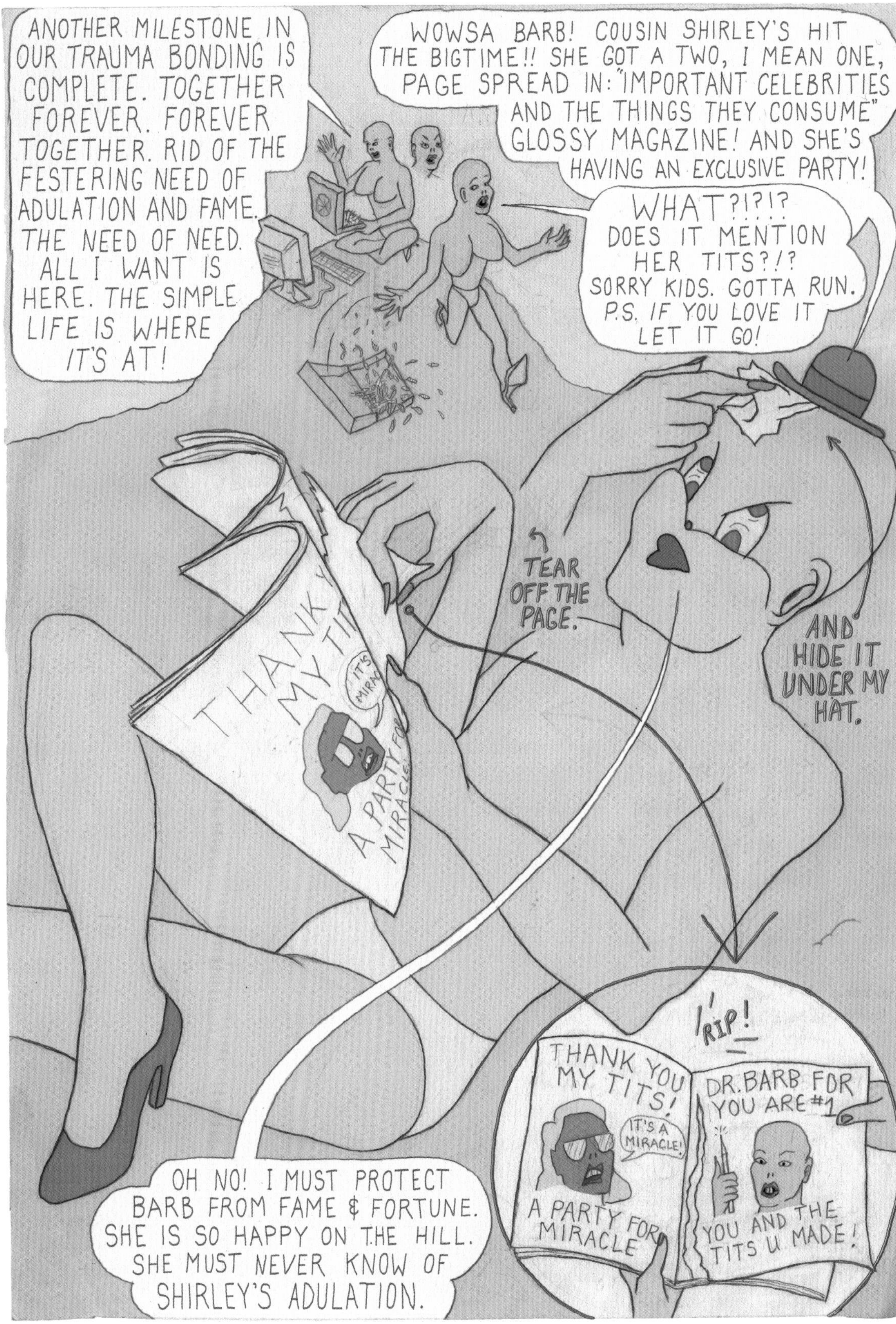
ANOTHER MILESTONE IN OUR TRAUMA BONDING IS COMPLETE. TOGETHER FOREVER. FOREVER TOGETHER. RID OF THE FESTERING NEED OF ADULATION AND FAME. THE NEED OF NEED. ALL I WANT IS HERE. THE SIMPLE LIFE IS WHERE IT'S AT!
WOWSA BARB! COUSIN SHIRLEY'S HIT THE BIGTIME!! SHE GOT A TWO, I MEAN ONE, PAGE SPREAD IN: "IMPORTANT CELEBRITIES AND THE THINGS THEY CONSUME" GLOSSY MAGAZINE! AND SHE'S HAVING AN EXCLUSIVE PARTY!
WHAT?!?!? DOES IT MENTION HER TITS?!? SORRY KIDS. GOTTA RUN. P.S. IF YOU LOVE IT LET IT GO!
TEAR OFF THE PAGE.
AND HIDE IT UNDER MY HAT.
IT'S A MIRAC
A PARTY FOR MIRACLE
RIP!
THANK YOU MY TITS!
IT'S A MIRACLE!
A PARTY FOR MIRACLE
DR. BARB FOR YOU ARE #1
YOU AND THE TITS U MADE!
OH NO! I MUST PROTECT BARB FROM FAME & FORTUNE. SHE IS SO HAPPY ON THE HILL. SHE MUST NEVER KNOW OF SHIRLEY'S ADULATION.

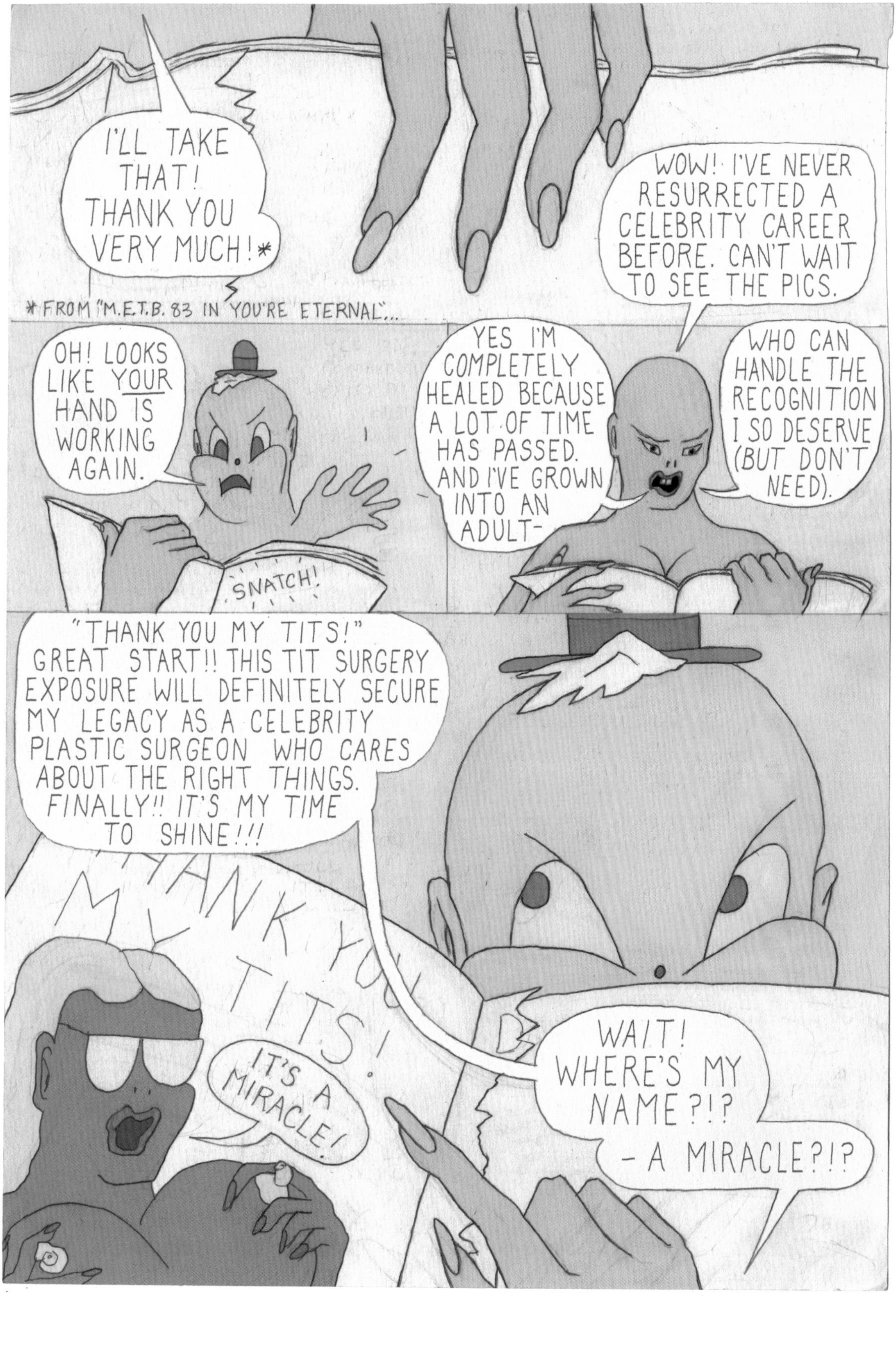
I'LL TAKE THAT! THANK YOU VERY MUCH!*
WOW! I'VE NEVER RESURRECTED A CELEBRITY CAREER BEFORE. CAN'T WAIT TO SEE THE PICS.
* FROM "M.E.T.B. 83 IN YOU'RE ETERNAL"...
OH! LOOKS LIKE YOUR HAND IS WORKING AGAIN.
YES I'M COMPLETELY HEALED BECAUSE A LOT OF TIME HAS PASSED. AND I'VE GROWN INTO AN ADULT-
WHO CAN HANDLE THE RECOGNITION I SO DESERVE (BUT DON'T NEED).
SNATCH!
"THANK YOU MY TITS!" GREAT START!! THIS TIT SURGERY EXPOSURE WILL DEFINITELY SECURE MY LEGACY AS A CELEBRITY PLASTIC SURGEON WHO CARES ABOUT THE RIGHT THINGS. FINALLY!! IT'S MY TIME TO SHINE!!!
THANK YOU MY TITS!
IT'S A MIRACLE!
WAIT! WHERE'S MY NAME?!? - A MIRACLE?!?

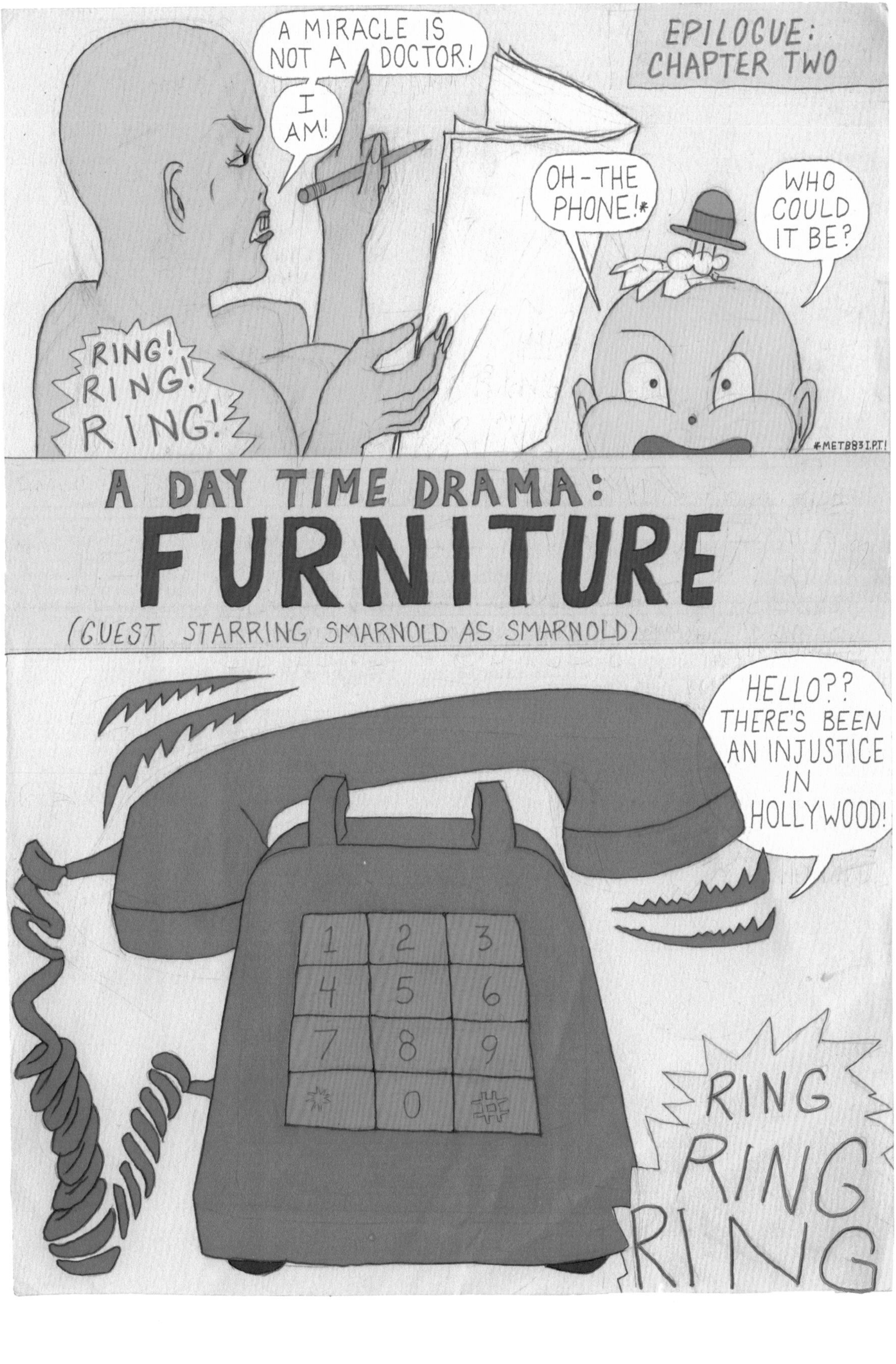
EPILOGUE: CHAPTER TWO
A MIRACLE IS NOT A DOCTOR!
I AM!
OH-THE PHONE!*
WHO COULD IT BE?
RING! RING! RING!
*METB83I.P.T!
A DAY TIME DRAMA:
FURNITURE
(GUEST STARRING SMARNOLD AS SMARNOLD)
HELLO?? THERE'S BEEN AN INJUSTICE IN HOLLYWOOD!
1 2 3 4 5 6 7 8 9 * 0 #
RING RING RING

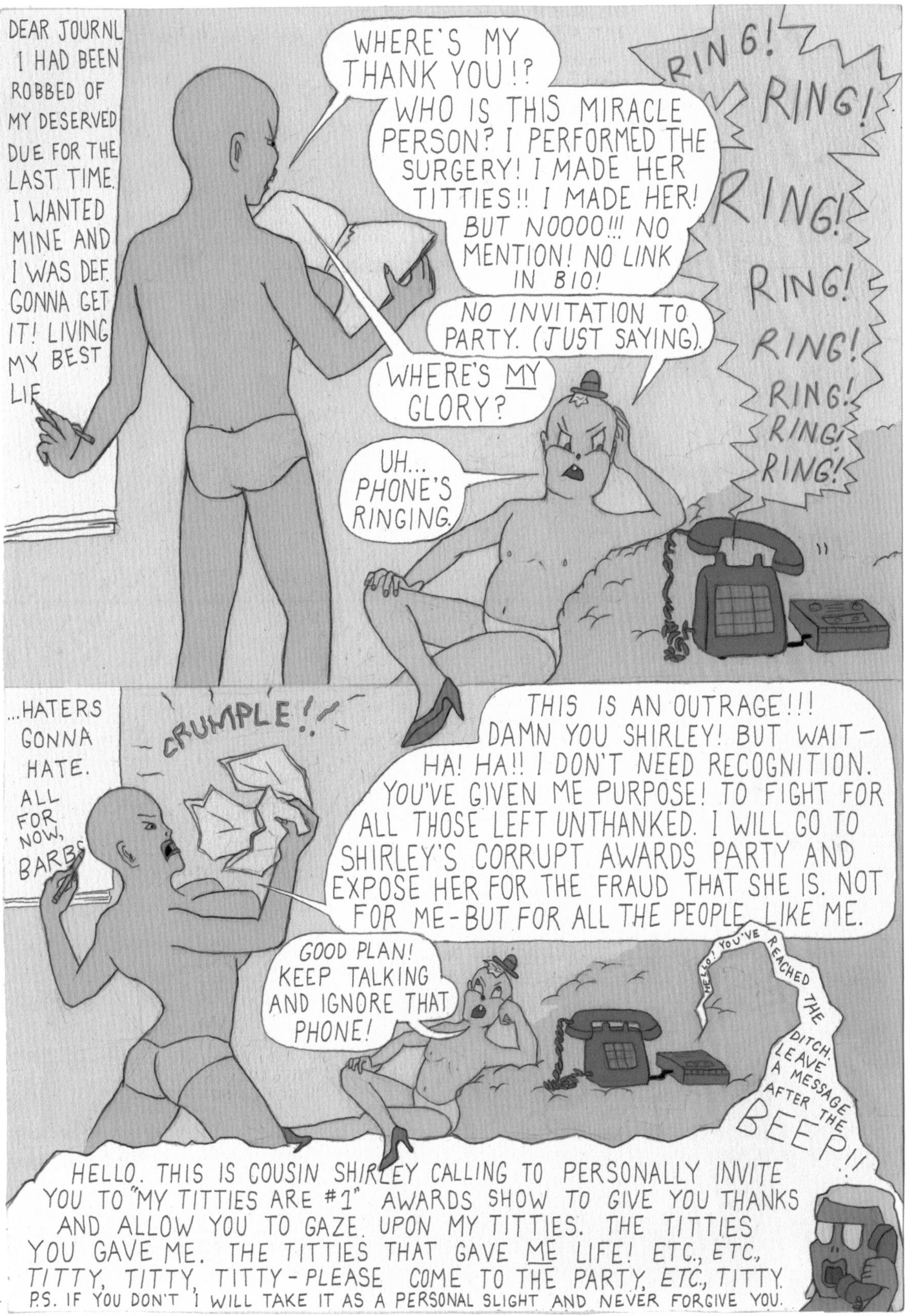
DEAR JOURNL I HAD BEEN ROBBED OF MY DESERVED DUE FOR THE LAST TIME. I WANTED MINE AND I WAS DEF. GONNA GET IT! LIVING MY BEST LIF
WHERE'S MY THANK YOU!?
WHO IS THIS MIRACLE PERSON? I PERFORMED THE SURGERY! I MADE HER TITTIES!! I MADE HER! BUT NOOOO!!! NO MENTION! NO LINK IN BIO!
NO INVITATION TO PARTY. (JUST SAYING).
WHERE'S MY GLORY?
RING! RING! RING! RING! RING! RING! RING! RING!
UH... PHONE'S RINGING.
...HATERS GONNA HATE. ALL FOR NOW, BARBS
CRUMPLE!!
THIS IS AN OUTRAGE!!! DAMN YOU SHIRLEY! BUT WAIT— HA! HA!! I DON'T NEED RECOGNITION. YOU'VE GIVEN ME PURPOSE! TO FIGHT FOR ALL THOSE LEFT UNTHANKED. I WILL GO TO SHIRLEY'S CORRUPT AWARDS PARTY AND EXPOSE HER FOR THE FRAUD THAT SHE IS. NOT FOR ME-BUT FOR ALL THE PEOPLE LIKE ME.
GOOD PLAN! KEEP TALKING AND IGNORE THAT PHONE!
HELLO! YOU'VE REACHED THE DITCH. LEAVE A MESSAGE AFTER THE BEEP!!
HELLO. THIS IS COUSIN SHIRLEY CALLING TO PERSONALLY INVITE YOU TO "MY TITTIES ARE #1" AWARDS SHOW TO GIVE YOU THANKS AND ALLOW YOU TO GAZE UPON MY TITTIES. THE TITTIES YOU GAVE ME. THE TITTIES THAT GAVE ME LIFE! ETC., ETC., TITTY, TITTY, TITTY-PLEASE COME TO THE PARTY, ETC., TITTY.
P.S. IF YOU DON'T I WILL TAKE IT AS A PERSONAL SLIGHT AND NEVER FORGIVE YOU.

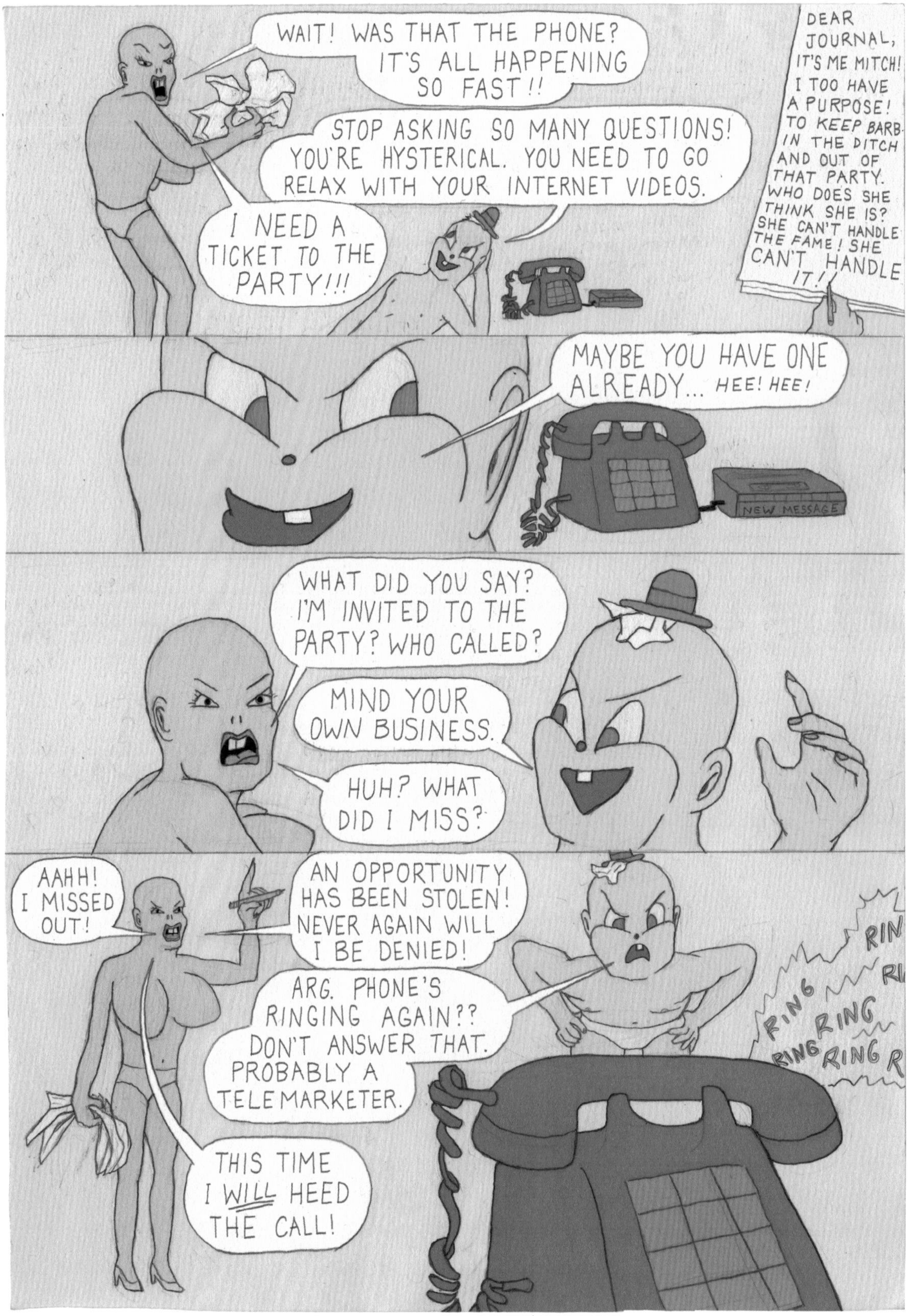
WAIT! WAS THAT THE PHONE? IT'S ALL HAPPENING SO FAST!!
STOP ASKING SO MANY QUESTIONS! YOU'RE HYSTERICAL. YOU NEED TO GO RELAX WITH YOUR INTERNET VIDEOS.
I NEED A TICKET TO THE PARTY!!!
DEAR JOURNAL, IT'S ME MITCH! I TOO HAVE A PURPOSE! TO KEEP BARB IN THE DITCH AND OUT OF THAT PARTY. WHO DOES SHE THINK SHE IS? SHE CAN'T HANDLE THE FAME! SHE CAN'T HANDLE IT!!
MAYBE YOU HAVE ONE ALREADY... HEE! HEE!
NEW MESSAGE
WHAT DID YOU SAY? I'M INVITED TO THE PARTY? WHO CALLED?
MIND YOUR OWN BUSINESS.
HUH? WHAT DID I MISS?
AAHH! I MISSED OUT!
AN OPPORTUNITY HAS BEEN STOLEN! NEVER AGAIN WILL I BE DENIED!
ARG. PHONE'S RINGING AGAIN?? DON'T ANSWER THAT. PROBABLY A TELEMARKETER.
THIS TIME I WILL HEED THE CALL!
RING RING RING RING RING

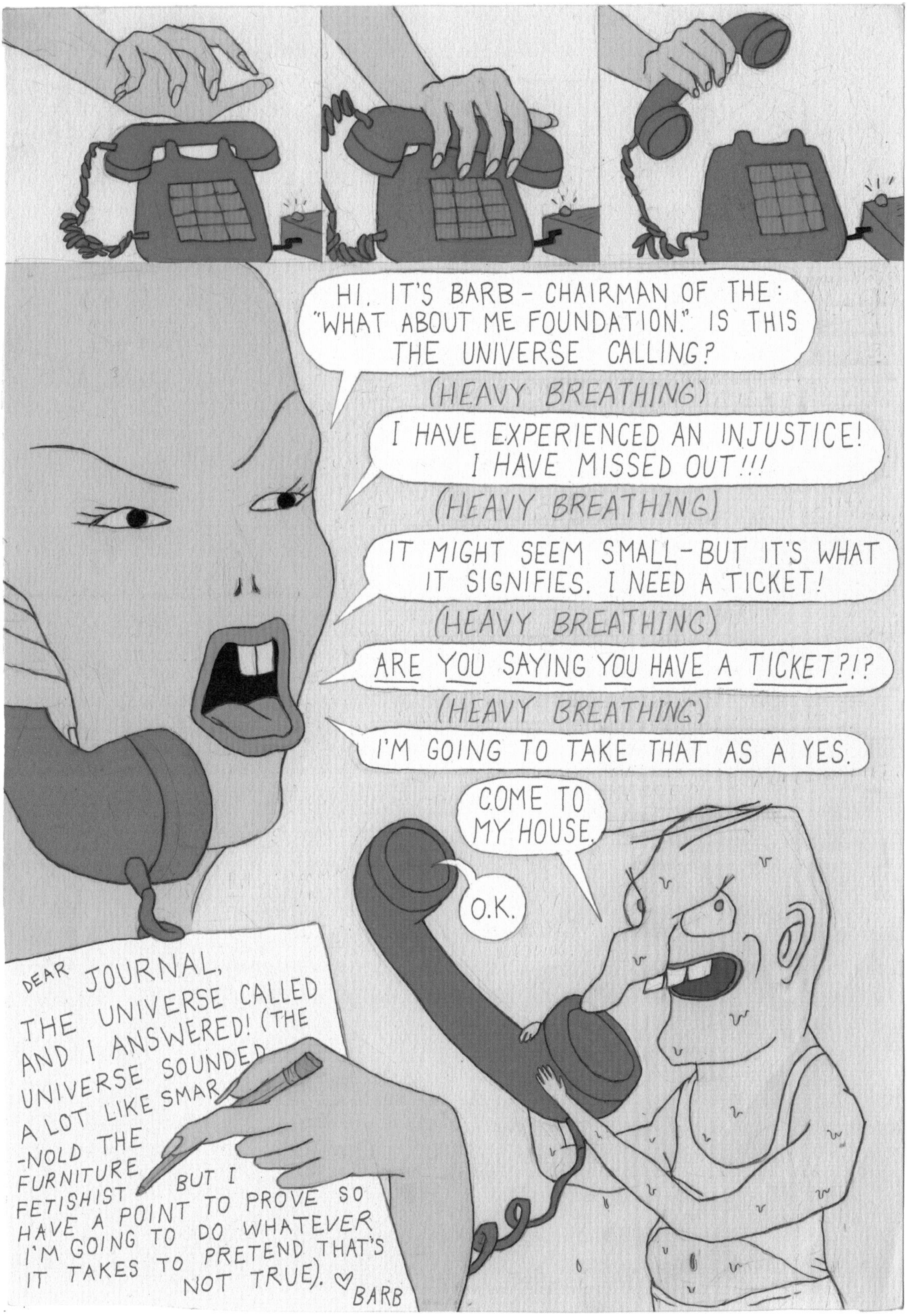
HI. IT'S BARB - CHAIRMAN OF THE: "WHAT ABOUT ME FOUNDATION." IS THIS THE UNIVERSE CALLING?
(HEAVY BREATHING)
I HAVE EXPERIENCED AN INJUSTICE! I HAVE MISSED OUT!!!
(HEAVY BREATHING)
IT MIGHT SEEM SMALL - BUT IT'S WHAT IT SIGNIFIES. I NEED A TICKET!
(HEAVY BREATHING)
ARE YOU SAYING YOU HAVE A TICKET?!?
(HEAVY BREATHING)
I'M GOING TO TAKE THAT AS A YES.
COME TO MY HOUSE.
O.K.
DEAR JOURNAL, THE UNIVERSE CALLED AND I ANSWERED! (THE UNIVERSE SOUNDED A LOT LIKE SMAR -NOLD THE FURNITURE FETISHIST BUT I HAVE A POINT TO PROVE SO I'M GOING TO DO WHATEVER IT TAKES TO PRETEND THAT'S NOT TRUE). ♡ BARB

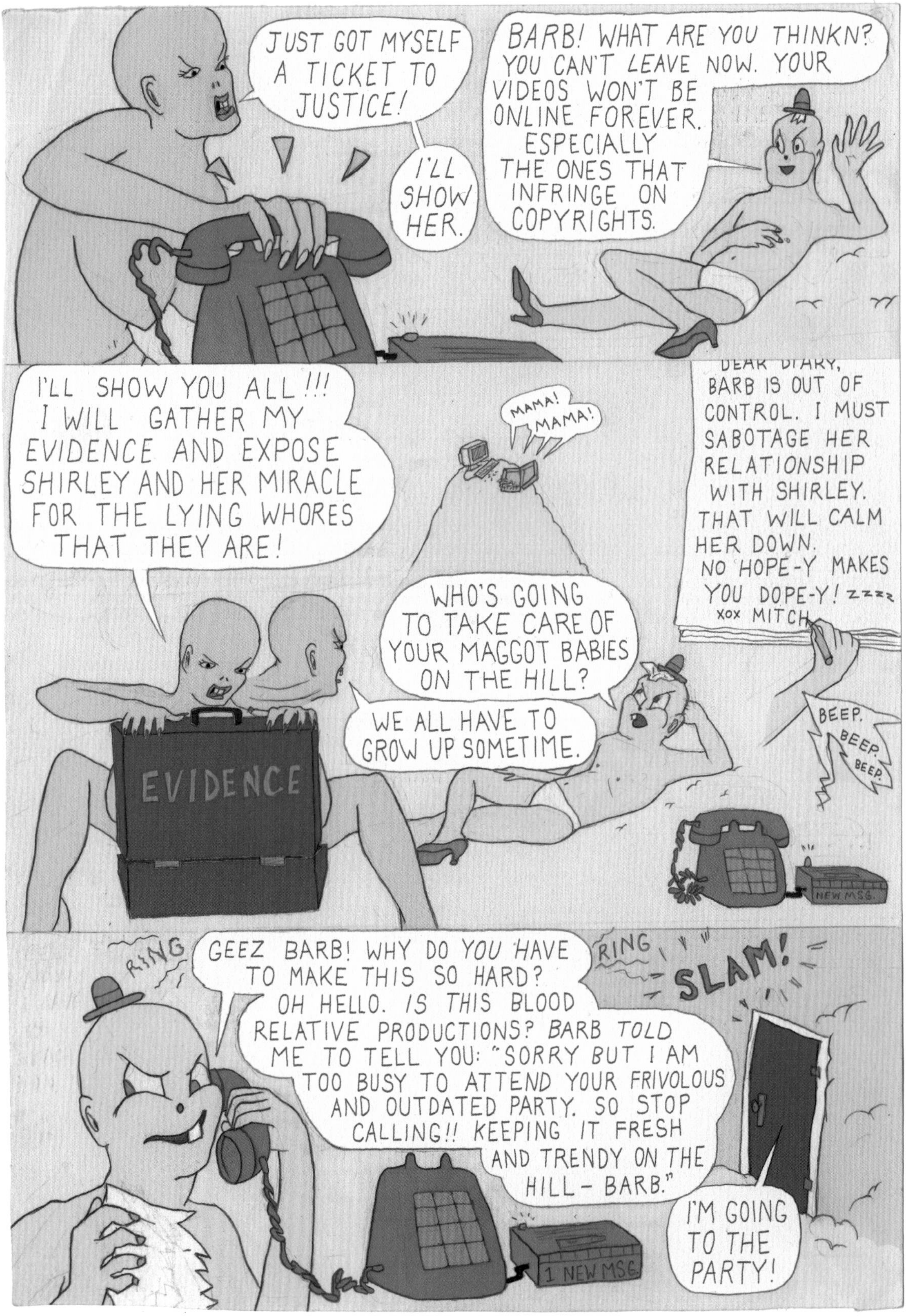

JUST GOT MYSELF A TICKET TO JUSTICE!
I'LL SHOW HER.
BARB! WHAT ARE YOU THINKN? YOU CAN'T LEAVE NOW. YOUR VIDEOS WON'T BE ONLINE FOREVER. ESPECIALLY THE ONES THAT INFRINGE ON COPYRIGHTS.
I'LL SHOW YOU ALL!!! I WILL GATHER MY EVIDENCE AND EXPOSE SHIRLEY AND HER MIRACLE FOR THE LYING WHORES THAT THEY ARE!
MAMA! MAMA!
DEAR DIARY, BARB IS OUT OF CONTROL. I MUST SABOTAGE HER RELATIONSHIP WITH SHIRLEY. THAT WILL CALM HER DOWN. NO HOPE-Y MAKES YOU DOPE-Y! zzzz
XOX MITCH
WHO'S GOING TO TAKE CARE OF YOUR MAGGOT BABIES ON THE HILL?
WE ALL HAVE TO GROW UP SOMETIME.
EVIDENCE
BEEP. BEEP. BEEP.
NEW MSG.
RING
GEEZ BARB! WHY DO YOU HAVE TO MAKE THIS SO HARD? OH HELLO. IS THIS BLOOD RELATIVE PRODUCTIONS? BARB TOLD ME TO TELL YOU: "SORRY BUT I AM TOO BUSY TO ATTEND YOUR FRIVOLOUS AND OUTDATED PARTY. SO STOP CALLING!! KEEPING IT FRESH AND TRENDY ON THE HILL - BARB."
RING
SLAM!
1 NEW MSG.
I'M GOING TO THE PARTY!

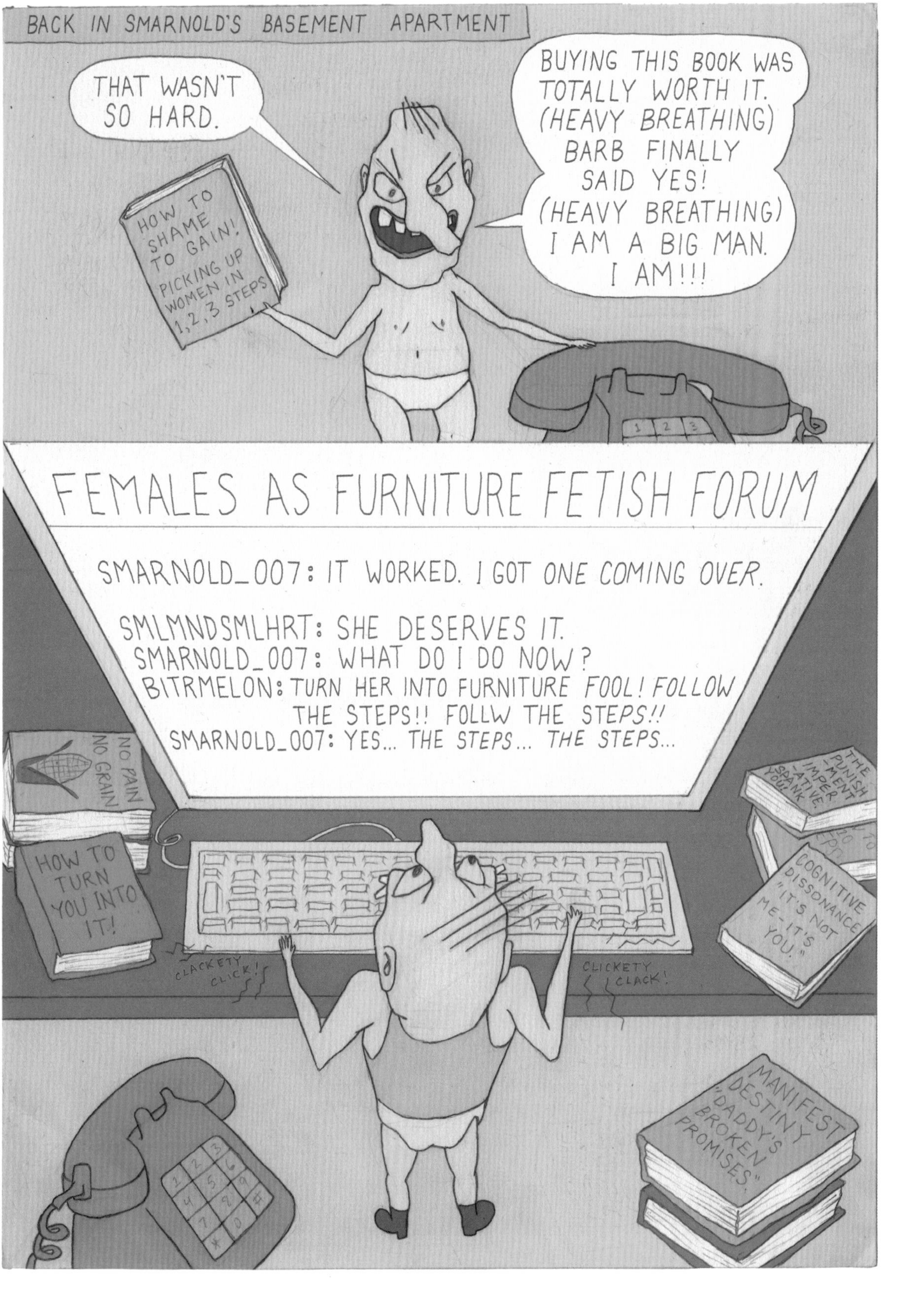
BACK IN SMARNOLD'S BASEMENT APARTMENT
THAT WASN'T SO HARD.
HOW TO SHAME TO GAIN! PICKING UP WOMEN IN 1,2,3 STEPS
BUYING THIS BOOK WAS TOTALLY WORTH IT. (HEAVY BREATHING) BARB FINALLY SAID YES! (HEAVY BREATHING) I AM A BIG MAN. I AM!!!
FEMALES AS FURNITURE FETISH FORUM
SMARNOLD_007: IT WORKED. I GOT ONE COMING OVER.
SMLMNDSMLHRT: SHE DESERVES IT.
SMARNOLD_007: WHAT DO I DO NOW?
BITRMELON: TURN HER INTO FURNITURE FOOL! FOLLOW THE STEPS!! FOLLW THE STEPS!!
SMARNOLD_007: YES... THE STEPS... THE STEPS...
NO PAIN NO GRAIN
HOW TO TURN YOU INTO IT!
THE PUNISH-MENT IMPER-ATIVE. SPANK YOU!
COGNITIVE DISSONANCE "IT'S NOT ME-IT'S YOU."
CLACKETY CLICK!
CLICKETY CLACK!
MANIFEST DESTINY "DADDY'S BROKEN PROMISES"

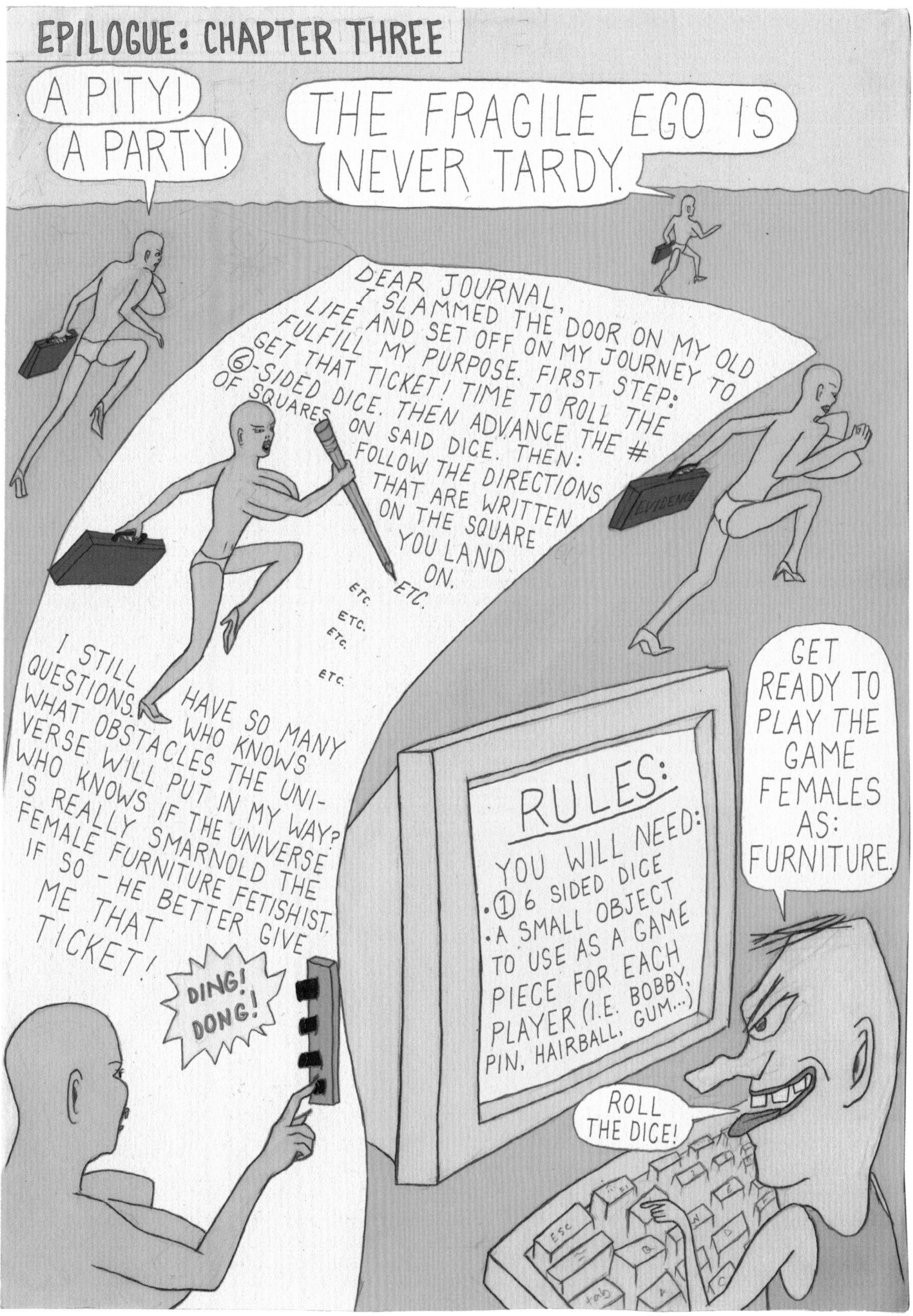
EPILOGUE: CHAPTER THREE
A PITY! A PARTY!
THE FRAGILE EGO IS NEVER TARDY.
DEAR JOURNAL, I SLAMMED THE DOOR ON MY OLD LIFE AND SET OFF ON MY JOURNEY TO FULFILL MY PURPOSE. FIRST STEP: GET THAT TICKET! TIME TO ROLL THE ⑥-SIDED DICE. THEN ADVANCE THE # OF SQUARES ON SAID DICE. THEN: FOLLOW THE DIRECTIONS THAT ARE WRITTEN ON THE SQUARE YOU LAND ON. ETC. ETC. ETC. ETC. ETC.
I STILL HAVE SO MANY QUESTIONS. WHO KNOWS WHAT OBSTACLES THE UNIVERSE WILL PUT IN MY WAY? WHO KNOWS IF THE UNIVERSE IS REALLY SMARNOLD THE FEMALE FURNITURE FETISHIST. IF SO - HE BETTER GIVE ME THAT TICKET!
EVIDENCE
GET READY TO PLAY THE GAME FEMALES AS: FURNITURE.
RULES:
YOU WILL NEED:
• ① 6 SIDED DICE
• A SMALL OBJECT TO USE AS A GAME PIECE FOR EACH PLAYER (I.E. BOBBY PIN, HAIRBALL, GUM...)
DING! DONG!
ROLL THE DICE!

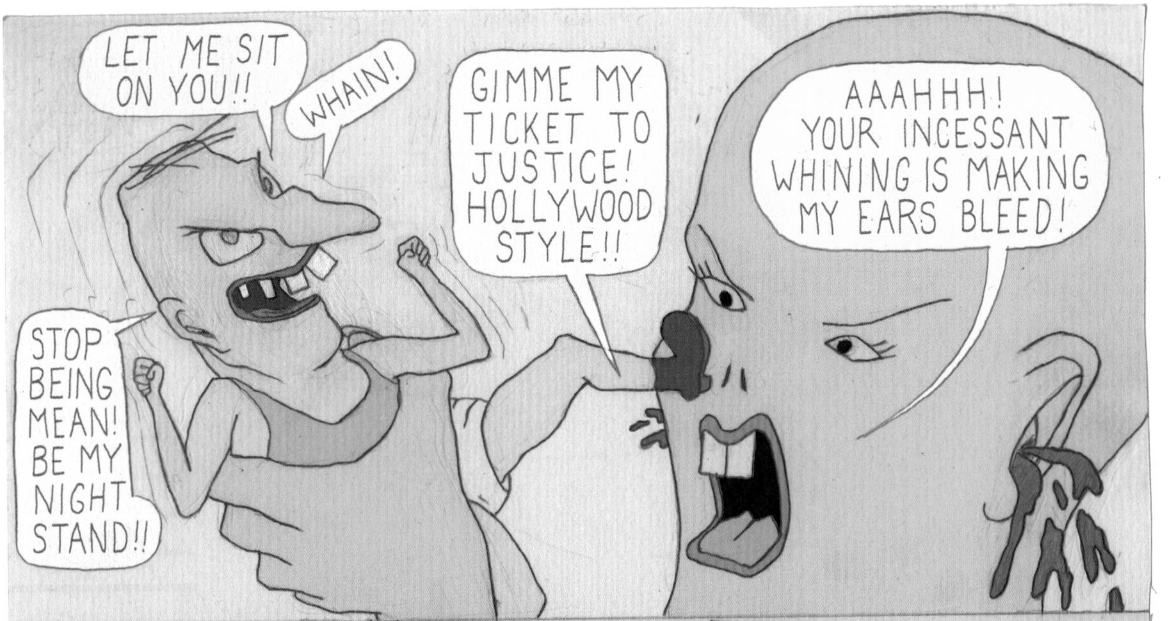
LET ME SIT ON YOU!!
WHAIN!
STOP BEING MEAN! BE MY NIGHT STAND!!
GIMME MY TICKET TO JUSTICE! HOLLYWOOD STYLE!!
AAAHHH! YOUR INCESSANT WHINING IS MAKING MY EARS BLEED!

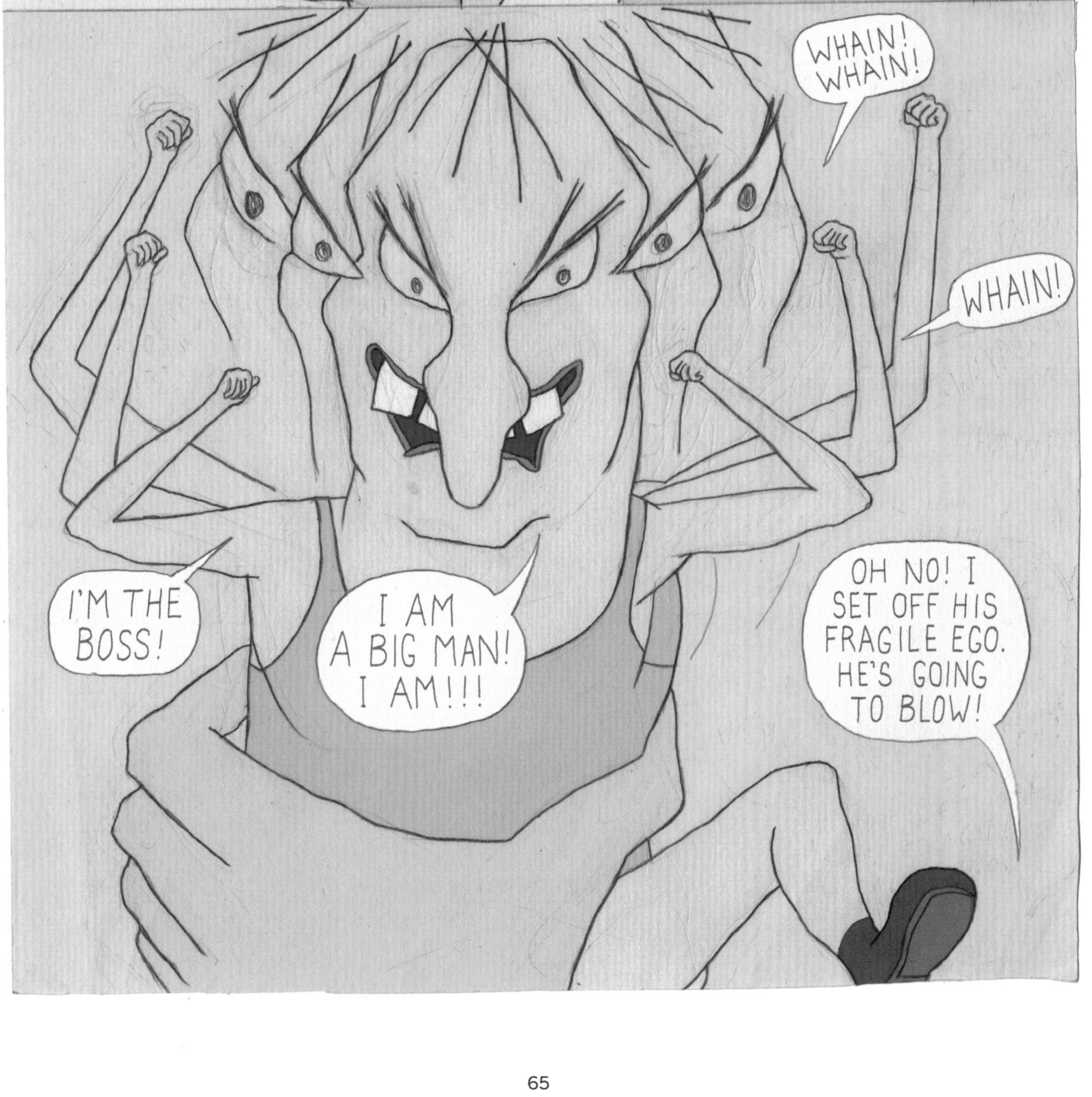
WHAIN! WHAIN!
WHAIN!
I'M THE BOSS!
I AM A BIG MAN! I AM!!!
OH NO! I SET OFF HIS FRAGILE EGO. HE'S GOING TO BLOW!

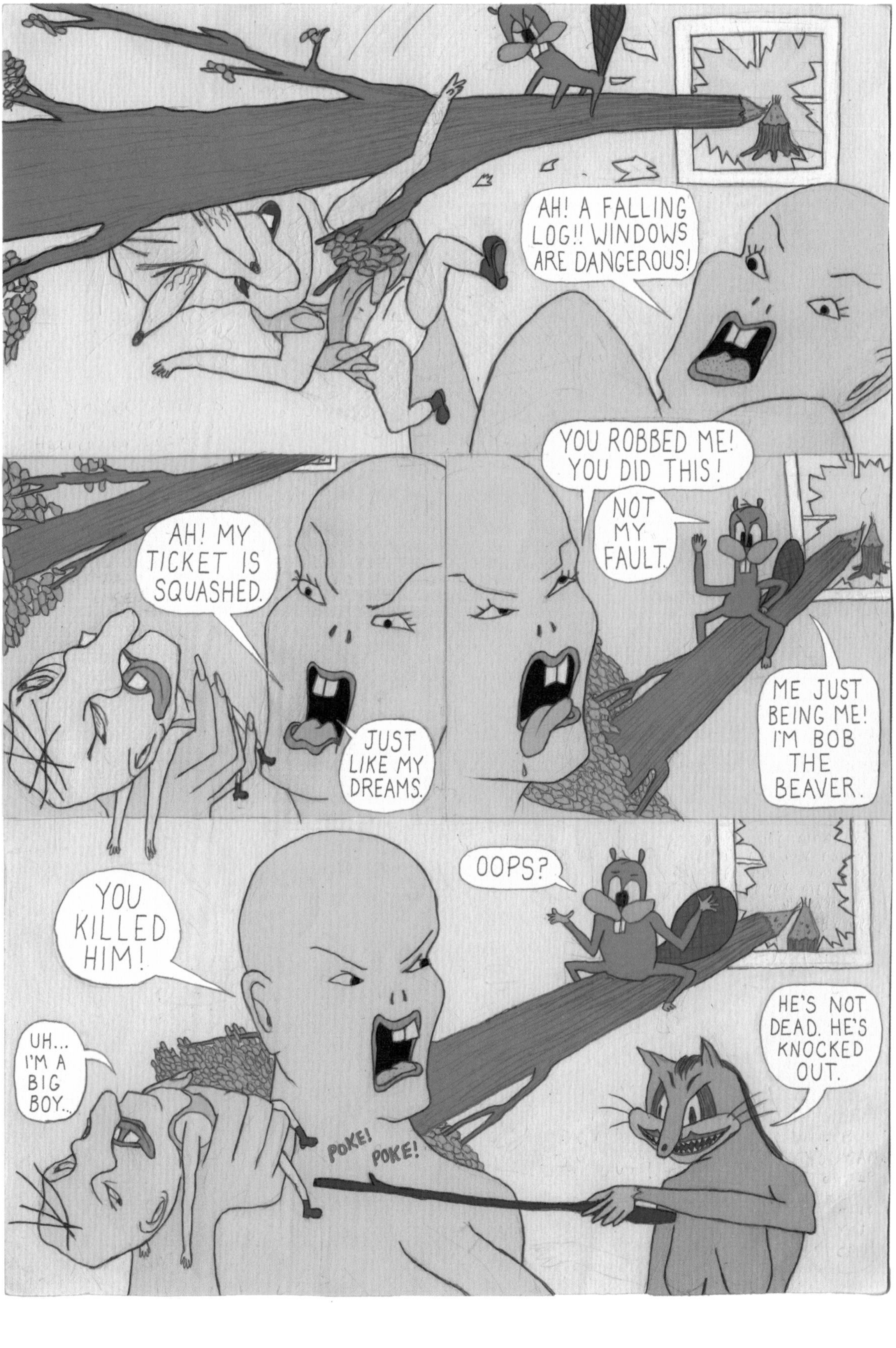
AH! A FALLING LOG!! WINDOWS ARE DANGEROUS!
AH! MY TICKET IS SQUASHED.
JUST LIKE MY DREAMS.
YOU ROBBED ME! YOU DID THIS!
NOT MY FAULT.
ME JUST BEING ME! I'M BOB THE BEAVER.
YOU KILLED HIM!
OOPS?
UH... I'M A BIG BOY...
HE'S NOT DEAD. HE'S KNOCKED OUT.
POKE! POKE!

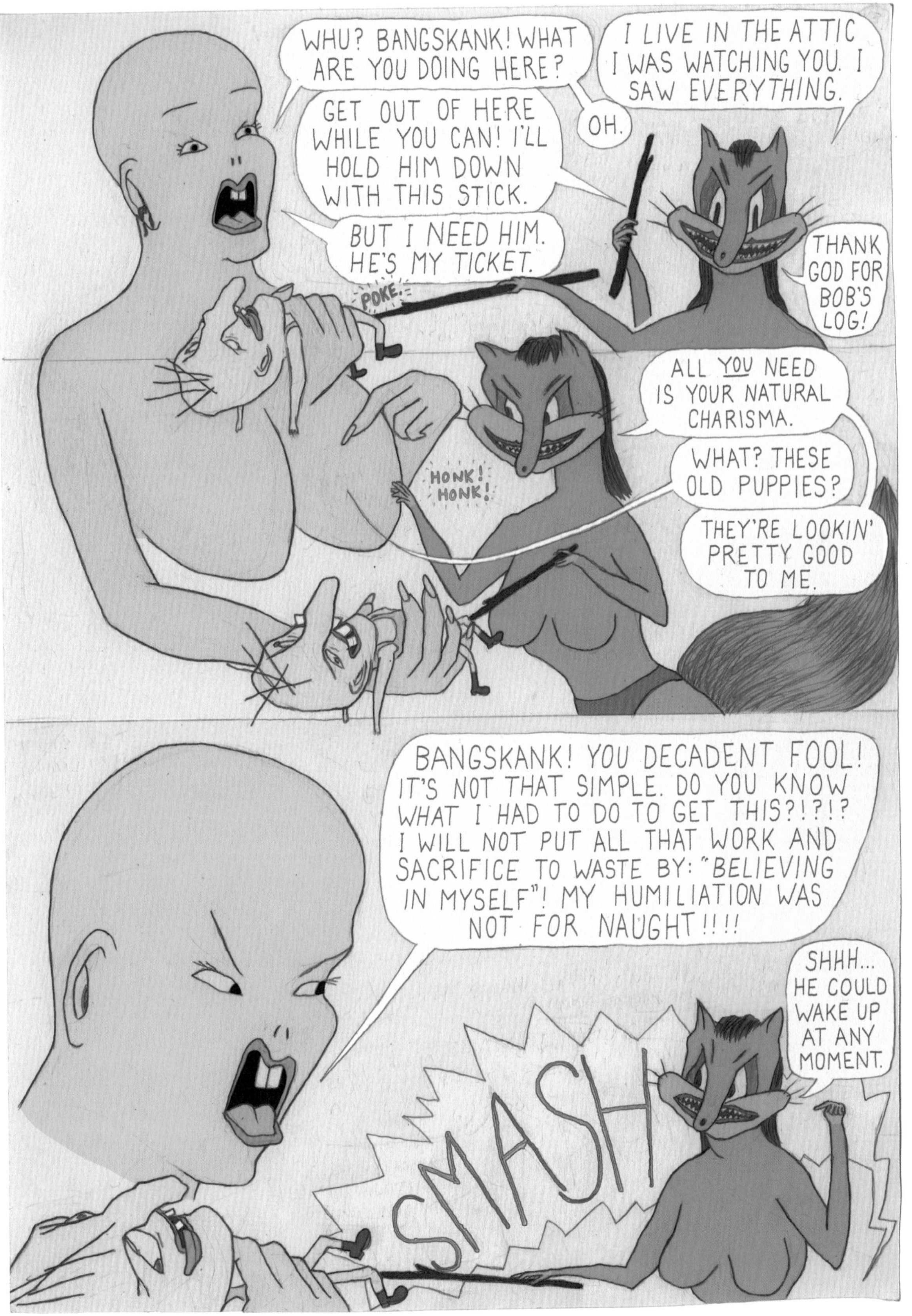
WHU? BANGSKANK! WHAT ARE YOU DOING HERE?
I LIVE IN THE ATTIC I WAS WATCHING YOU. I SAW EVERYTHING.
OH.
GET OUT OF HERE WHILE YOU CAN! I'LL HOLD HIM DOWN WITH THIS STICK.
BUT I NEED HIM. HE'S MY TICKET.
POKE
THANK GOD FOR BOB'S LOG!
ALL YOU NEED IS YOUR NATURAL CHARISMA.
WHAT? THESE OLD PUPPIES?
HONK! HONK!
THEY'RE LOOKIN' PRETTY GOOD TO ME.
BANGSKANK! YOU DECADENT FOOL! IT'S NOT THAT SIMPLE. DO YOU KNOW WHAT I HAD TO DO TO GET THIS?!?!? I WILL NOT PUT ALL THAT WORK AND SACRIFICE TO WASTE BY: "BELIEVING IN MYSELF"! MY HUMILIATION WAS NOT FOR NAUGHT!!!!
SHHH... HE COULD WAKE UP AT ANY MOMENT.
SMASH

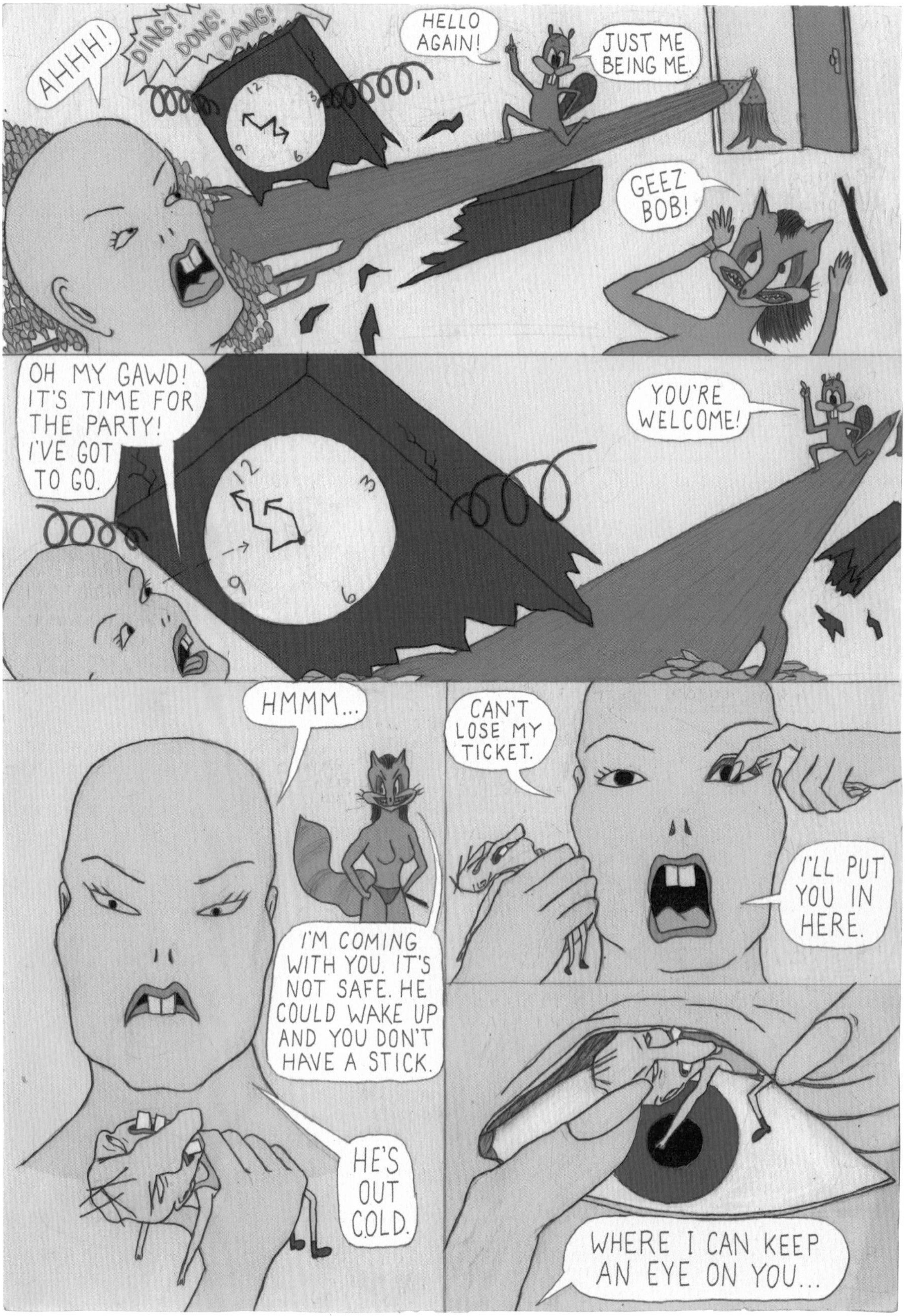
AHHH!
DING! DONG! DANG!
HELLO AGAIN!
JUST ME BEING ME.
GEEZ BOB!
OH MY GAWD! IT'S TIME FOR THE PARTY! I'VE GOT TO GO.
YOU'RE WELCOME!
HMMM...
I'M COMING WITH YOU. IT'S NOT SAFE. HE COULD WAKE UP AND YOU DON'T HAVE A STICK.
HE'S OUT COLD.
CAN'T LOSE MY TICKET.
I'LL PUT YOU IN HERE.
WHERE I CAN KEEP AN EYE ON YOU...

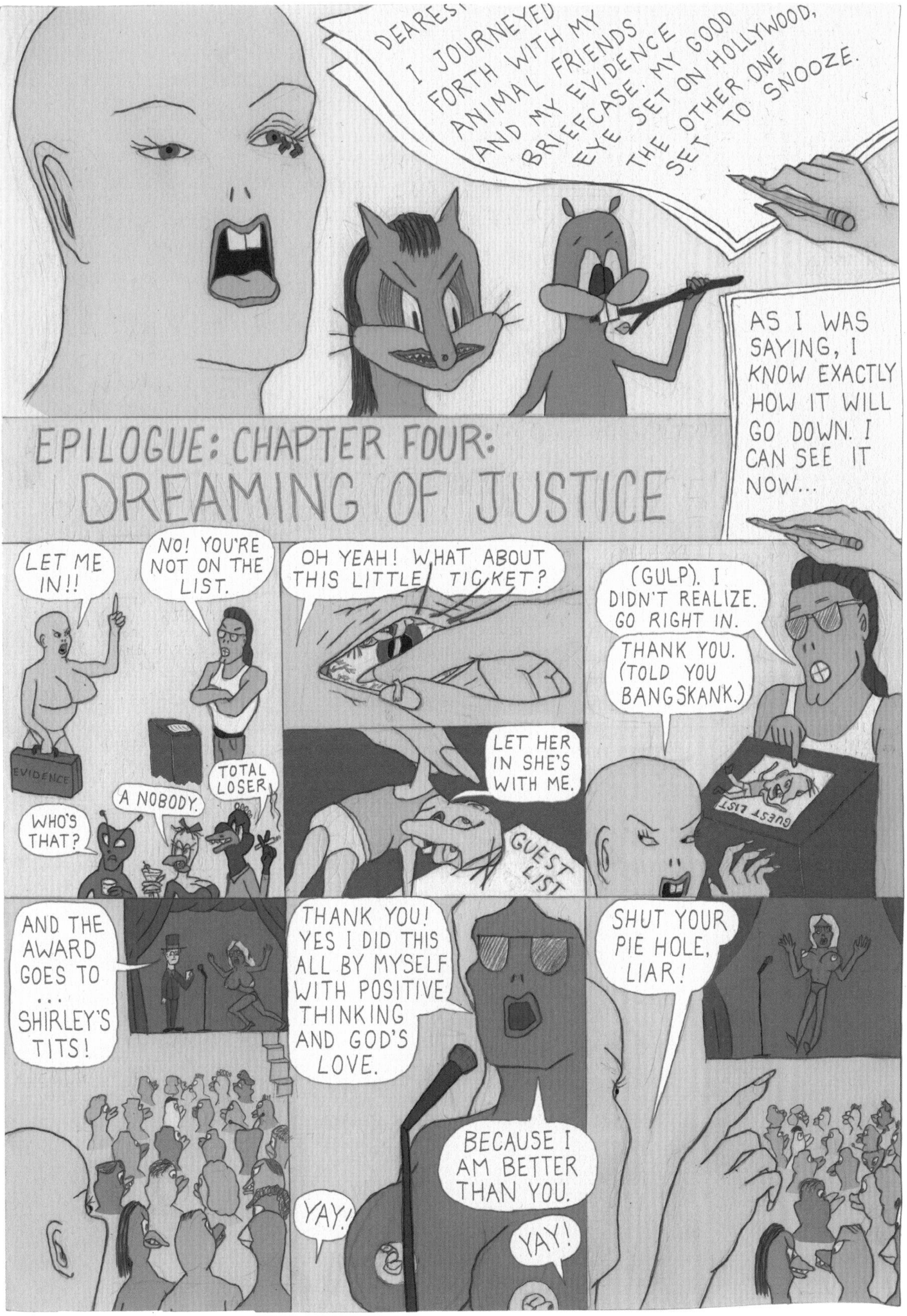
DEAREST
I JOURNEYED FORTH WITH MY ANIMAL FRIENDS AND MY EVIDENCE BRIEFCASE. MY GOOD EYE SET ON HOLLYWOOD, THE OTHER ONE SET TO SNOOZE.
AS I WAS SAYING, I KNOW EXACTLY HOW IT WILL GO DOWN. I CAN SEE IT NOW...
EPILOGUE: CHAPTER FOUR:
DREAMING OF JUSTICE
LET ME IN!!
NO! YOU'RE NOT ON THE LIST.
EVIDENCE
TOTAL LOSER
A NOBODY.
WHO'S THAT?
OH YEAH! WHAT ABOUT THIS LITTLE TICKET?
LET HER IN SHE'S WITH ME.
GUEST LIST
(GULP). I DIDN'T REALIZE. GO RIGHT IN.
THANK YOU. (TOLD YOU BANGSKANK.)
GUEST LIST
AND THE AWARD GOES TO ... SHIRLEY'S TITS!
THANK YOU! YES I DID THIS ALL BY MYSELF WITH POSITIVE THINKING AND GOD'S LOVE.
BECAUSE I AM BETTER THAN YOU.
YAY!
YAY!
SHUT YOUR PIE HOLE, LIAR!

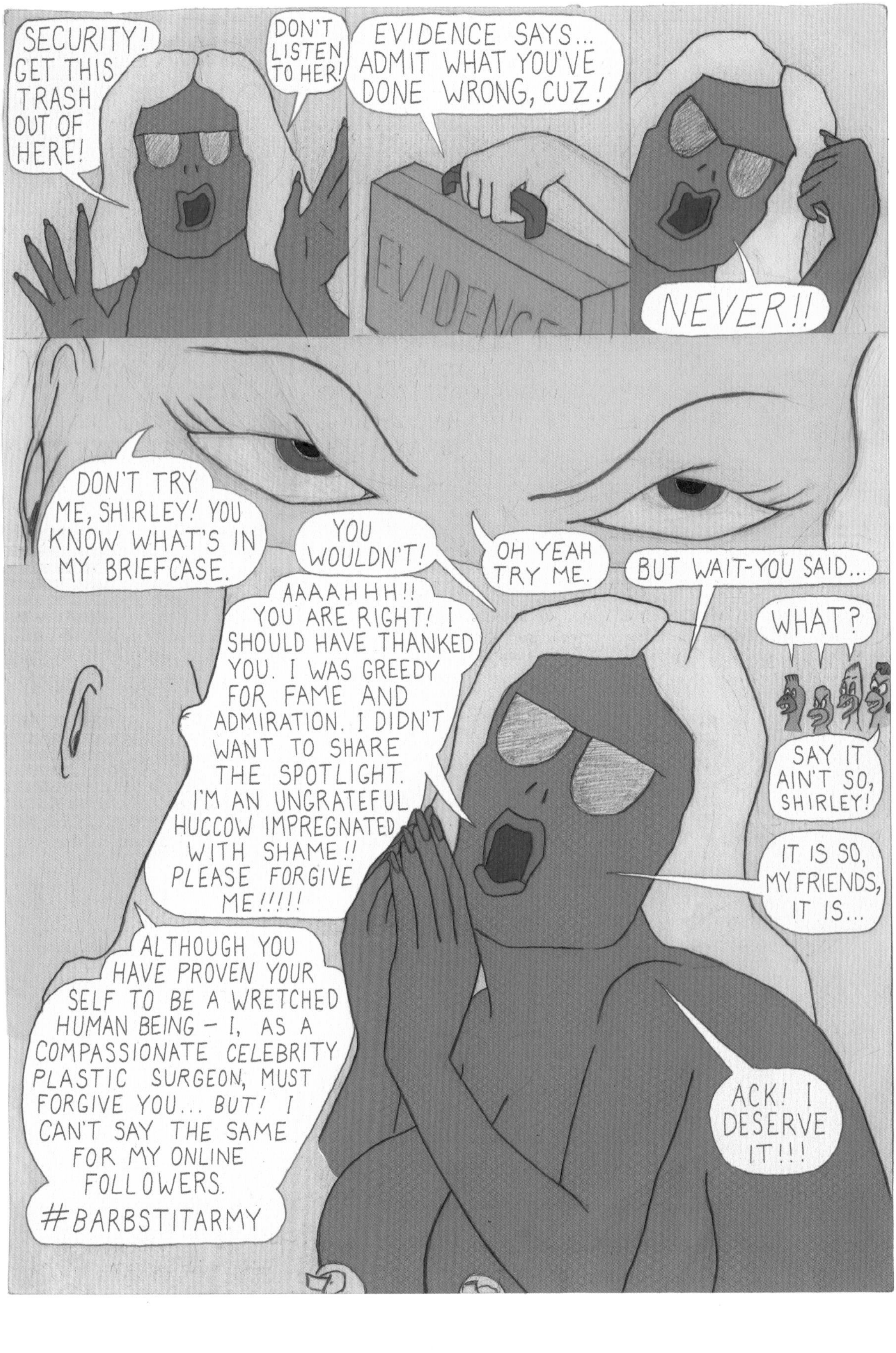
SECURITY! GET THIS TRASH OUT OF HERE!
DON'T LISTEN TO HER!
EVIDENCE SAYS... ADMIT WHAT YOU'VE DONE WRONG, CUZ!
EVIDENCE
NEVER!!
DON'T TRY ME, SHIRLEY! YOU KNOW WHAT'S IN MY BRIEFCASE.
YOU WOULDN'T!
OH YEAH TRY ME.
BUT WAIT-YOU SAID...
AAAAHHH!! YOU ARE RIGHT! I SHOULD HAVE THANKED YOU. I WAS GREEDY FOR FAME AND ADMIRATION. I DIDN'T WANT TO SHARE THE SPOTLIGHT. I'M AN UNGRATEFUL HUCCOW IMPREGNATED WITH SHAME!! PLEASE FORGIVE ME!!!!!
WHAT?
SAY IT AIN'T SO, SHIRLEY!
IT IS SO, MY FRIENDS, IT IS...
ALTHOUGH YOU HAVE PROVEN YOUR SELF TO BE A WRETCHED HUMAN BEING – I, AS A COMPASSIONATE CELEBRITY PLASTIC SURGEON, MUST FORGIVE YOU... BUT! I CAN'T SAY THE SAME FOR MY ONLINE FOLLOWERS.
#BARBSTITARMY
ACK! I DESERVE IT!!!

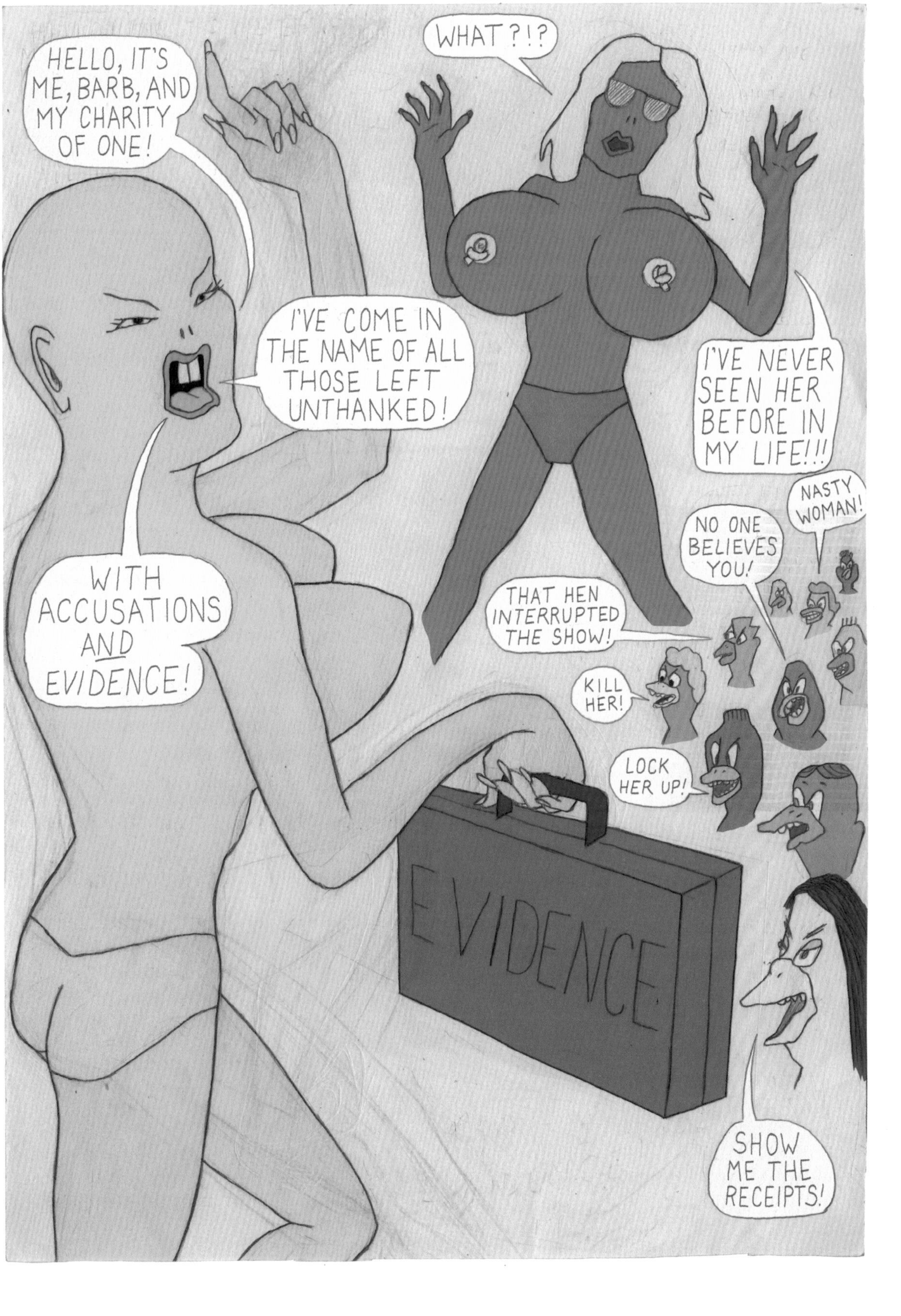
HELLO, IT'S ME, BARB, AND MY CHARITY OF ONE!
WHAT?!?
I'VE COME IN THE NAME OF ALL THOSE LEFT UNTHANKED!
WITH ACCUSATIONS AND EVIDENCE!
I'VE NEVER SEEN HER BEFORE IN MY LIFE!!!
NASTY WOMAN!
NO ONE BELIEVES YOU!
THAT HEN INTERRUPTED THE SHOW!
KILL HER!
LOCK HER UP!
EVIDENCE
SHOW ME THE RECEIPTS!

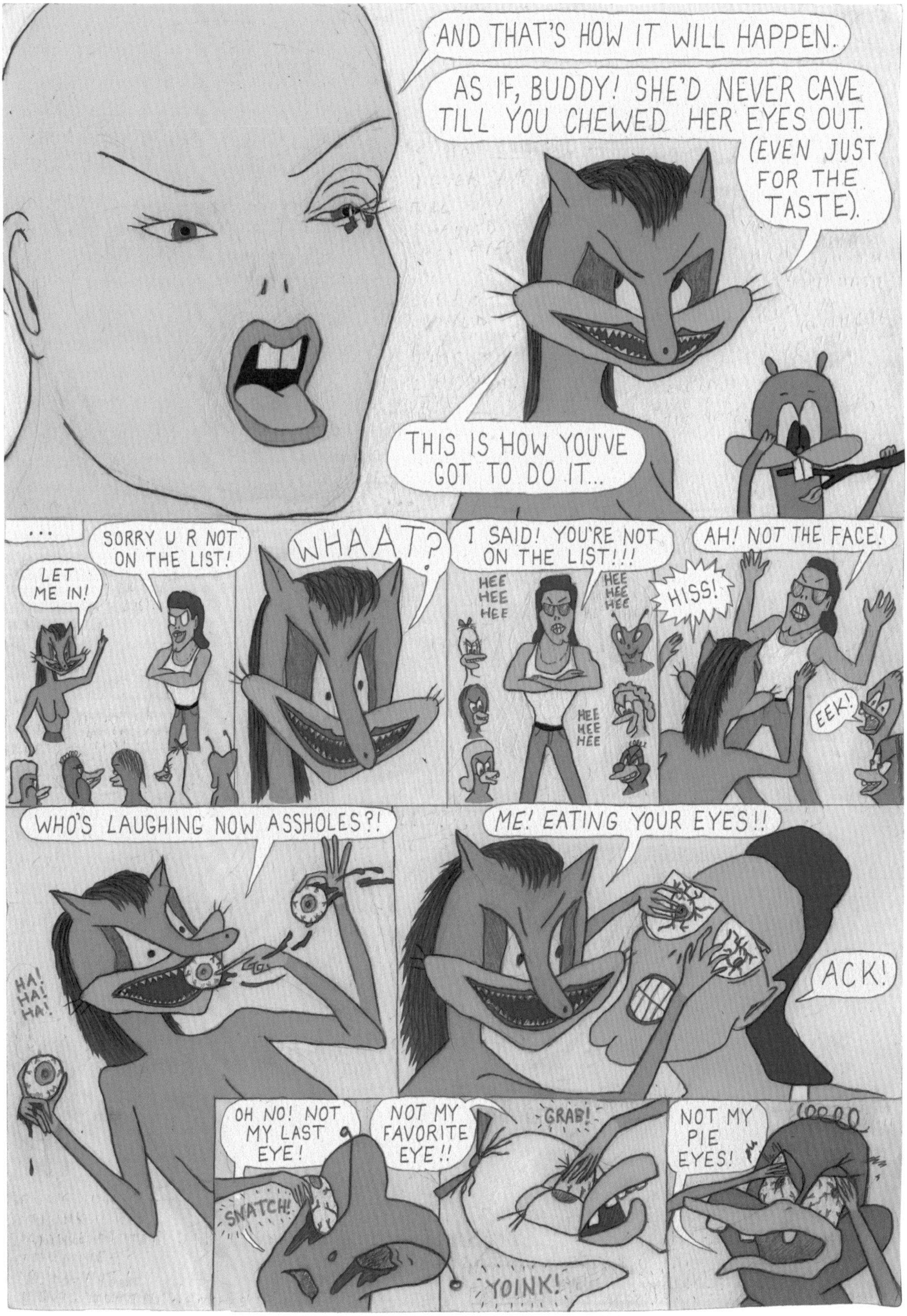
AND THAT'S HOW IT WILL HAPPEN.
AS IF, BUDDY! SHE'D NEVER CAVE TILL YOU CHEWED HER EYES OUT.
(EVEN JUST FOR THE TASTE).
THIS IS HOW YOU'VE GOT TO DO IT...
...
LET ME IN!
SORRY U R NOT ON THE LIST!
WHAAT?
I SAID! YOU'RE NOT ON THE LIST!!!
HEE HEE HEE
HEE HEE HEE
HEE HEE HEE
AH! NOT THE FACE!
HISS!
EEK!
WHO'S LAUGHING NOW ASSHOLES?!
HA! HA! HA!
ME! EATING YOUR EYES!!
ACK!
OH NO! NOT MY LAST EYE!
SNATCH!
NOT MY FAVORITE EYE!!
GRAB!
YOINK!
NOT MY PIE EYES!

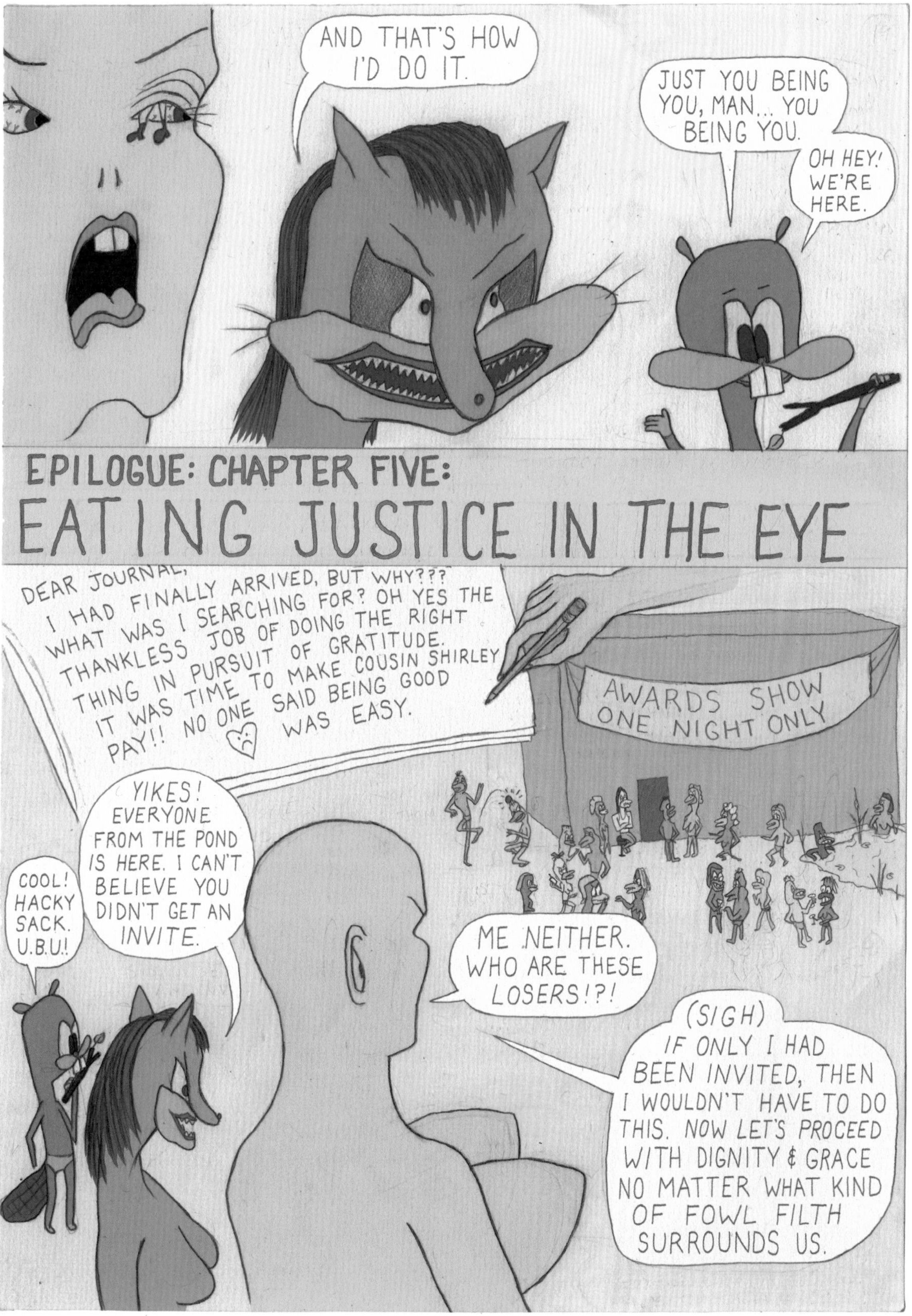
AND THAT'S HOW I'D DO IT.
JUST YOU BEING YOU, MAN... YOU BEING YOU.
OH HEY! WE'RE HERE.
EPILOGUE: CHAPTER FIVE:
EATING JUSTICE IN THE EYE
DEAR JOURNAL, I HAD FINALLY ARRIVED, BUT WHY??? WHAT WAS I SEARCHING FOR? OH YES THE THANKLESS JOB OF DOING THE RIGHT THING IN PURSUIT OF GRATITUDE. IT WAS TIME TO MAKE COUSIN SHIRLEY PAY!! NO ONE SAID BEING GOOD WAS EASY.
AWARDS SHOW ONE NIGHT ONLY
COOL! HACKY SACK. U.B.U.!
YIKES! EVERYONE FROM THE POND IS HERE. I CAN'T BELIEVE YOU DIDN'T GET AN INVITE.
ME NEITHER. WHO ARE THESE LOSERS!?!
(SIGH) IF ONLY I HAD BEEN INVITED, THEN I WOULDN'T HAVE TO DO THIS. NOW LET'S PROCEED WITH DIGNITY & GRACE NO MATTER WHAT KIND OF FOWL FILTH SURROUNDS US.

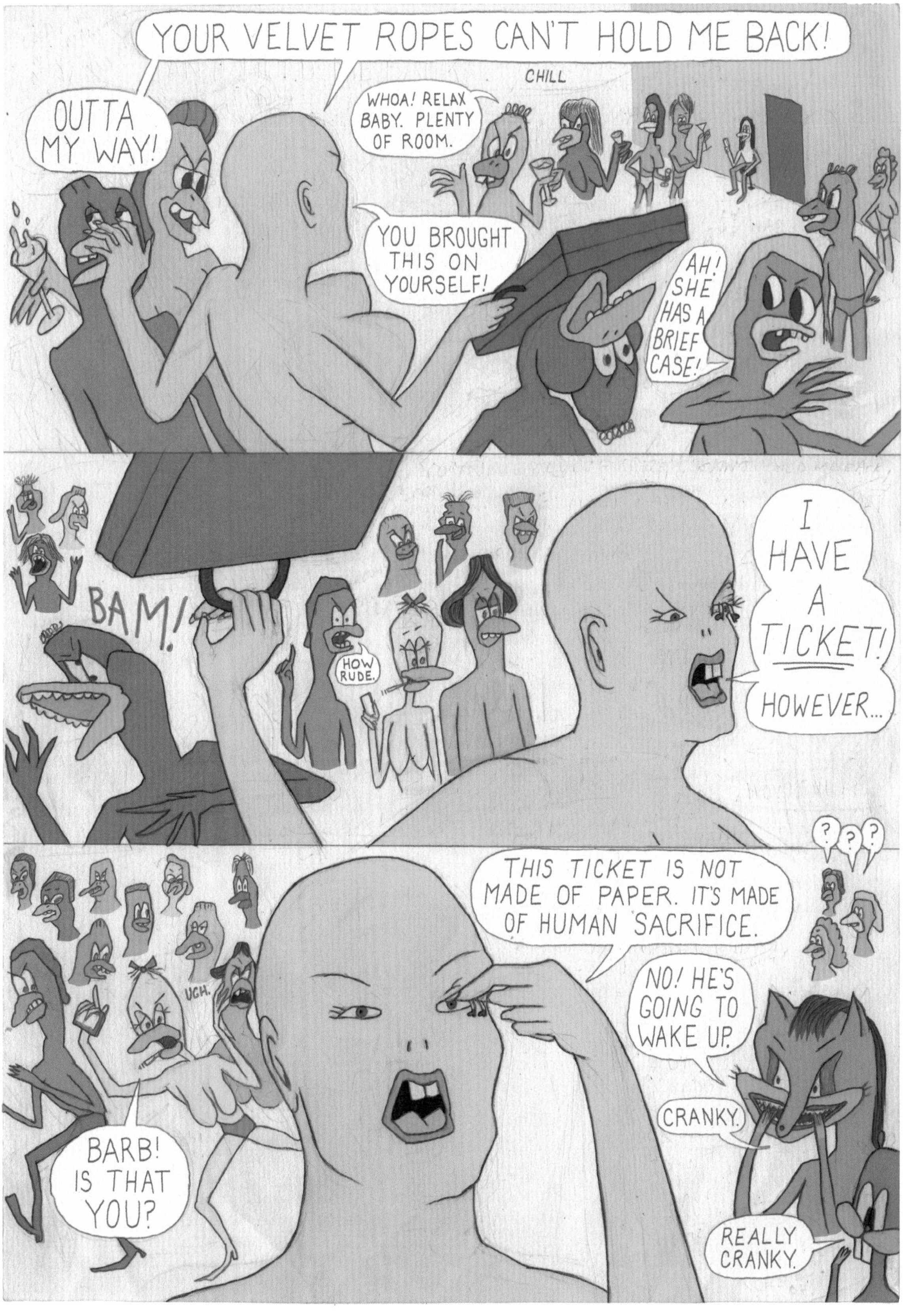
YOUR VELVET ROPES CAN'T HOLD ME BACK!
OUTTA MY WAY!
WHOA! RELAX BABY. PLENTY OF ROOM.
CHILL
YOU BROUGHT THIS ON YOURSELF!
AH! SHE HAS A BRIEF CASE!
BAM!
HOW RUDE.
I HAVE A TICKET!
HOWEVER...
THIS TICKET IS NOT MADE OF PAPER. IT'S MADE OF HUMAN SACRIFICE.
? ? ?
UGH.
NO! HE'S GOING TO WAKE UP.
CRANKY.
BARB! IS THAT YOU?
REALLY CRANKY.

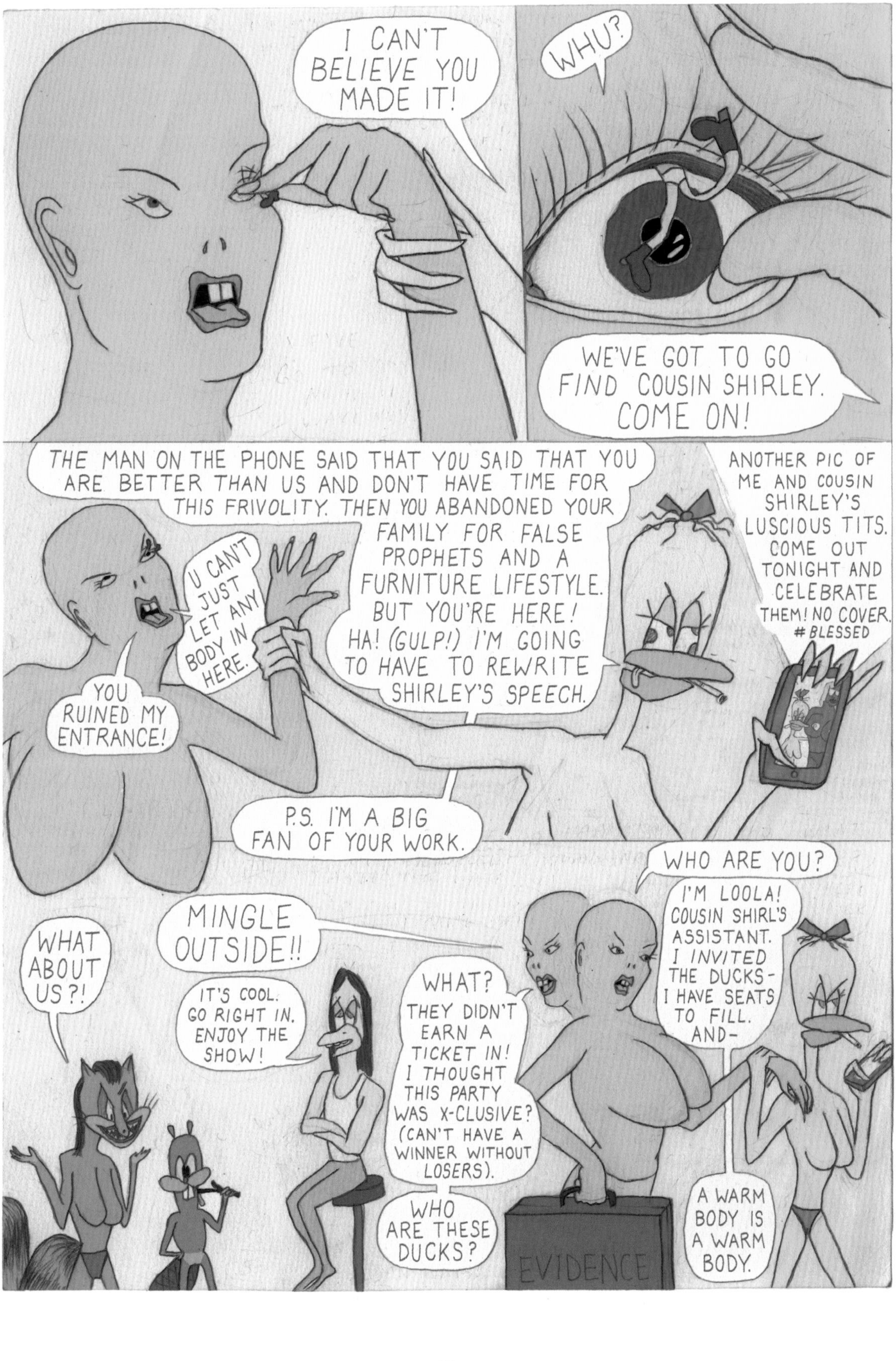
I CAN'T BELIEVE YOU MADE IT!
WHU?
WE'VE GOT TO GO FIND COUSIN SHIRLEY. COME ON!
THE MAN ON THE PHONE SAID THAT YOU SAID THAT YOU ARE BETTER THAN US AND DON'T HAVE TIME FOR THIS FRIVOLITY. THEN YOU ABANDONED YOUR FAMILY FOR FALSE PROPHETS AND A FURNITURE LIFESTYLE. BUT YOU'RE HERE! HA! (GULP!) I'M GOING TO HAVE TO REWRITE SHIRLEY'S SPEECH.
ANOTHER PIC OF ME AND COUSIN SHIRLEY'S LUSCIOUS TITS. COME OUT TONIGHT AND CELEBRATE THEM! NO COVER. #BLESSED
U CAN'T JUST LET ANY BODY IN HERE.
YOU RUINED MY ENTRANCE!
P.S. I'M A BIG FAN OF YOUR WORK.
WHO ARE YOU?
I'M LOOLA! COUSIN SHIRL'S ASSISTANT. I INVITED THE DUCKS - I HAVE SEATS TO FILL. AND-
MINGLE OUTSIDE!!
WHAT ABOUT US?!
IT'S COOL. GO RIGHT IN. ENJOY THE SHOW!
WHAT? THEY DIDN'T EARN A TICKET IN! I THOUGHT THIS PARTY WAS X-CLUSIVE? (CAN'T HAVE A WINNER WITHOUT LOSERS).
WHO ARE THESE DUCKS?
EVIDENCE
A WARM BODY IS A WARM BODY.

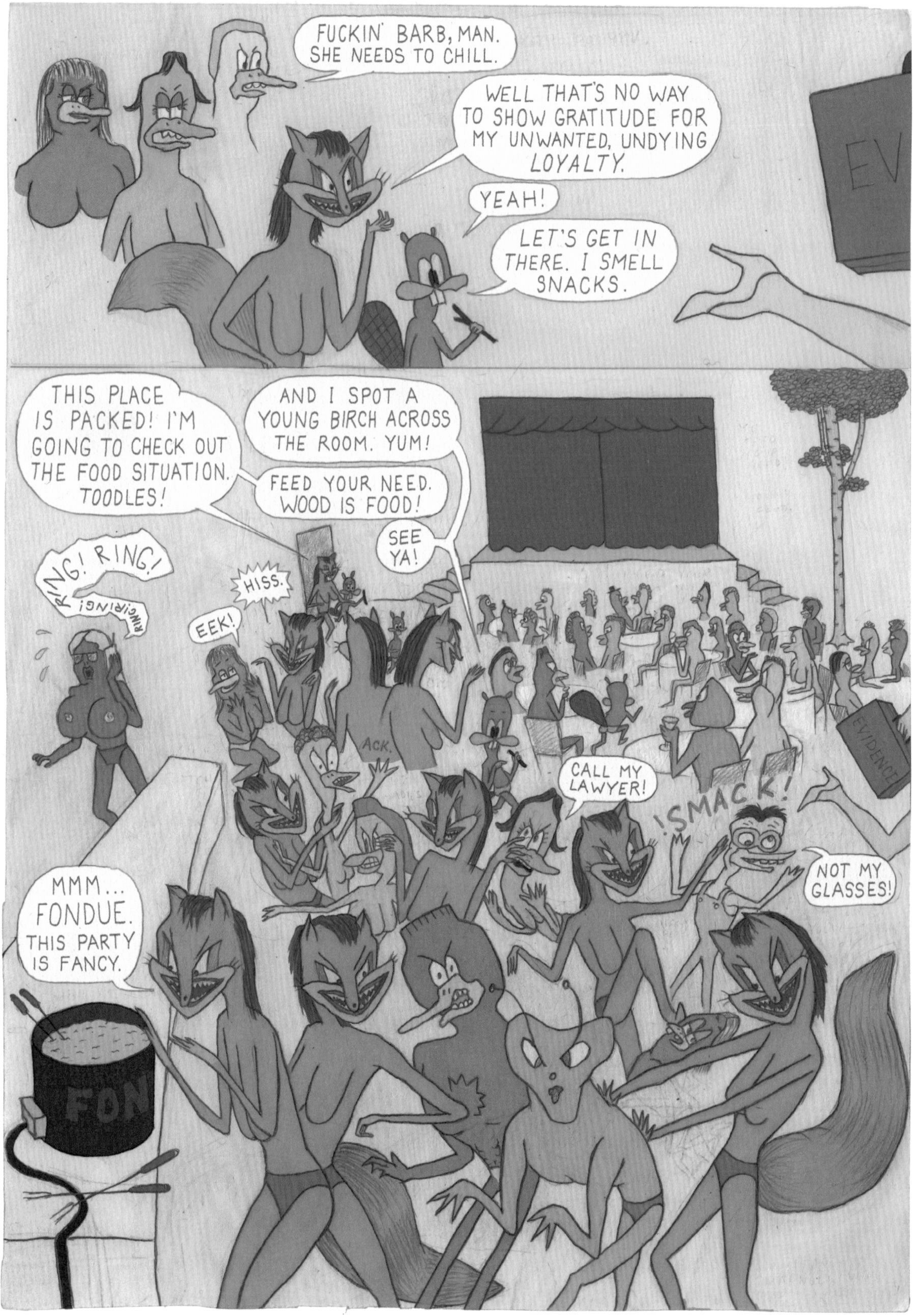
FUCKIN' BARB, MAN. SHE NEEDS TO CHILL.
WELL THAT'S NO WAY TO SHOW GRATITUDE FOR MY UNWANTED, UNDYING *LOYALTY.*
YEAH!
LET'S GET IN THERE. I SMELL SNACKS.
THIS PLACE IS PACKED! I'M GOING TO CHECK OUT THE FOOD SITUATION. TOODLES!
AND I SPOT A YOUNG BIRCH ACROSS THE ROOM. YUM!
FEED YOUR NEED. WOOD IS FOOD!
SEE YA!
RING! RING!
RINGRING!
HISS.
EEK!
ACK.
CALL MY LAWYER!
SMACK!
NOT MY GLASSES!
EVIDENCE
MMM... FONDUE. THIS PARTY IS FANCY.
FON

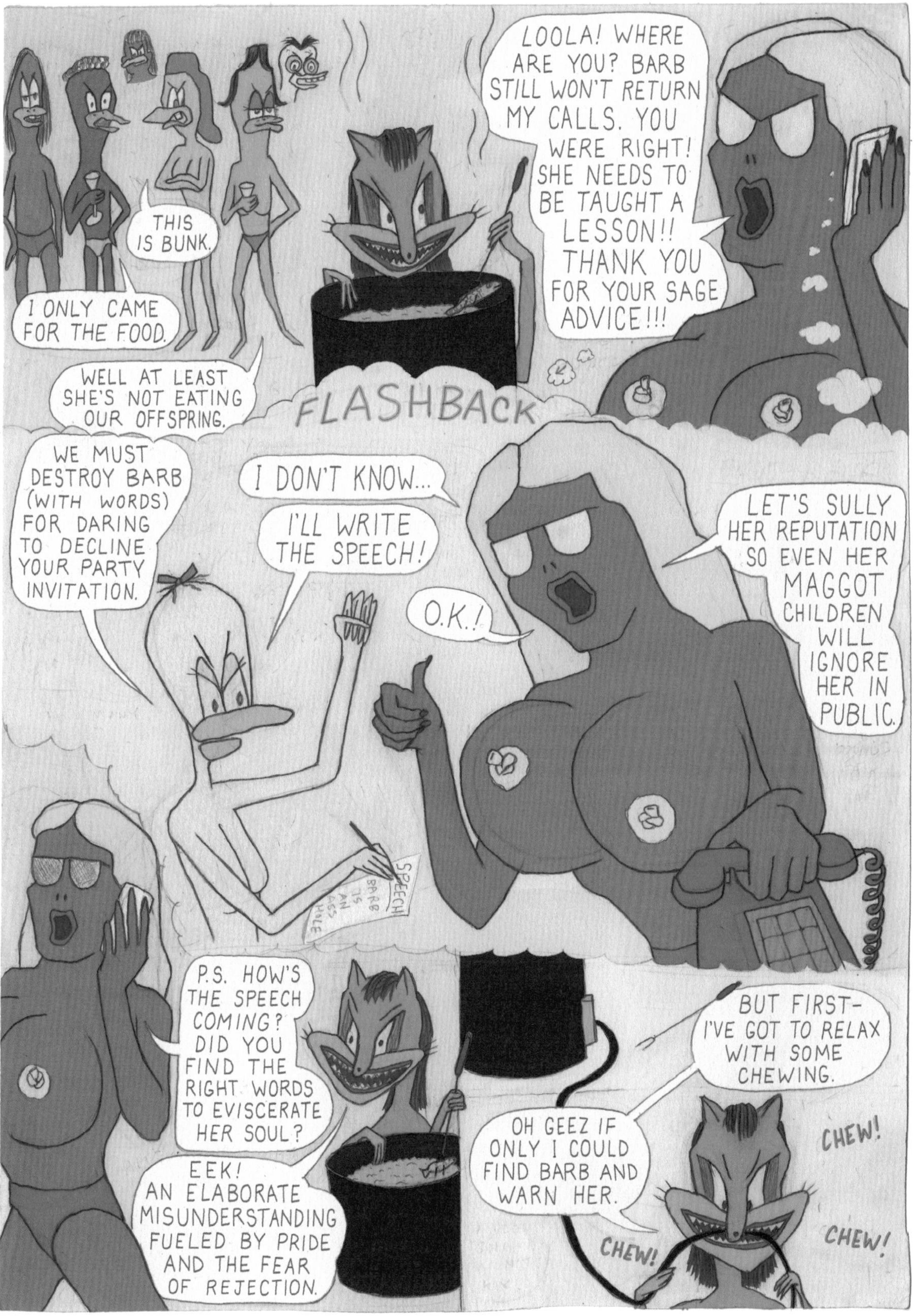

THIS IS BUNK.
I ONLY CAME FOR THE FOOD.
WELL AT LEAST SHE'S NOT EATING OUR OFFSPRING.
LOOLA! WHERE ARE YOU? BARB STILL WON'T RETURN MY CALLS. YOU WERE RIGHT! SHE NEEDS TO BE TAUGHT A LESSON!! THANK YOU FOR YOUR SAGE ADVICE!!!
FLASHBACK
WE MUST DESTROY BARB (WITH WORDS) FOR DARING TO DECLINE YOUR PARTY INVITATION.
I DON'T KNOW...
I'LL WRITE THE SPEECH!
O.K.!
LET'S SULLY HER REPUTATION SO EVEN HER MAGGOT CHILDREN WILL IGNORE HER IN PUBLIC.
SPEECH
BARB IS AN ASS HOLE
P.S. HOW'S THE SPEECH COMING? DID YOU FIND THE RIGHT WORDS TO EVISCERATE HER SOUL?
EEK! AN ELABORATE MISUNDERSTANDING FUELED BY PRIDE AND THE FEAR OF REJECTION.
BUT FIRST- I'VE GOT TO RELAX WITH SOME CHEWING.
OH GEEZ IF ONLY I COULD FIND BARB AND WARN HER.
CHEW!
CHEW!
CHEW!

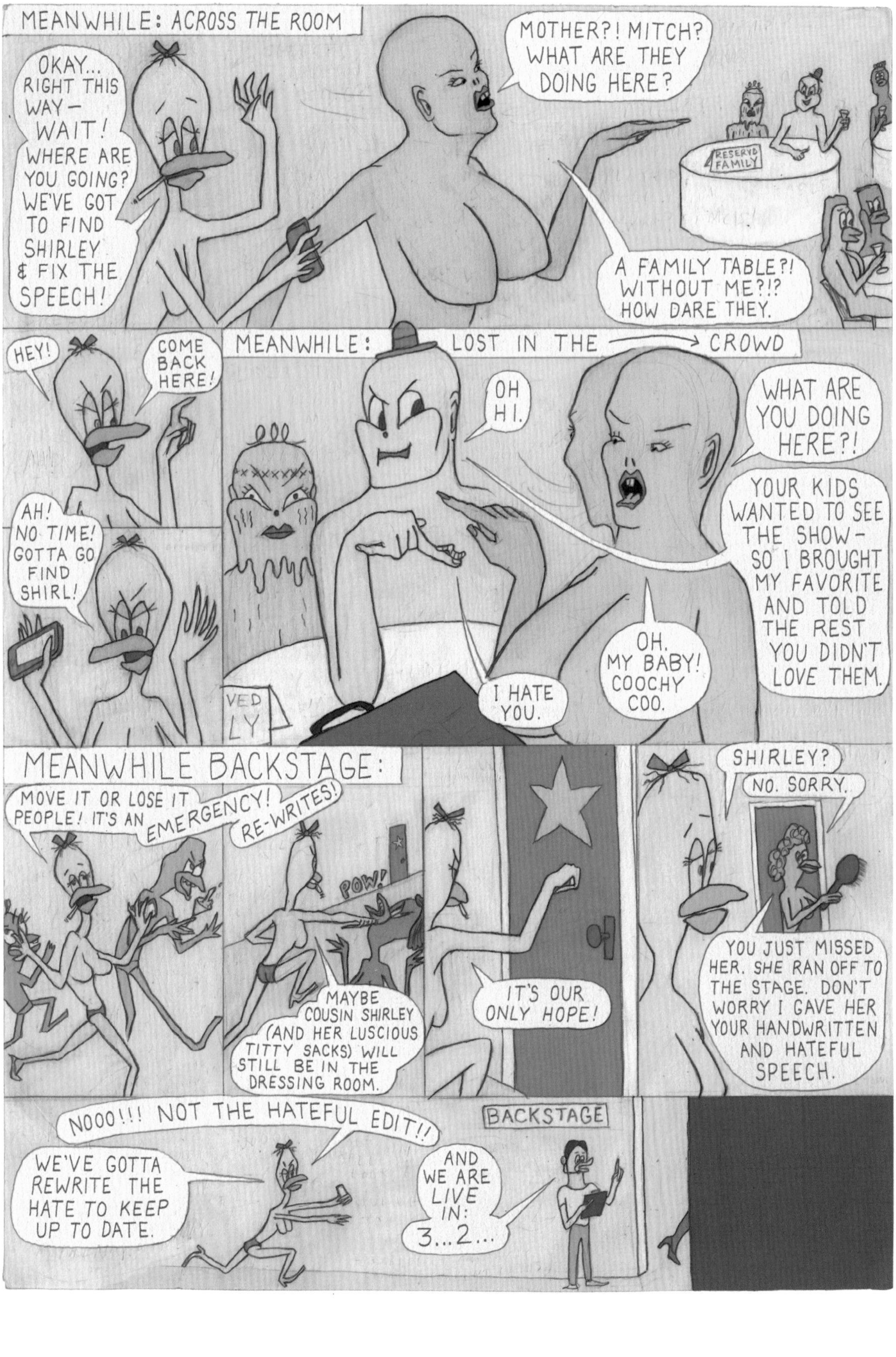
MEANWHILE: ACROSS THE ROOM
OKAY... RIGHT THIS WAY— WAIT! WHERE ARE YOU GOING? WE'VE GOT TO FIND SHIRLEY & FIX THE SPEECH!
MOTHER?! MITCH? WHAT ARE THEY DOING HERE?
RESERVD FAMILY
A FAMILY TABLE?! WITHOUT ME?!? HOW DARE THEY.
HEY!
COME BACK HERE!
AH! NO TIME! GOTTA GO FIND SHIRL!
MEANWHILE: LOST IN THE CROWD
OH HI.
WHAT ARE YOU DOING HERE?!
YOUR KIDS WANTED TO SEE THE SHOW— SO I BROUGHT MY FAVORITE AND TOLD THE REST YOU DIDN'T LOVE THEM.
OH. MY BABY! COOCHY COO.
I HATE YOU.
MEANWHILE BACKSTAGE:
MOVE IT OR LOSE IT PEOPLE! IT'S AN EMERGENCY! RE-WRITES!
POW!
MAYBE COUSIN SHIRLEY (AND HER LUSCIOUS TITTY SACKS) WILL STILL BE IN THE DRESSING ROOM.
IT'S OUR ONLY HOPE!
SHIRLEY?
NO. SORRY.
YOU JUST MISSED HER. SHE RAN OFF TO THE STAGE. DON'T WORRY I GAVE HER YOUR HANDWRITTEN AND HATEFUL SPEECH.
NOOO!!! NOT THE HATEFUL EDIT!!
WE'VE GOTTA REWRITE THE HATE TO KEEP UP TO DATE.
BACKSTAGE
AND WE ARE LIVE IN: 3...2...

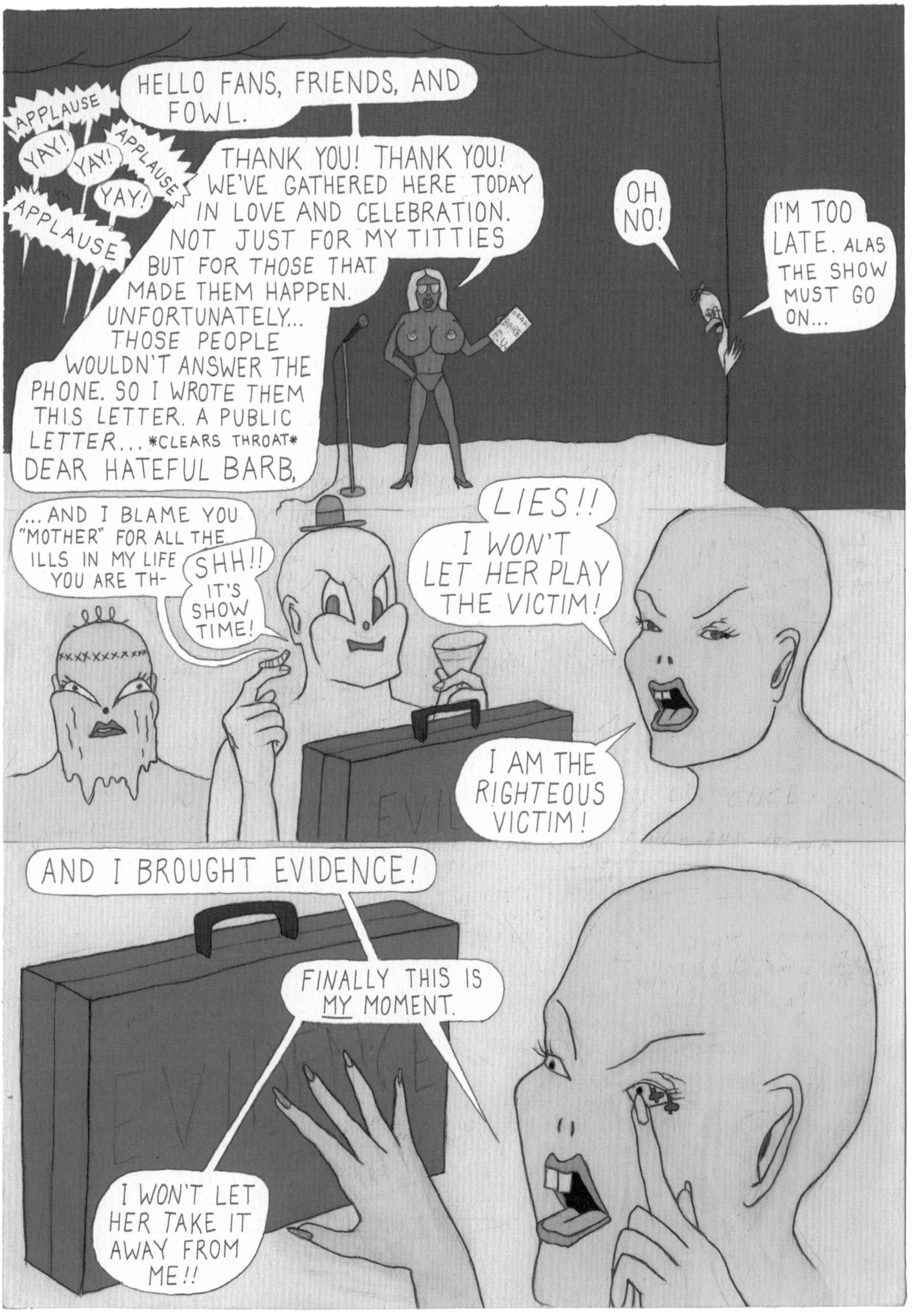

HELLO FANS, FRIENDS, AND FOWL.
APPLAUSE
YAY!
YAY!
APPLAUSE
YAY!
APPLAUSE
THANK YOU! THANK YOU! WE'VE GATHERED HERE TODAY IN LOVE AND CELEBRATION. NOT JUST FOR MY TITTIES BUT FOR THOSE THAT MADE THEM HAPPEN. UNFORTUNATELY... THOSE PEOPLE WOULDN'T ANSWER THE PHONE. SO I WROTE THEM THIS LETTER. A PUBLIC LETTER... *CLEARS THROAT* DEAR HATEFUL BARB,
OH NO!
I'M TOO LATE. ALAS THE SHOW MUST GO ON...
...AND I BLAME YOU "MOTHER" FOR ALL THE ILLS IN MY LIFE YOU ARE TH-
SHH!! IT'S SHOW TIME!
LIES!!
I WON'T LET HER PLAY THE VICTIM!
I AM THE RIGHTEOUS VICTIM!
EVIL
AND I BROUGHT EVIDENCE!
FINALLY THIS IS MY MOMENT.
I WON'T LET HER TAKE IT AWAY FROM ME!!

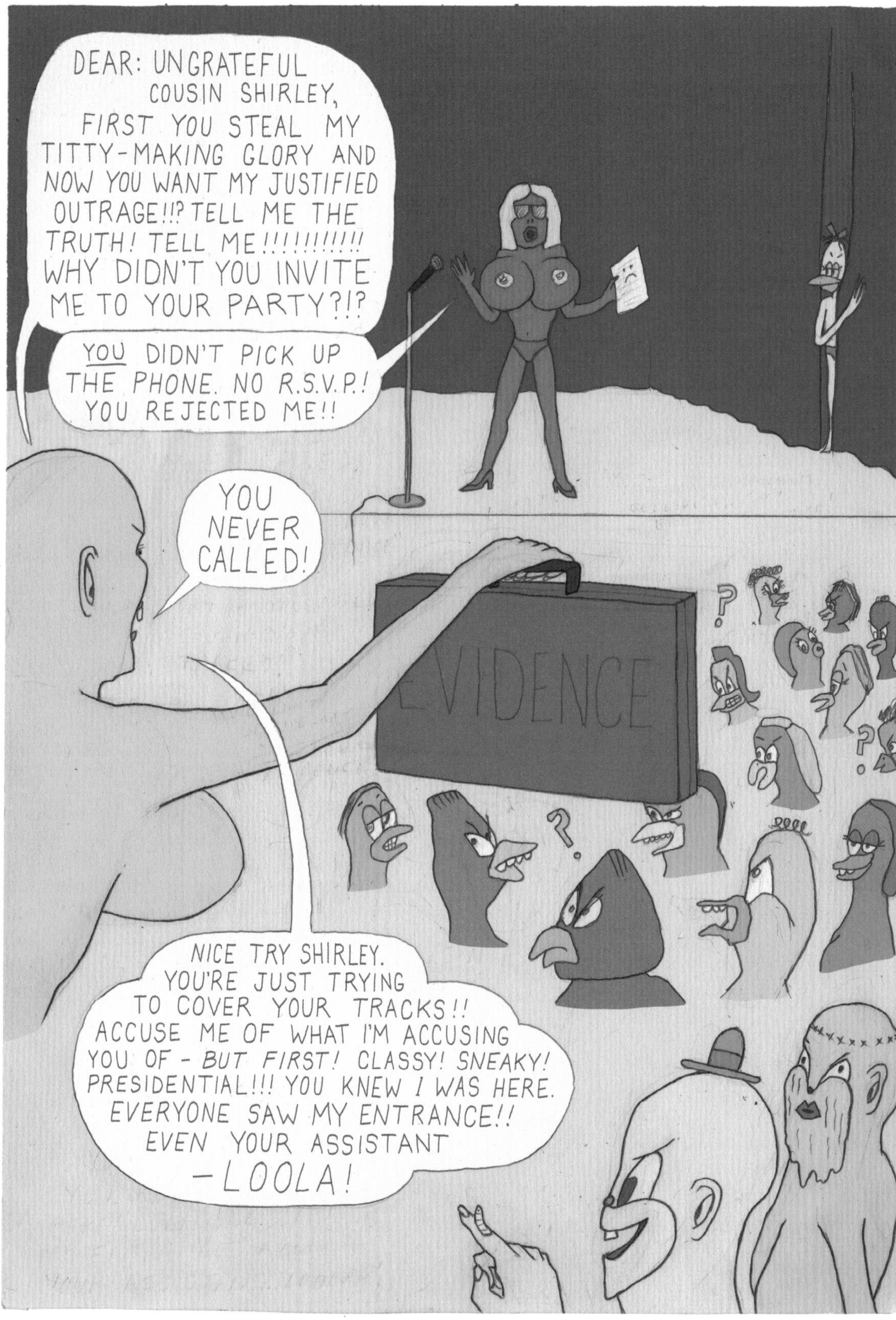
DEAR: UNGRATEFUL COUSIN SHIRLEY, FIRST YOU STEAL MY TITTY-MAKING GLORY AND NOW YOU WANT MY JUSTIFIED OUTRAGE!!? TELL ME THE TRUTH! TELL ME!!!!!!!!!!! WHY DIDN'T YOU INVITE ME TO YOUR PARTY?!?
YOU DIDN'T PICK UP THE PHONE. NO R.S.V.P.! YOU REJECTED ME!!
YOU NEVER CALLED!
EVIDENCE
NICE TRY SHIRLEY. YOU'RE JUST TRYING TO COVER YOUR TRACKS!! ACCUSE ME OF WHAT I'M ACCUSING YOU OF - BUT FIRST! CLASSY! SNEAKY! PRESIDENTIAL!!! YOU KNEW I WAS HERE. EVERYONE SAW MY ENTRANCE!! EVEN YOUR ASSISTANT -LOOLA!

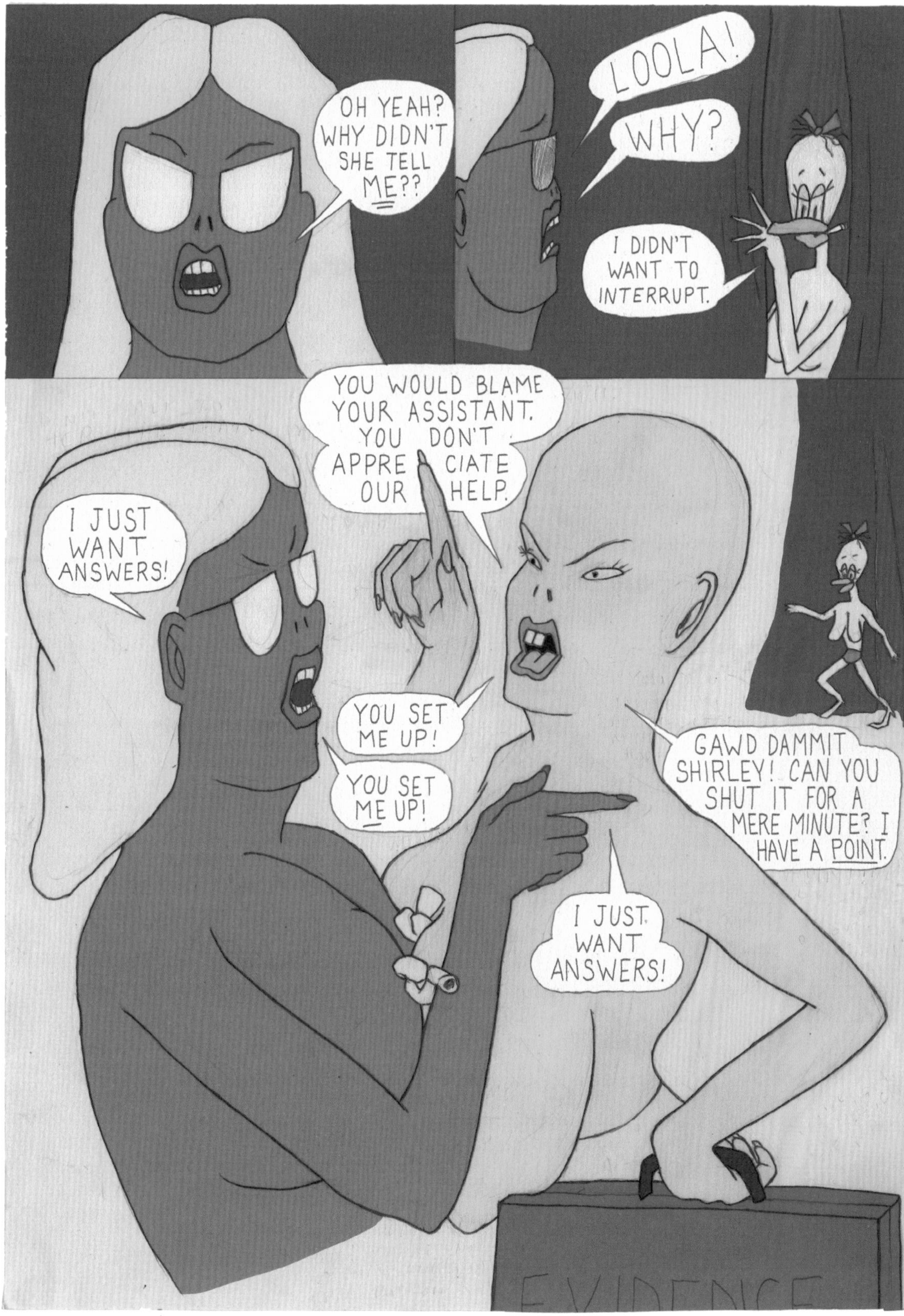
OH YEAH? WHY DIDN'T SHE TELL ME??
LOOLA!
WHY?
I DIDN'T WANT TO INTERRUPT.
YOU WOULD BLAME YOUR ASSISTANT. YOU DON'T APPRECIATE OUR HELP.
I JUST WANT ANSWERS!
YOU SET ME UP!
YOU SET ME UP!
GAWD DAMMIT SHIRLEY! CAN YOU SHUT IT FOR A MERE MINUTE? I HAVE A POINT.
I JUST WANT ANSWERS!
EVIDENCE

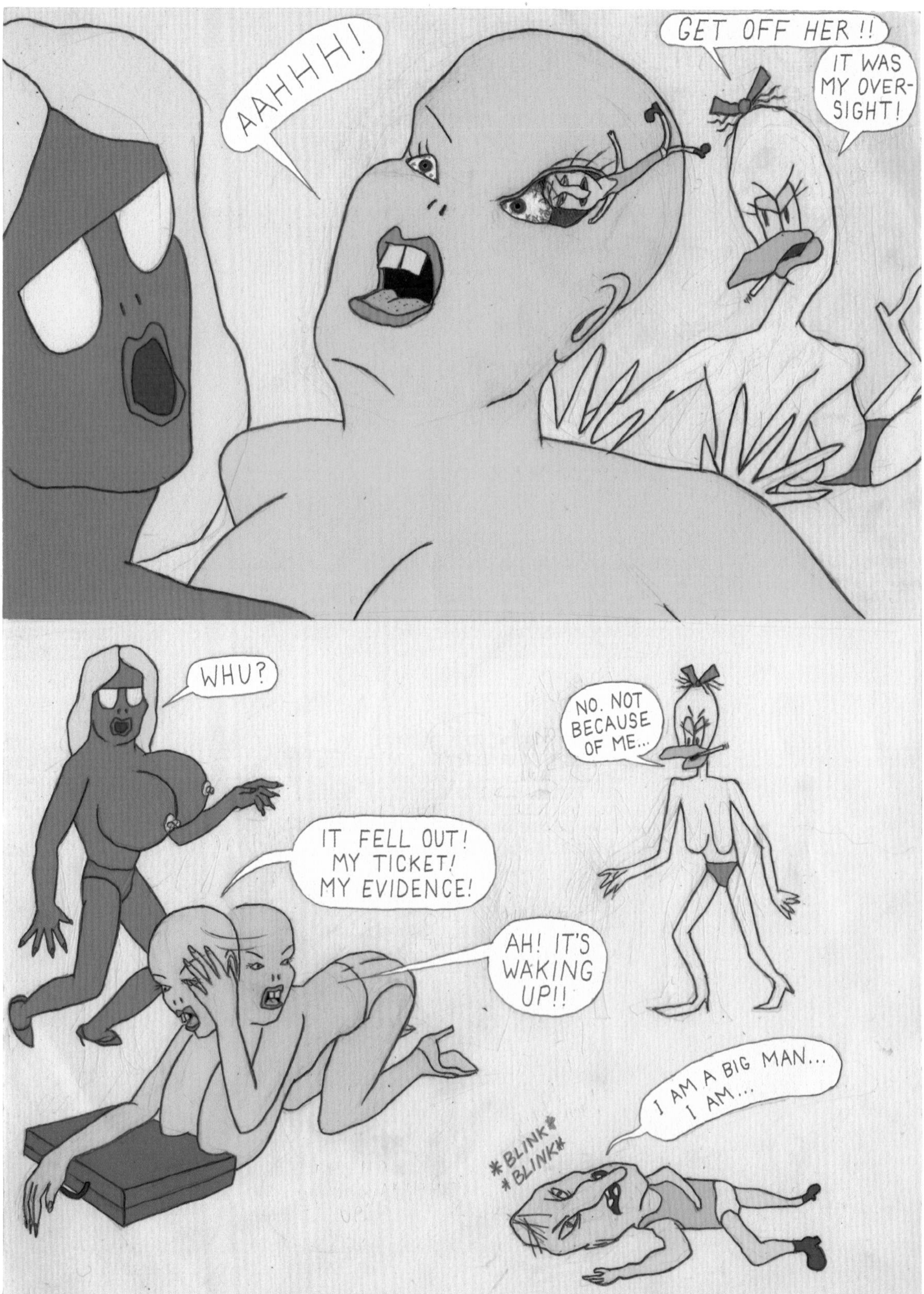
AAHHH!
GET OFF HER!!
IT WAS MY OVER-SIGHT!
WHU?
NO. NOT BECAUSE OF ME...
IT FELL OUT! MY TICKET! MY EVIDENCE!
AH! IT'S WAKING UP!!
I AM A BIG MAN... I AM...
BLINK *BLINK*

HUH?
DON'T LET IT WAKE UP!
NO!
HUH?
...I AM SMARNOLD... YOU ARE MY... YOU ARE...
NOT AGAIN!! NOT AGAIN!!

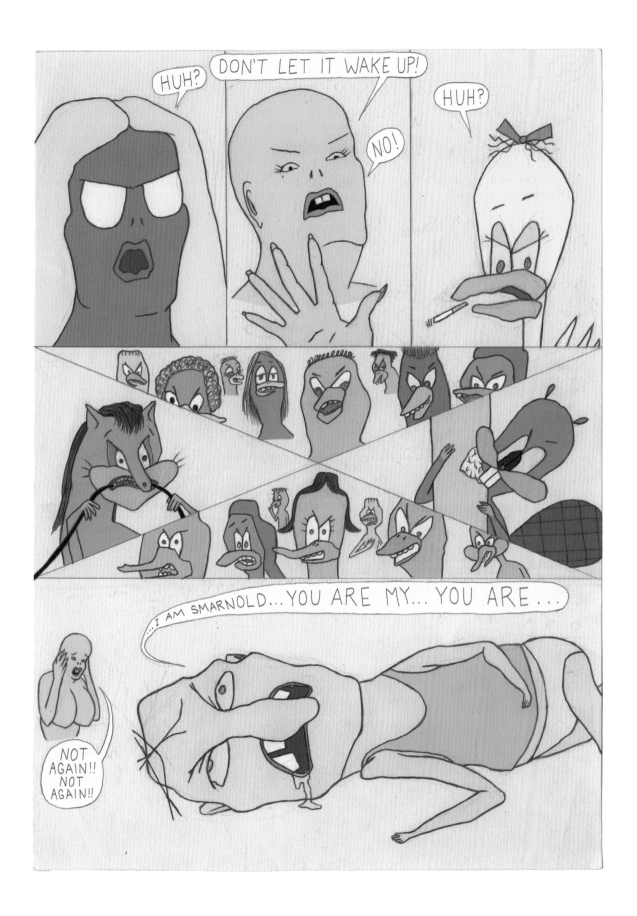

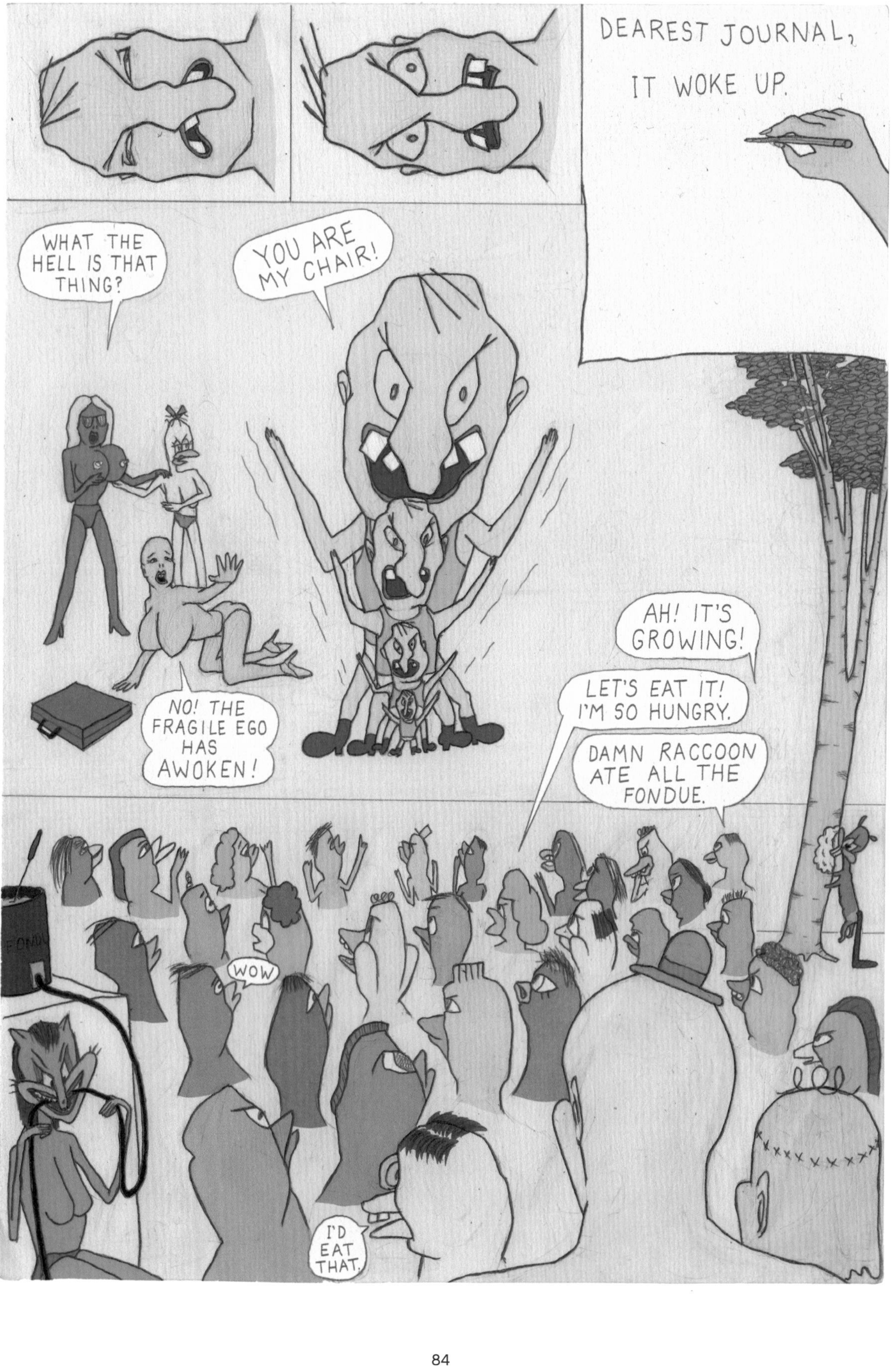
DEAREST JOURNAL,
IT WOKE UP.
WHAT THE HELL IS THAT THING?
YOU ARE MY CHAIR!
NO! THE FRAGILE EGO HAS AWOKEN!
AH! IT'S GROWING!
LET'S EAT IT! I'M SO HUNGRY.
DAMN RACCOON ATE ALL THE FONDUE.
WOW
I'D EAT THAT.

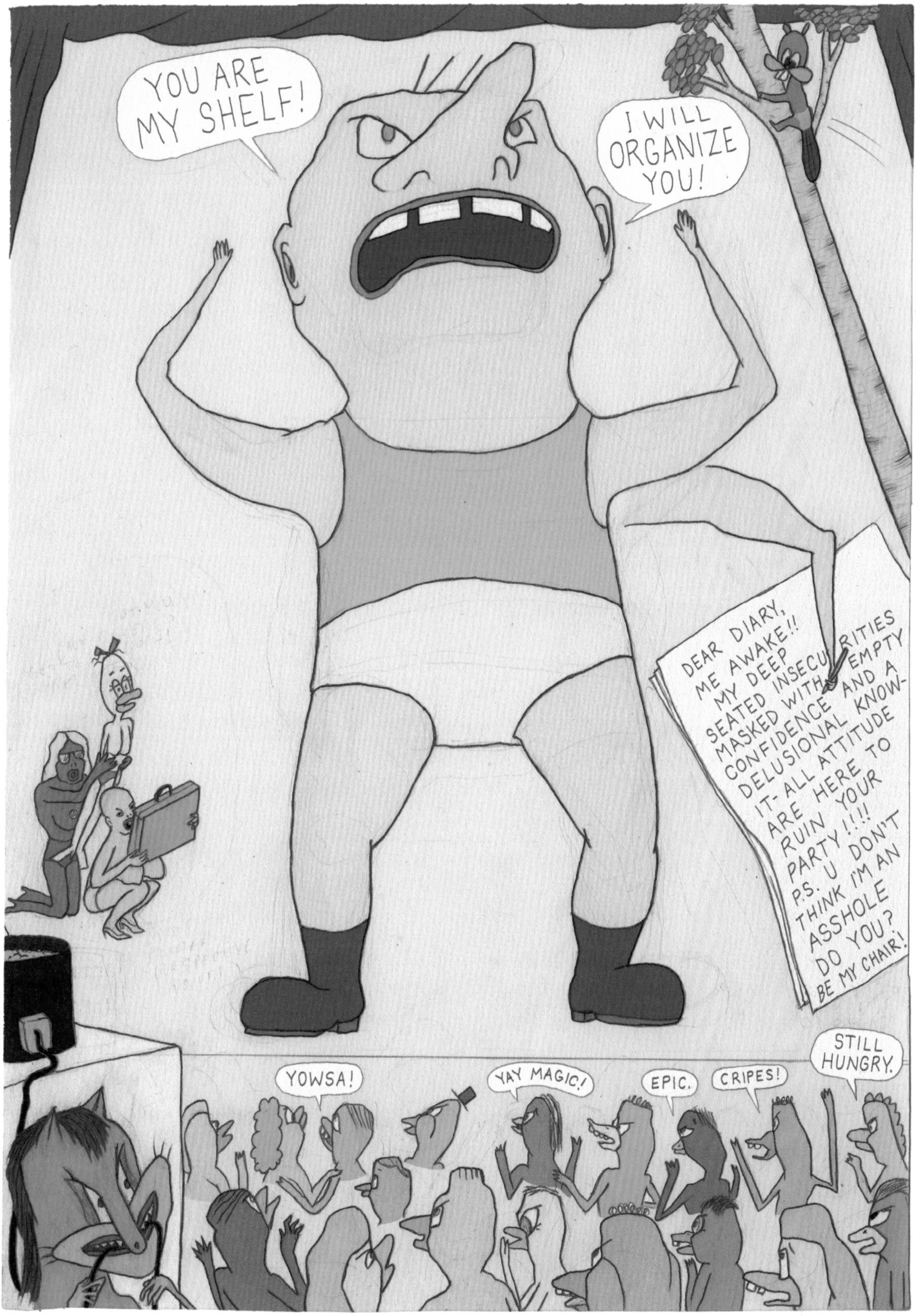

YOU ARE MY SHELF!
I WILL ORGANIZE YOU!
DEAR DIARY,
ME AWAKE!!
MY DEEP
SEATED INSECURITIES
MASKED WITH EMPTY
CONFIDENCE AND A
DELUSIONAL KNOW-
IT- ALL ATTITUDE
ARE HERE TO
RUIN YOUR
PARTY!!!!
P.S. U DON'T
THINK I'M AN
ASSHOLE
DO YOU?
BE MY CHAIR!
YOWSA!
YAY MAGIC!
EPIC.
CRIPES!
STILL HUNGRY.

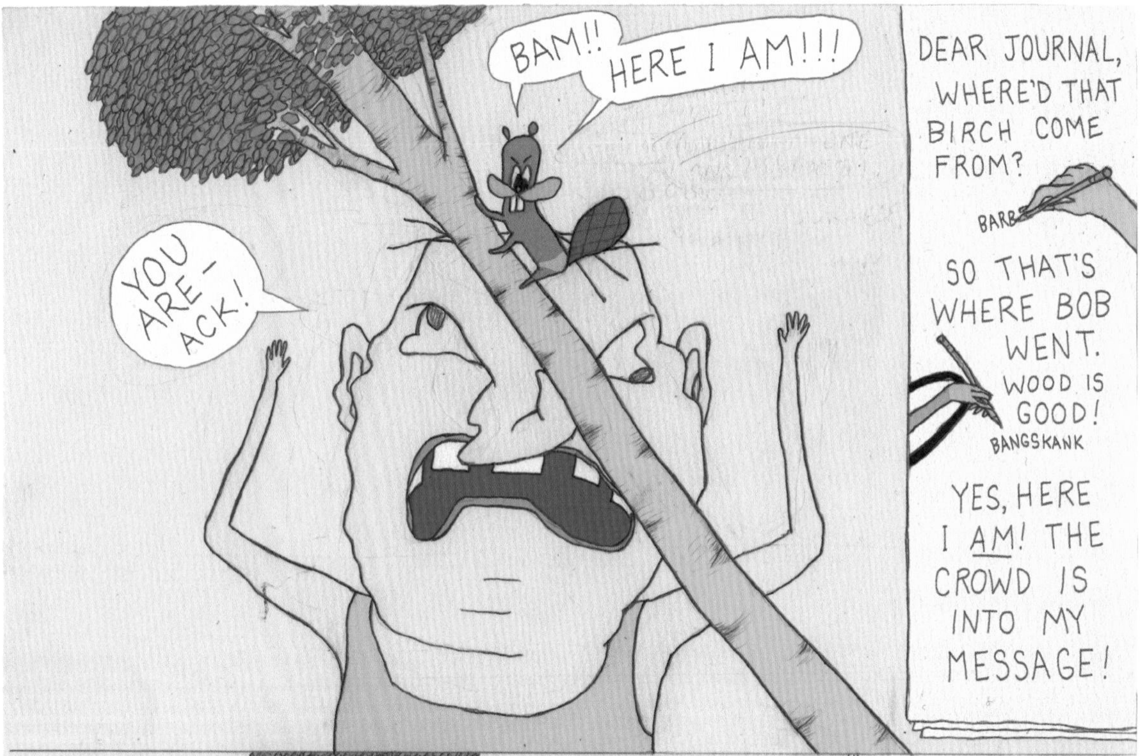
BAM!!
HERE I AM!!!
YOU ARE— ACK!
DEAR JOURNAL, WHERE'D THAT BIRCH COME FROM?
BARB
SO THAT'S WHERE BOB WENT.
WOOD IS GOOD!
BANGSKANK
YES, HERE I AM! THE CROWD IS INTO MY MESSAGE!

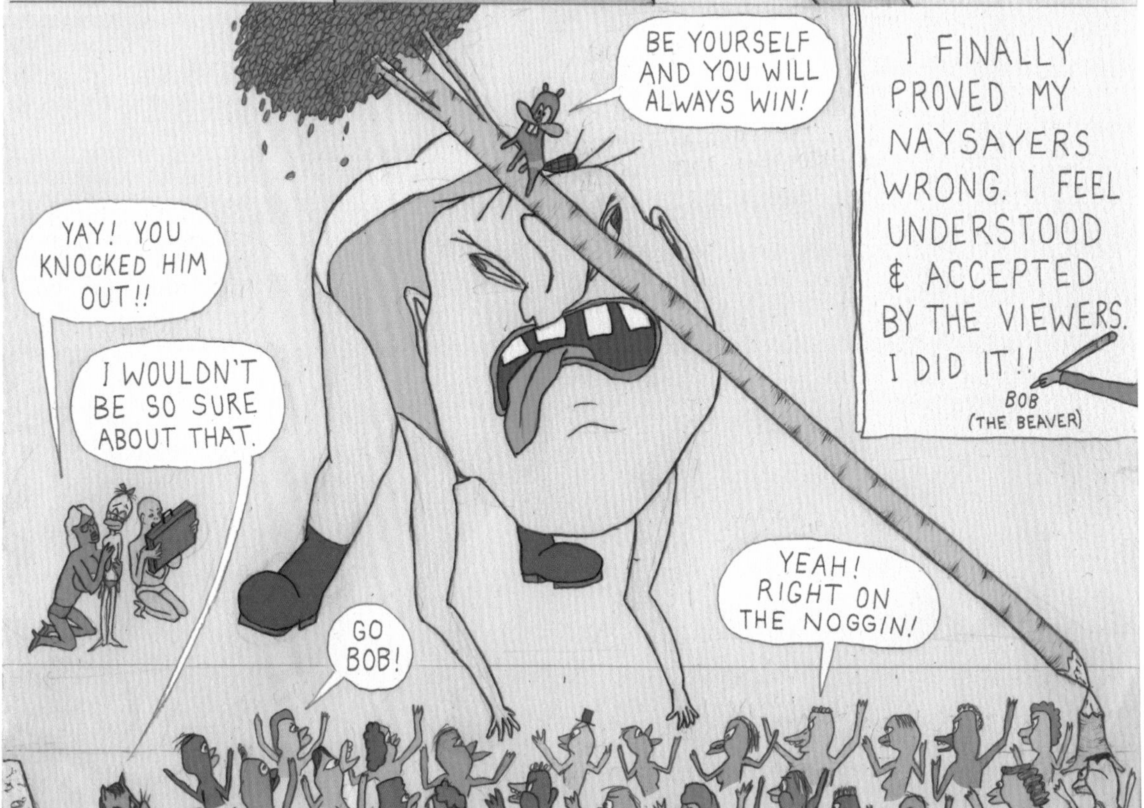
BE YOURSELF AND YOU WILL ALWAYS WIN!
I FINALLY PROVED MY NAYSAYERS WRONG. I FEEL UNDERSTOOD & ACCEPTED BY THE VIEWERS. I DID IT!!
BOB (THE BEAVER)
YAY! YOU KNOCKED HIM OUT!!
I WOULDN'T BE SO SURE ABOUT THAT.
YEAH! RIGHT ON THE NOGGIN!
GO BOB!

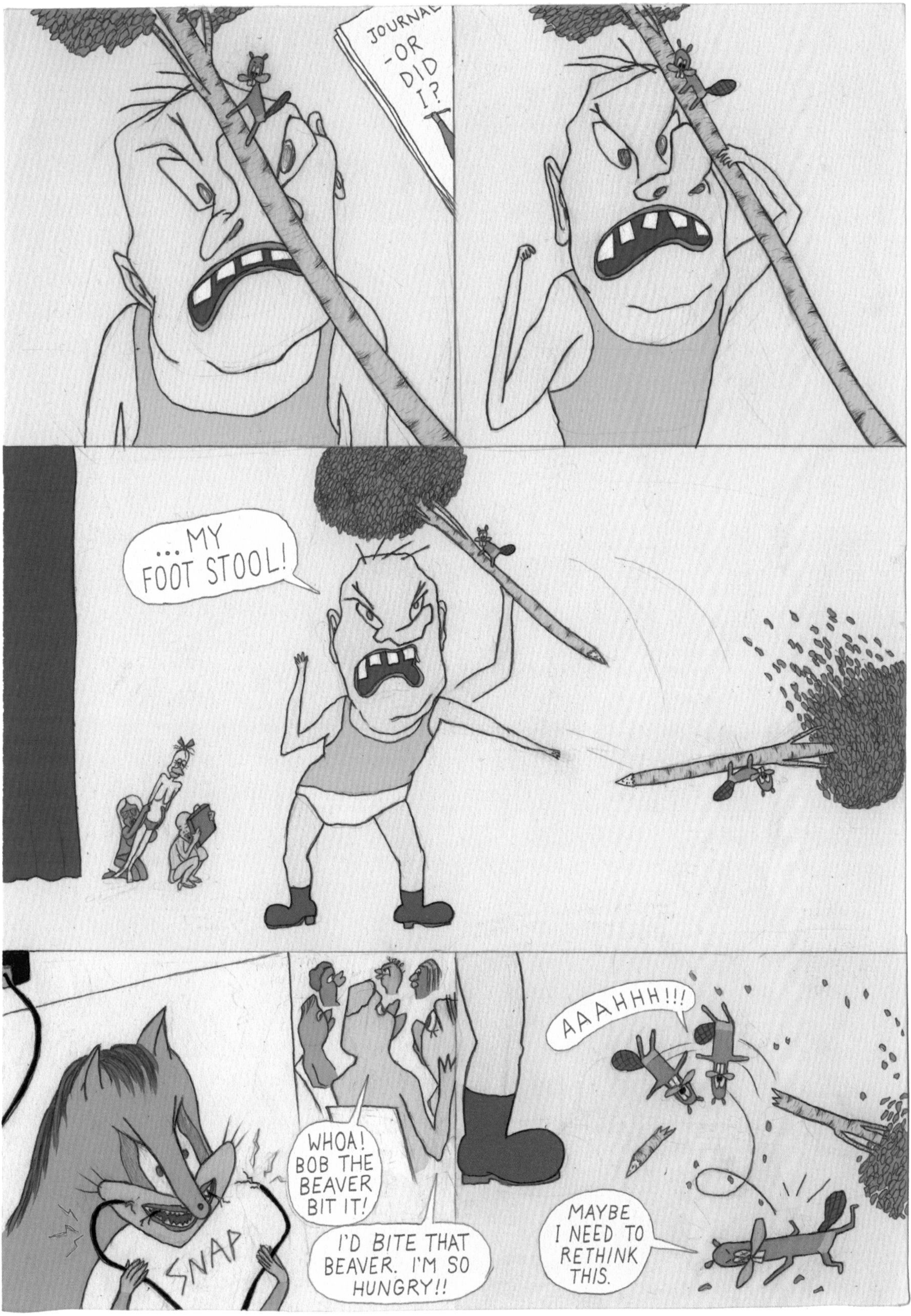
JOURNAL
-OR DID I?
...MY FOOT STOOL!
AAAHHH!!!
SNAP
WHOA! BOB THE BEAVER BIT IT!
I'D BITE THAT BEAVER. I'M SO HUNGRY!!
MAYBE I NEED TO RETHINK THIS.

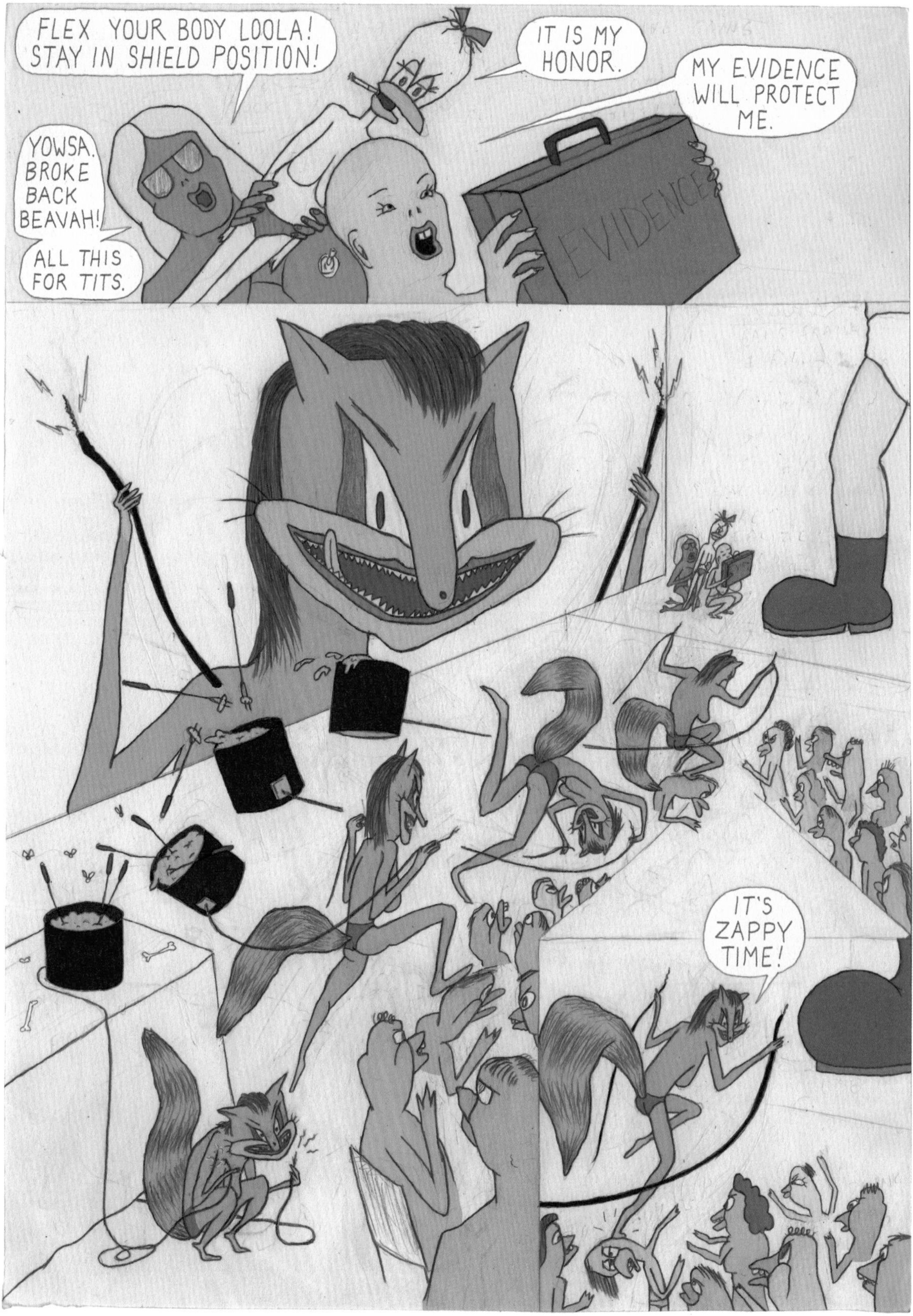
FLEX YOUR BODY LOOLA! STAY IN SHIELD POSITION!
YOWSA. BROKE BACK BEAVAH!
ALL THIS FOR TITS.
IT IS MY HONOR.
MY EVIDENCE WILL PROTECT ME.
EVIDENCE
IT'S ZAPPY TIME!

¡BANG!

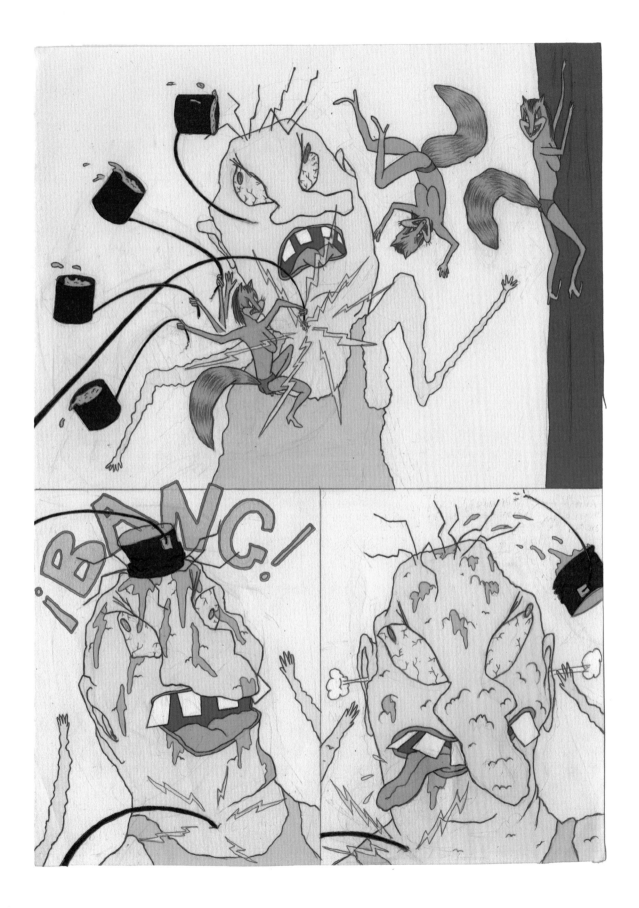

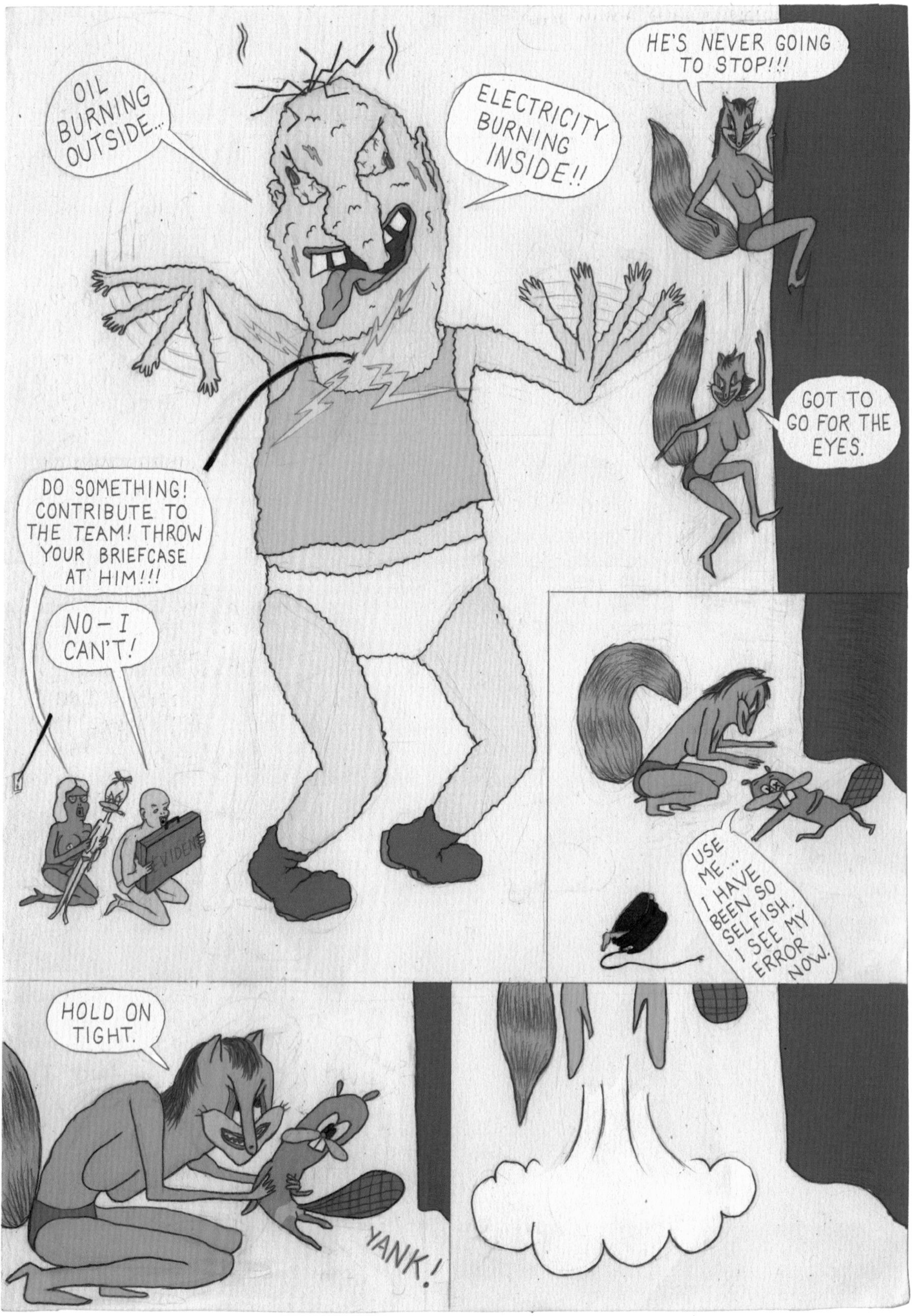
OIL BURNING OUTSIDE...
ELECTRICITY BURNING INSIDE!!
HE'S NEVER GOING TO STOP!!!
GOT TO GO FOR THE EYES.
DO SOMETHING! CONTRIBUTE TO THE TEAM! THROW YOUR BRIEFCASE AT HIM!!!
NO- I CAN'T!
USE ME... I HAVE BEEN SO SELFISH. I SEE MY ERROR NOW.
HOLD ON TIGHT.
YANK!

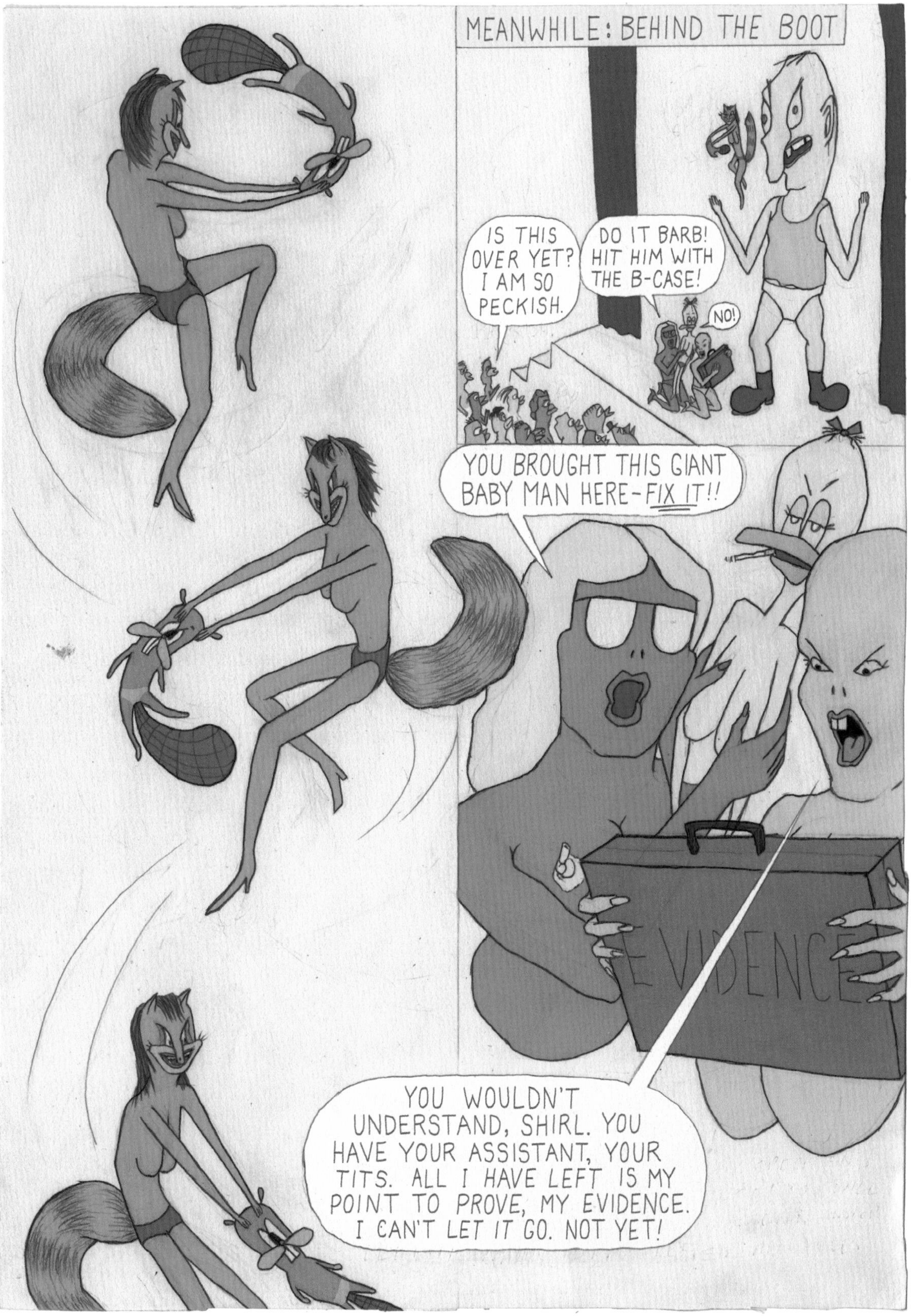
MEANWHILE: BEHIND THE BOOT
IS THIS OVER YET? I AM SO PECKISH.
DO IT BARB! HIT HIM WITH THE B-CASE!
NO!
YOU BROUGHT THIS GIANT BABY MAN HERE-FIX IT!!
EVIDENCE
YOU WOULDN'T UNDERSTAND, SHIRL. YOU HAVE YOUR ASSISTANT, YOUR TITS. ALL I HAVE LEFT IS MY POINT TO PROVE, MY EVIDENCE. I CAN'T LET IT GO. NOT YET!

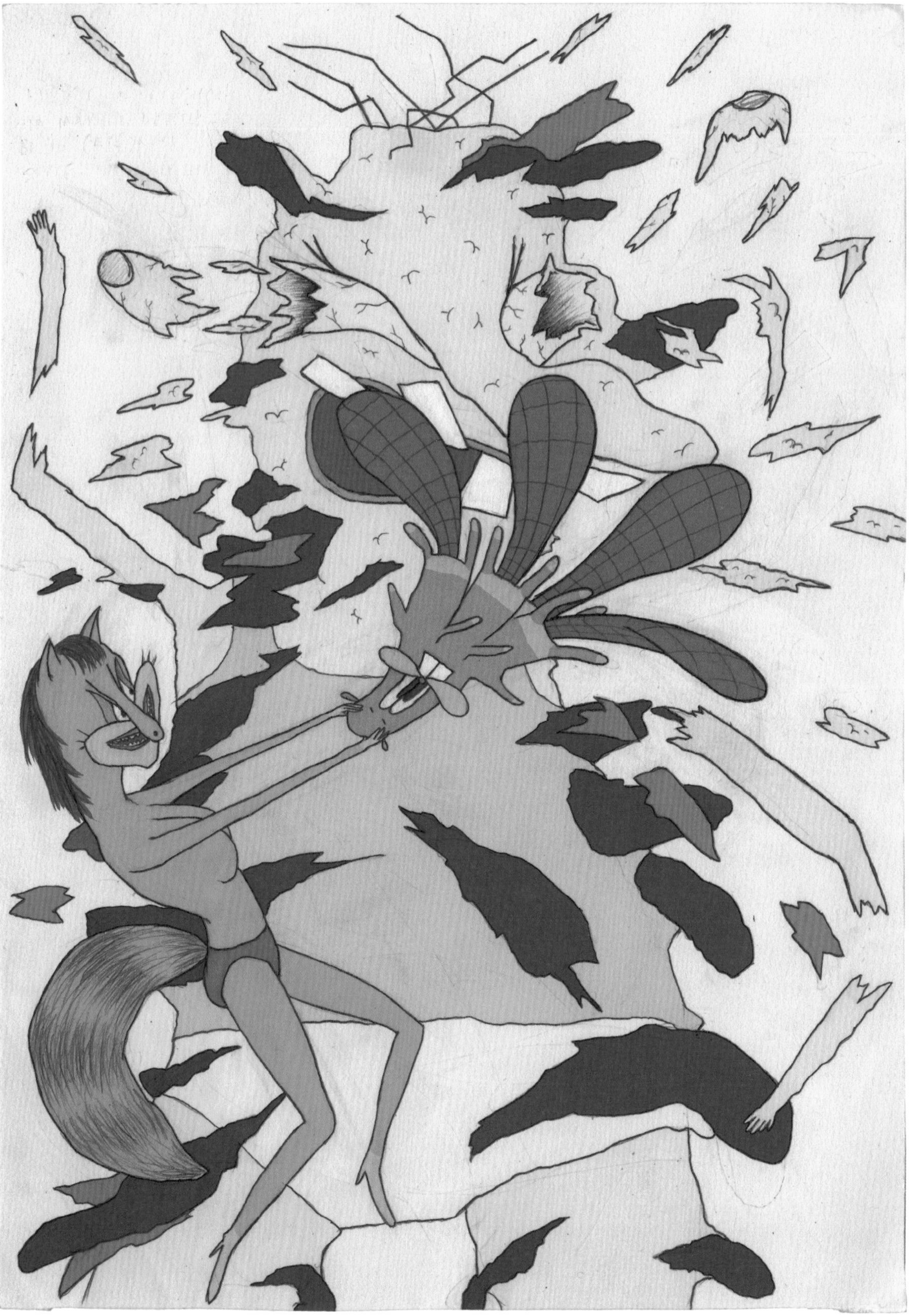

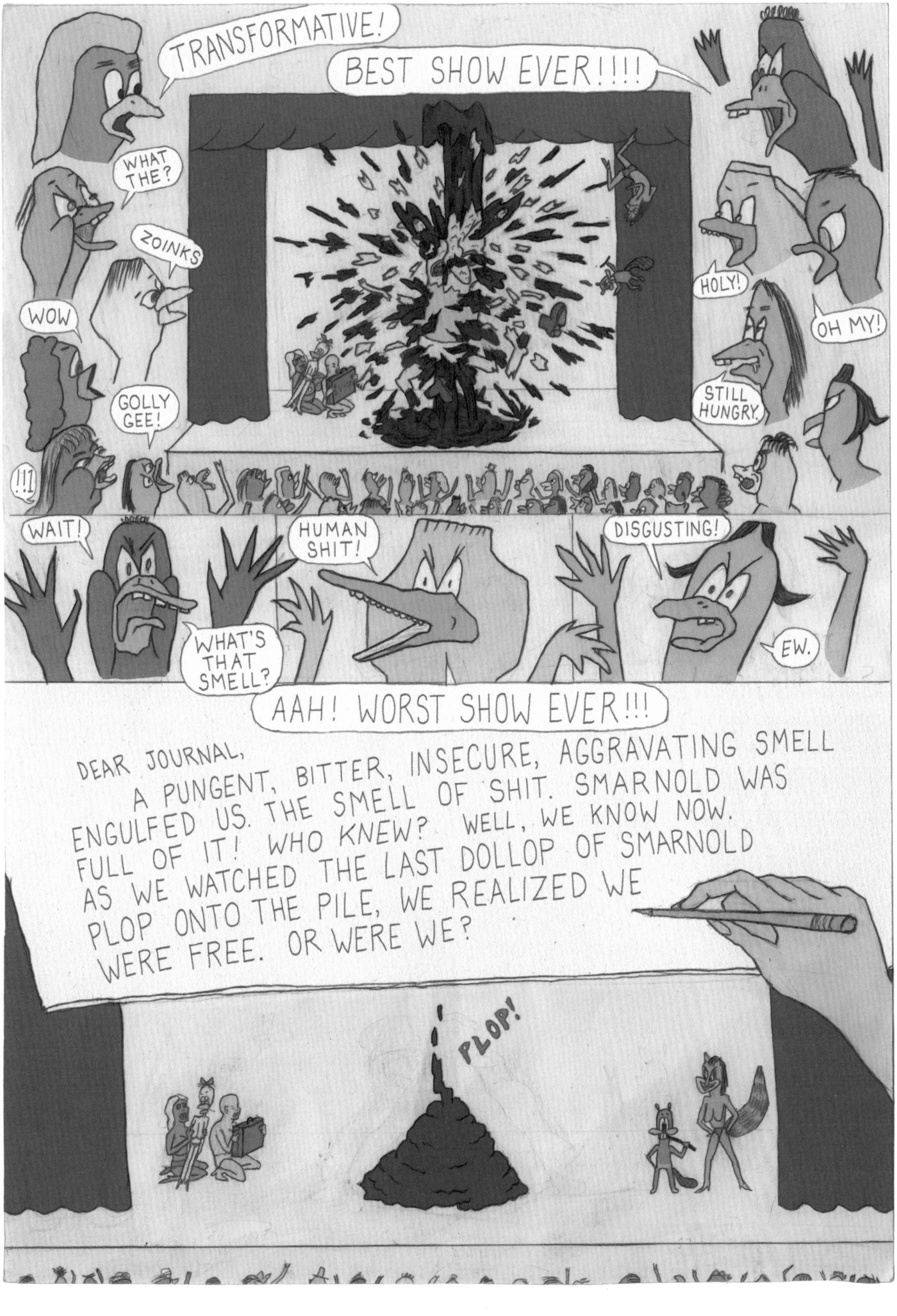
TRANSFORMATIVE!
BEST SHOW EVER!!!!
WHAT THE?
ZOINKS
WOW
GOLLY GEE!
!!!
HOLY!
OH MY!
STILL HUNGRY.
WAIT!
WHAT'S THAT SMELL?
HUMAN SHIT!
DISGUSTING!
EW.
AAH! WORST SHOW EVER!!!
DEAR JOURNAL,
A PUNGENT, BITTER, INSECURE, AGGRAVATING SMELL ENGULFED US. THE SMELL OF SHIT. SMARNOLD WAS FULL OF IT! WHO KNEW? WELL, WE KNOW NOW. AS WE WATCHED THE LAST DOLLOP OF SMARNOLD PLOP ONTO THE PILE, WE REALIZED WE WERE FREE. OR WERE WE?
PLOP!

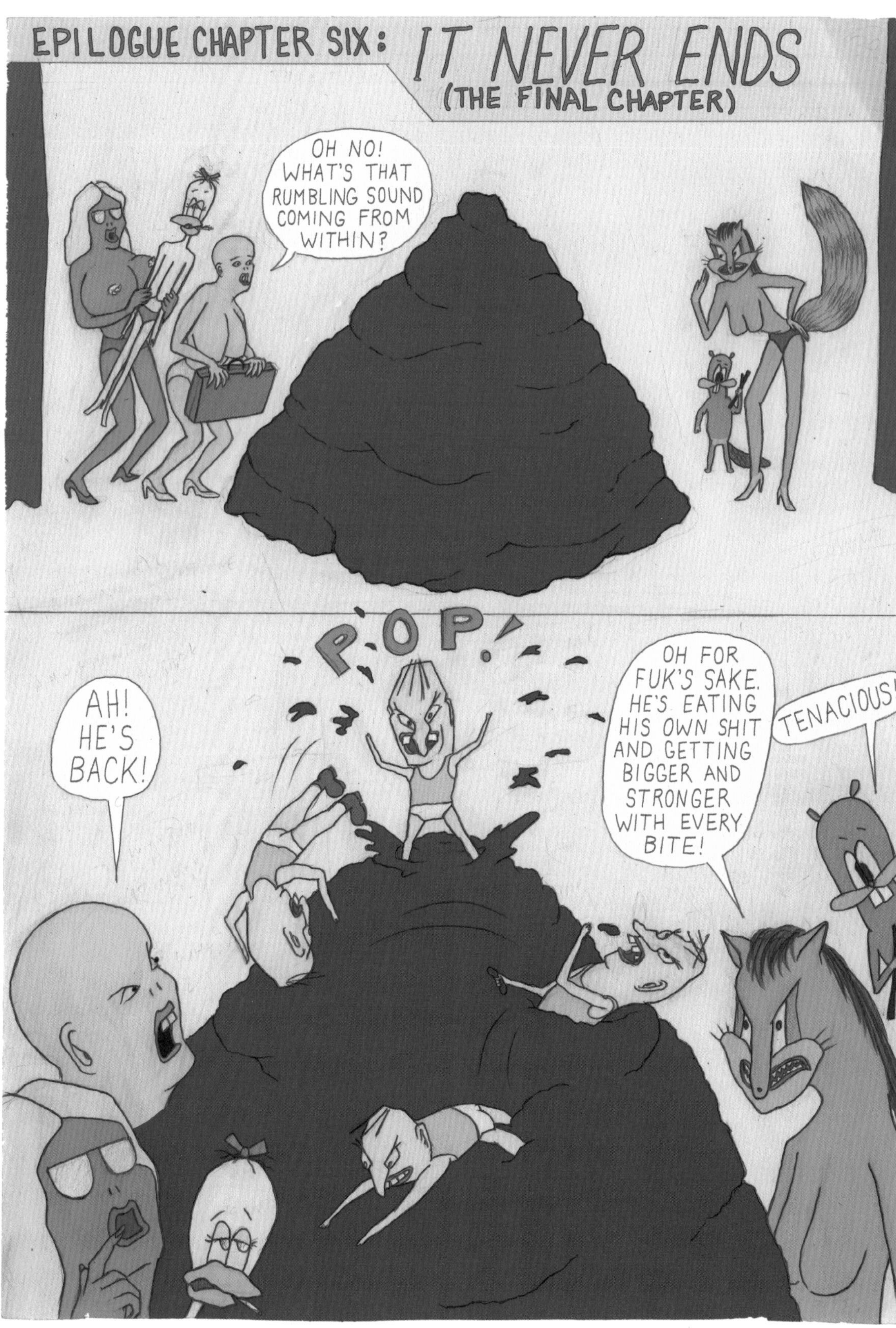
EPILOGUE CHAPTER SIX: IT NEVER ENDS
(THE FINAL CHAPTER)
OH NO! WHAT'S THAT RUMBLING SOUND COMING FROM WITHIN?
POP!
AH! HE'S BACK!
OH FOR FUK'S SAKE. HE'S EATING HIS OWN SHIT AND GETTING BIGGER AND STRONGER WITH EVERY BITE!
TENACIOUS!

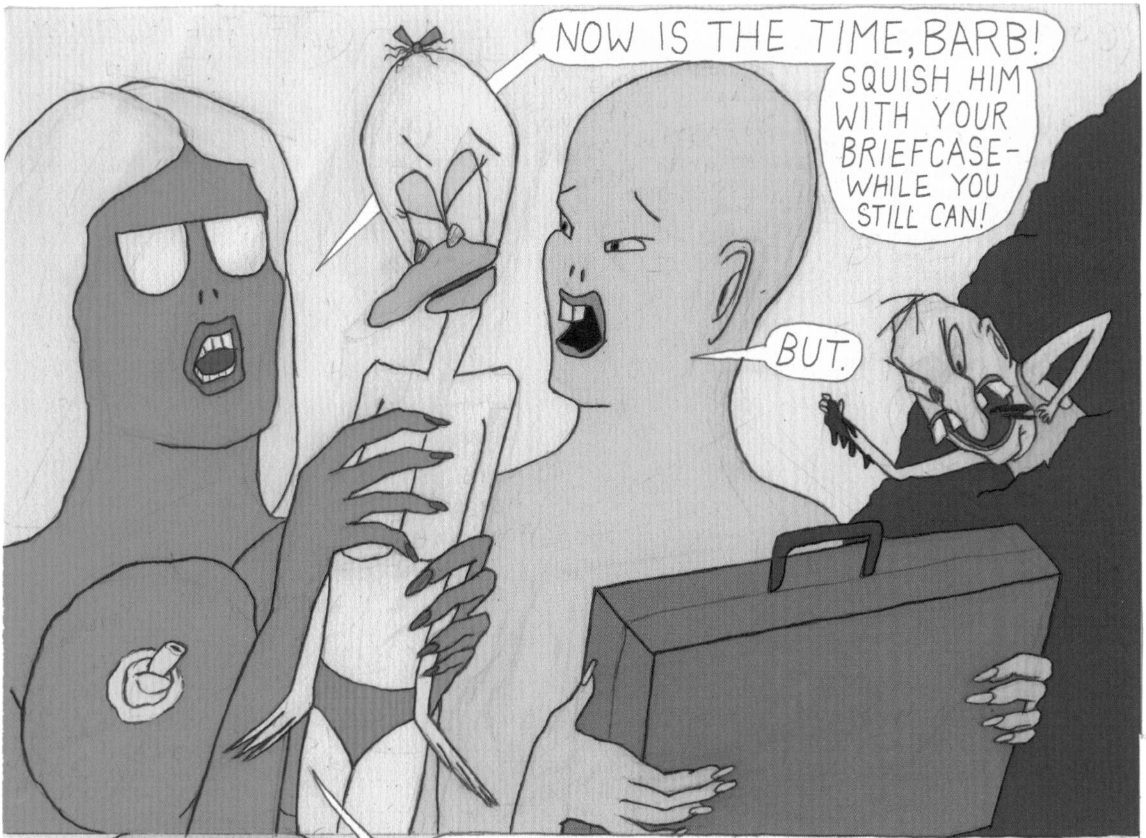
NOW IS THE TIME, BARB! SQUISH HIM WITH YOUR BRIEFCASE- WHILE YOU STILL CAN!
BUT.

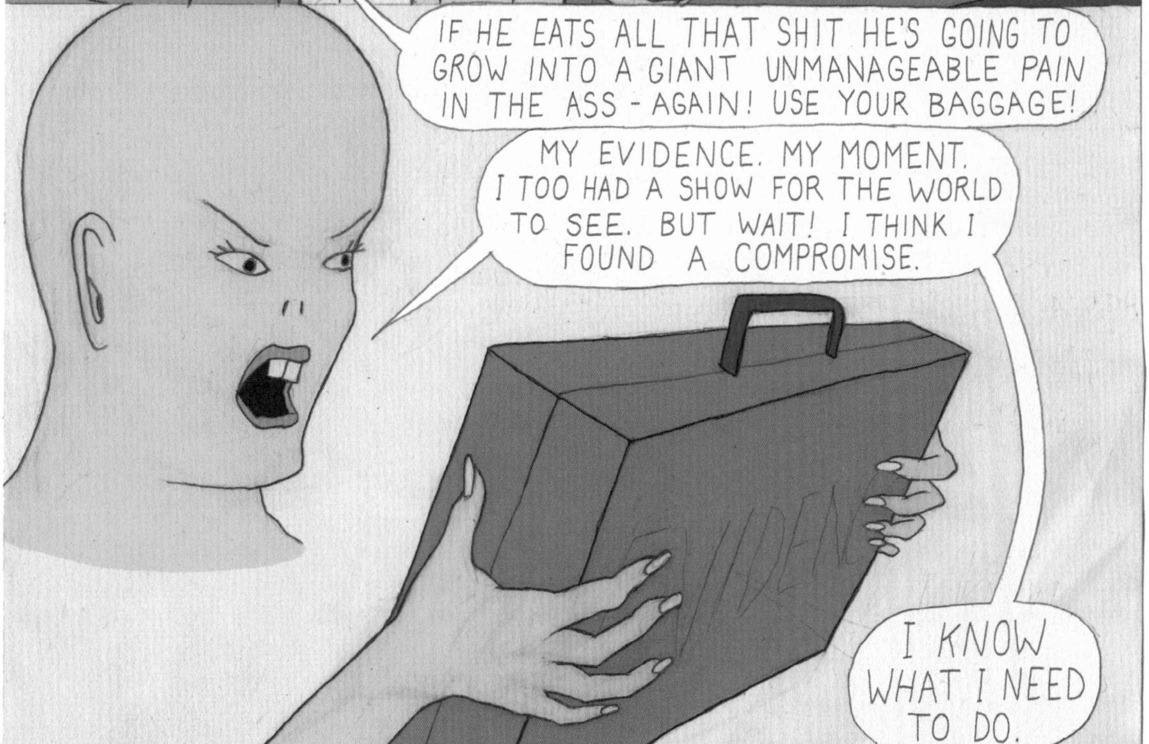
IF HE EATS ALL THAT SHIT HE'S GOING TO GROW INTO A GIANT UNMANAGEABLE PAIN IN THE ASS - AGAIN! USE YOUR BAGGAGE!
MY EVIDENCE. MY MOMENT. I TOO HAD A SHOW FOR THE WORLD TO SEE. BUT WAIT! I THINK I FOUND A COMPROMISE.
I KNOW WHAT I NEED TO DO.

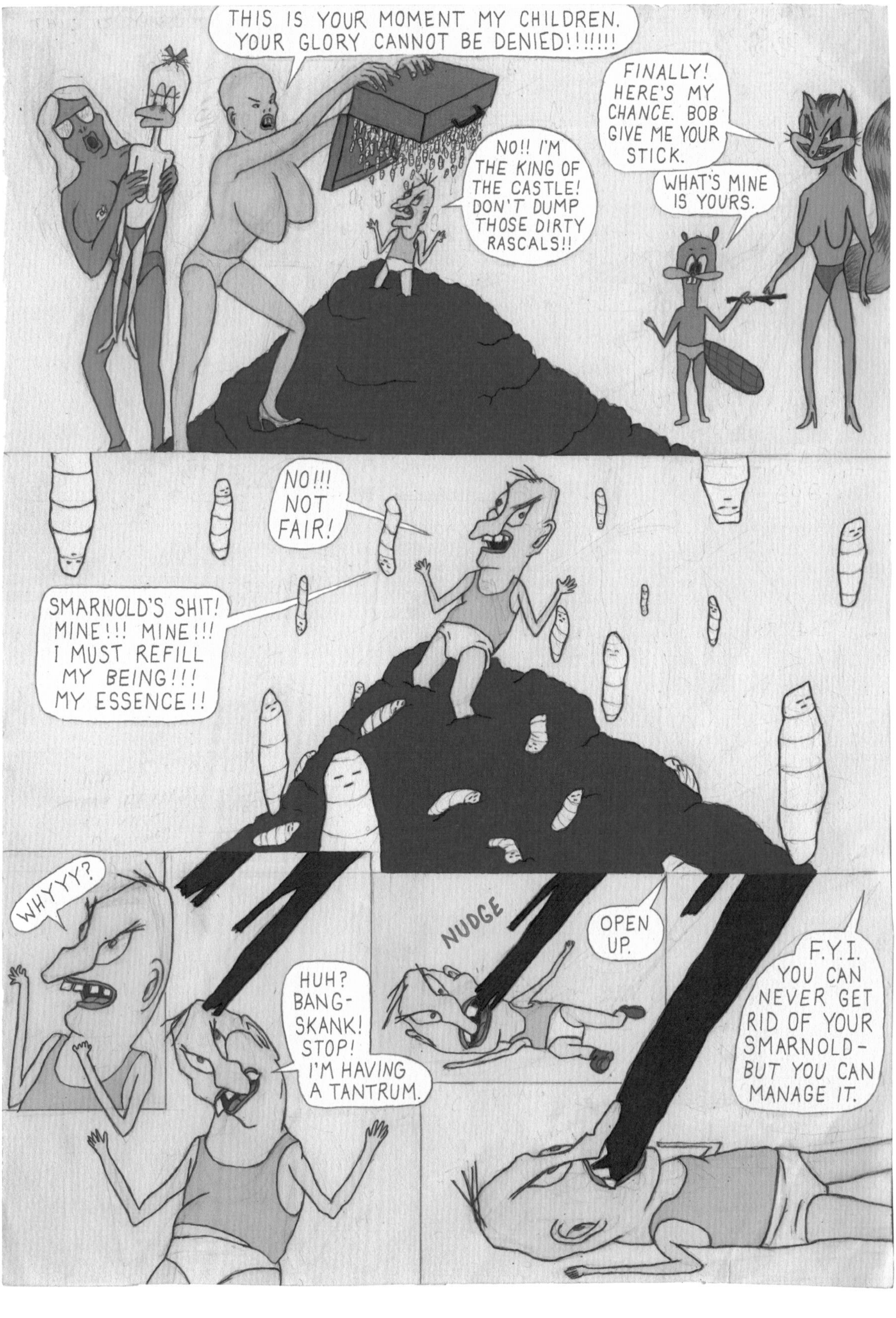
THIS IS YOUR MOMENT MY CHILDREN. YOUR GLORY CANNOT BE DENIED!!!!!!!
NO!! I'M THE KING OF THE CASTLE! DON'T DUMP THOSE DIRTY RASCALS!!
FINALLY! HERE'S MY CHANCE. BOB GIVE ME YOUR STICK.
WHAT'S MINE IS YOURS.
NO!!! NOT FAIR!
SMARNOLD'S SHIT! MINE!!! MINE!!! I MUST REFILL MY BEING!!! MY ESSENCE!!
WHYYY?
HUH? BANG-SKANK! STOP! I'M HAVING A TANTRUM.
NUDGE
OPEN UP.
F.Y.I. YOU CAN NEVER GET RID OF YOUR SMARNOLD- BUT YOU CAN MANAGE IT.

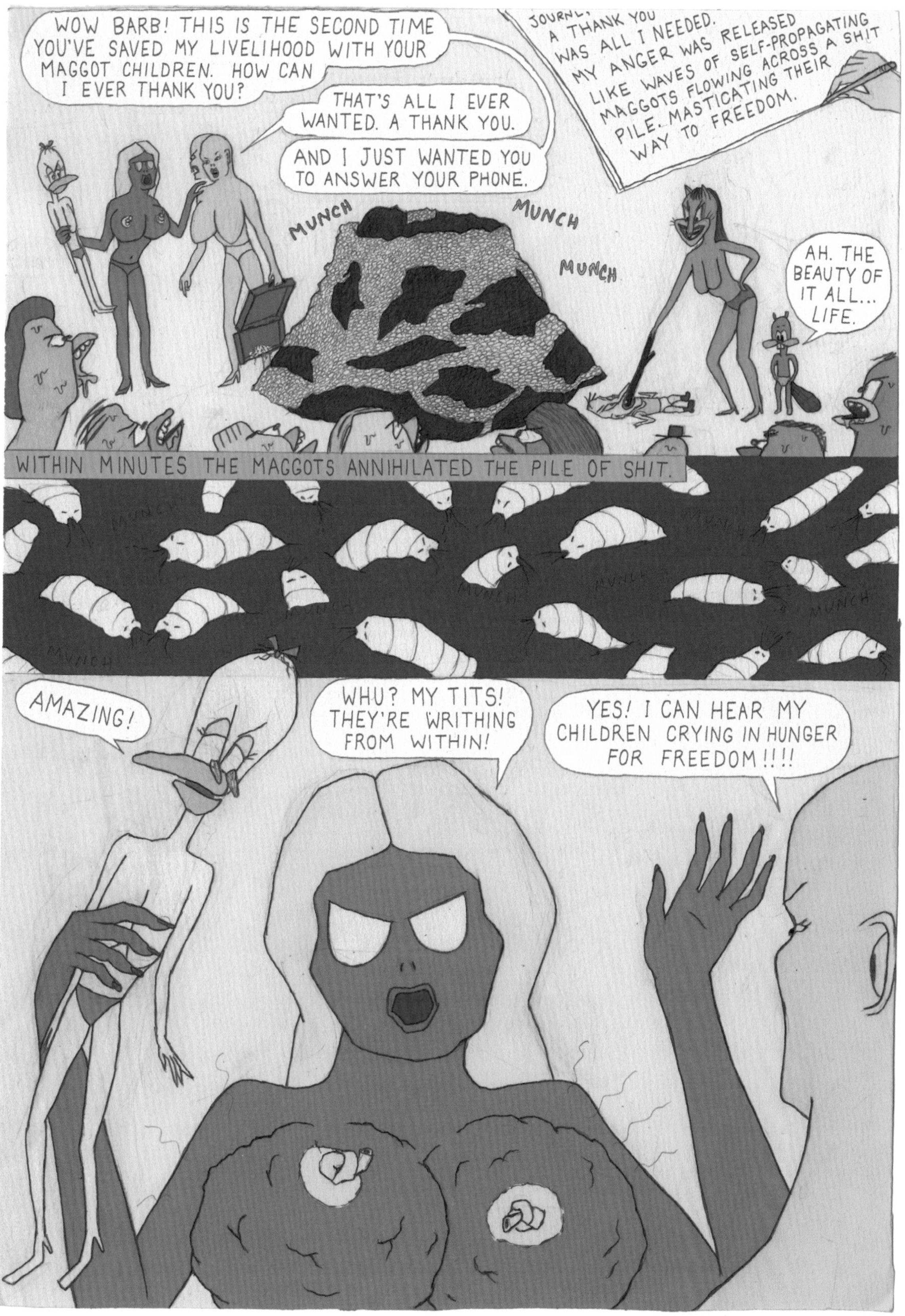
WOW BARB! THIS IS THE SECOND TIME YOU'VE SAVED MY LIVELIHOOD WITH YOUR MAGGOT CHILDREN. HOW CAN I EVER THANK YOU?
THAT'S ALL I EVER WANTED. A THANK YOU.
AND I JUST WANTED YOU TO ANSWER YOUR PHONE.
A THANK YOU WAS ALL I NEEDED. MY ANGER WAS RELEASED LIKE WAVES OF SELF-PROPAGATING MAGGOTS FLOWING ACROSS A SHIT PILE, MASTICATING THEIR WAY TO FREEDOM.
MUNCH
MUNCH
MUNCH
AH. THE BEAUTY OF IT ALL... LIFE.
WITHIN MINUTES THE MAGGOTS ANNIHILATED THE PILE OF SHIT.
MUNCH
MUNCH
AMAZING!
WHU? MY TITS! THEY'RE WRITHING FROM WITHIN!
YES! I CAN HEAR MY CHILDREN CRYING IN HUNGER FOR FREEDOM!!!!

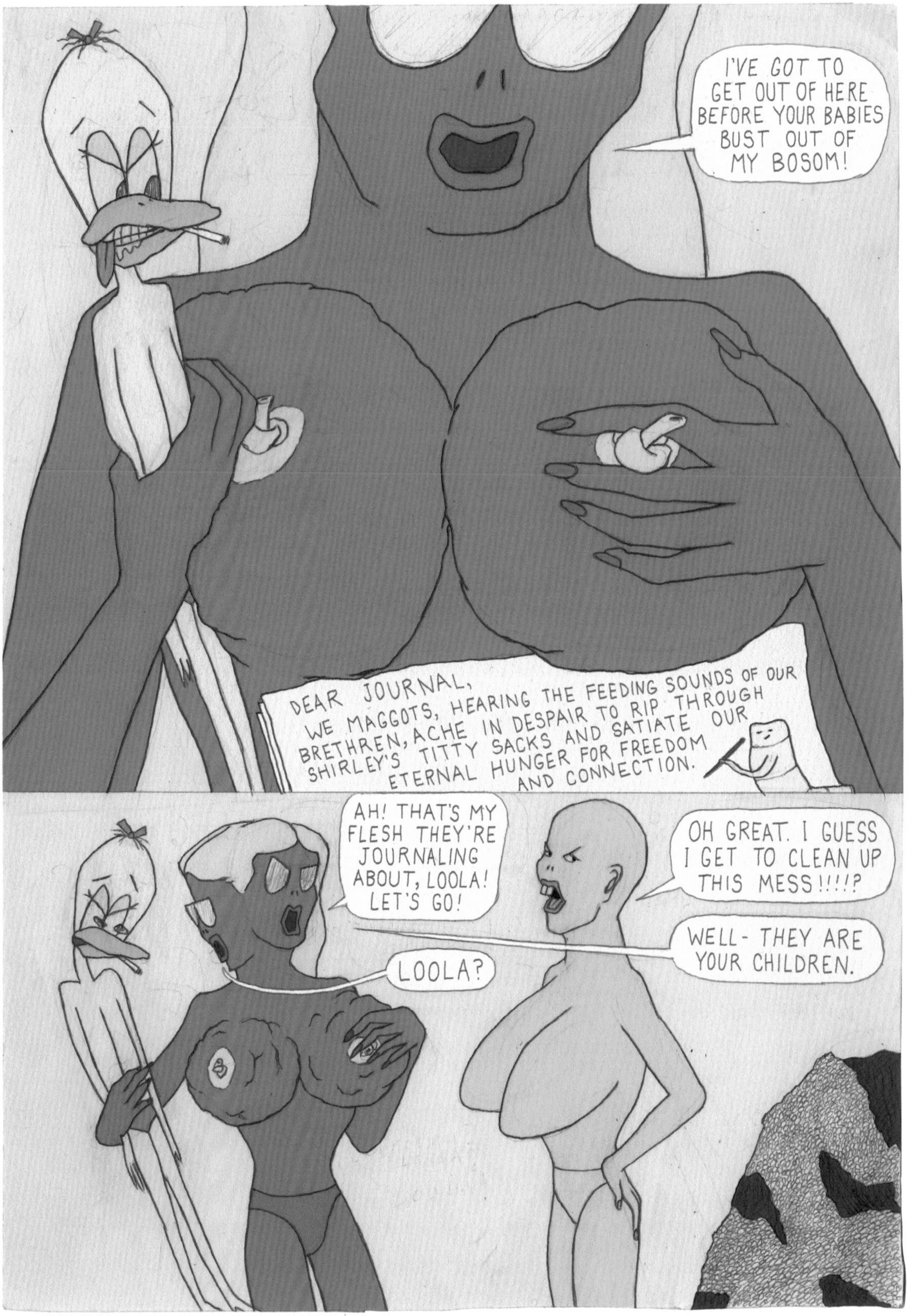
I'VE GOT TO GET OUT OF HERE BEFORE YOUR BABIES BUST OUT OF MY BOSOM!
DEAR JOURNAL, WE MAGGOTS, HEARING THE FEEDING SOUNDS OF OUR BRETHREN, ACHE IN DESPAIR TO RIP THROUGH SHIRLEY'S TITTY SACKS AND SATIATE OUR ETERNAL HUNGER FOR FREEDOM AND CONNECTION.
AH! THAT'S MY FLESH THEY'RE JOURNALING ABOUT, LOOLA! LET'S GO!
OH GREAT. I GUESS I GET TO CLEAN UP THIS MESS!!!!?
LOOLA?
WELL- THEY ARE YOUR CHILDREN.

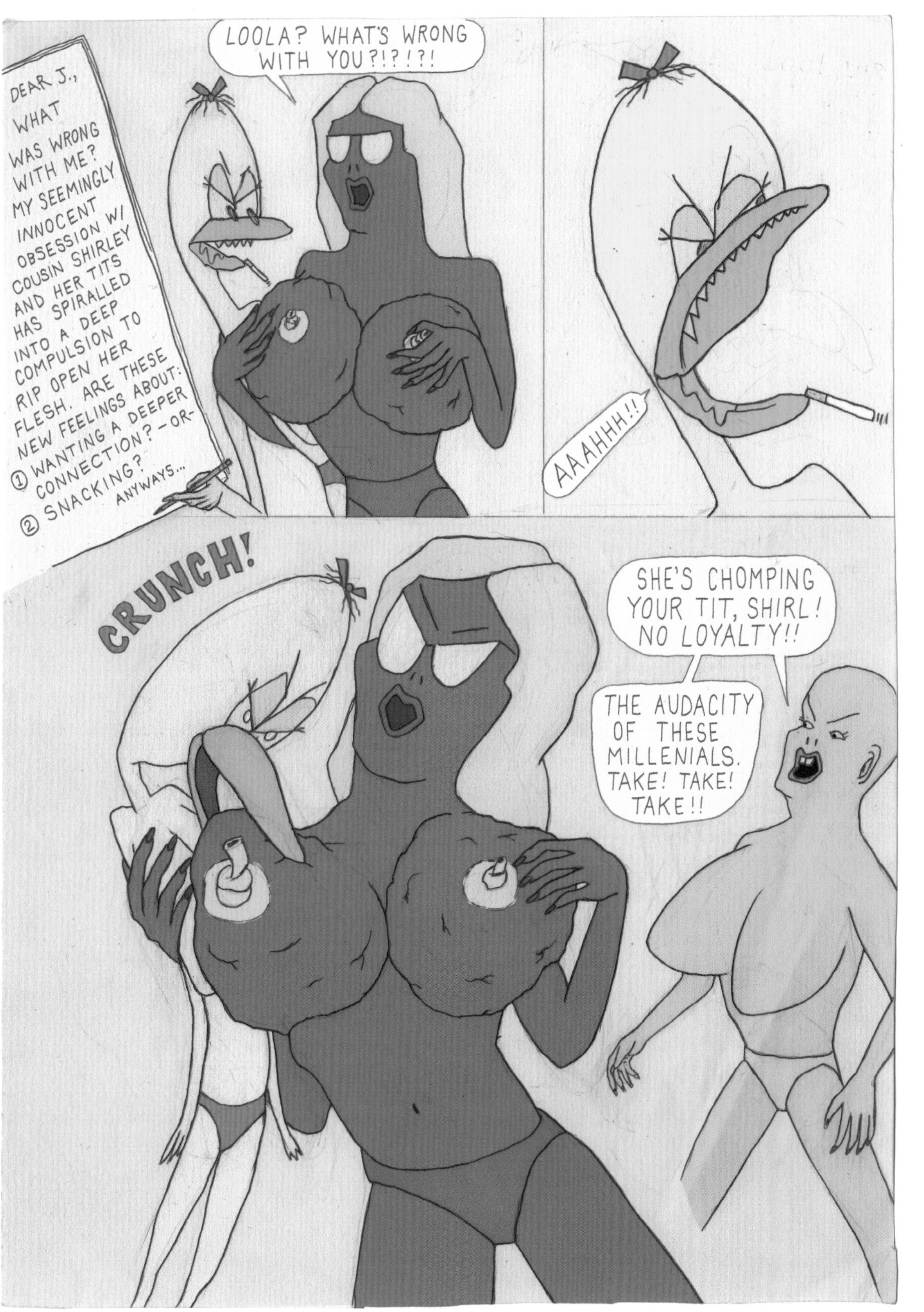
DEAR J., WHAT WAS WRONG WITH ME? MY SEEMINGLY INNOCENT OBSESSION W/ COUSIN SHIRLEY AND HER TITS HAS SPIRALLED INTO A DEEP COMPULSION TO RIP OPEN HER FLESH. ARE THESE NEW FEELINGS ABOUT: ① WANTING A DEEPER CONNECTION? -OR- ② SNACKING? ANYWAYS...
LOOLA? WHAT'S WRONG WITH YOU?!?!?!
AAAHHH!!
CRUNCH!
SHE'S CHOMPING YOUR TIT, SHIRL! NO LOYALTY!!
THE AUDACITY OF THESE MILLENIALS. TAKE! TAKE! TAKE!!

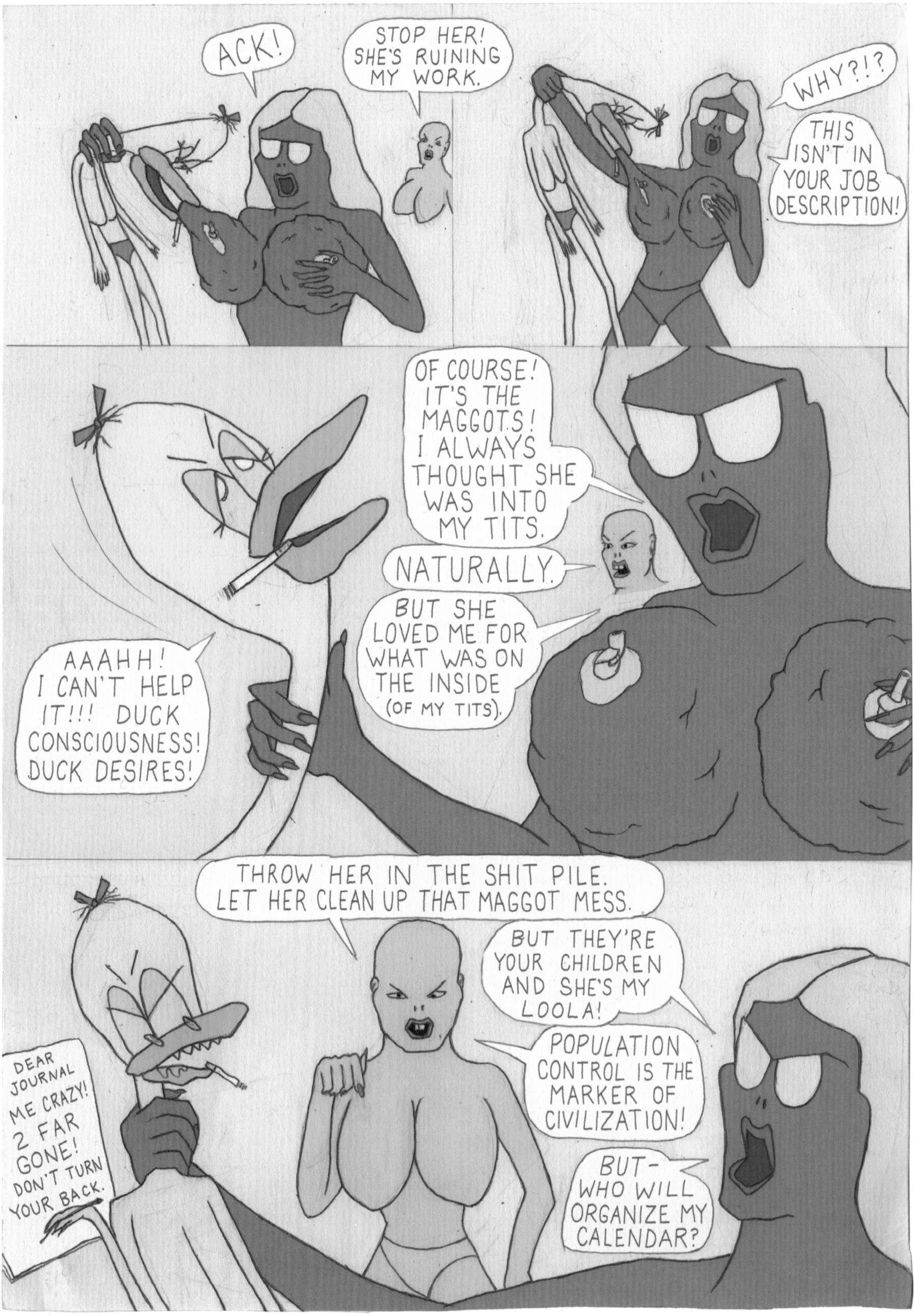
ACK!
STOP HER! SHE'S RUINING MY WORK.
WHY?!?
THIS ISN'T IN YOUR JOB DESCRIPTION!
OF COURSE! IT'S THE MAGGOTS! I ALWAYS THOUGHT SHE WAS INTO MY TITS.
NATURALLY.
BUT SHE LOVED ME FOR WHAT WAS ON THE INSIDE (OF MY TITS).
AAAHH! I CAN'T HELP IT!!! DUCK CONSCIOUSNESS! DUCK DESIRES!
THROW HER IN THE SHIT PILE. LET HER CLEAN UP THAT MAGGOT MESS.
BUT THEY'RE YOUR CHILDREN AND SHE'S MY LOOLA!
POPULATION CONTROL IS THE MARKER OF CIVILIZATION!
BUT- WHO WILL ORGANIZE MY CALENDAR?
DEAR JOURNAL ME CRAZY! 2 FAR GONE! DON'T TURN YOUR BACK.

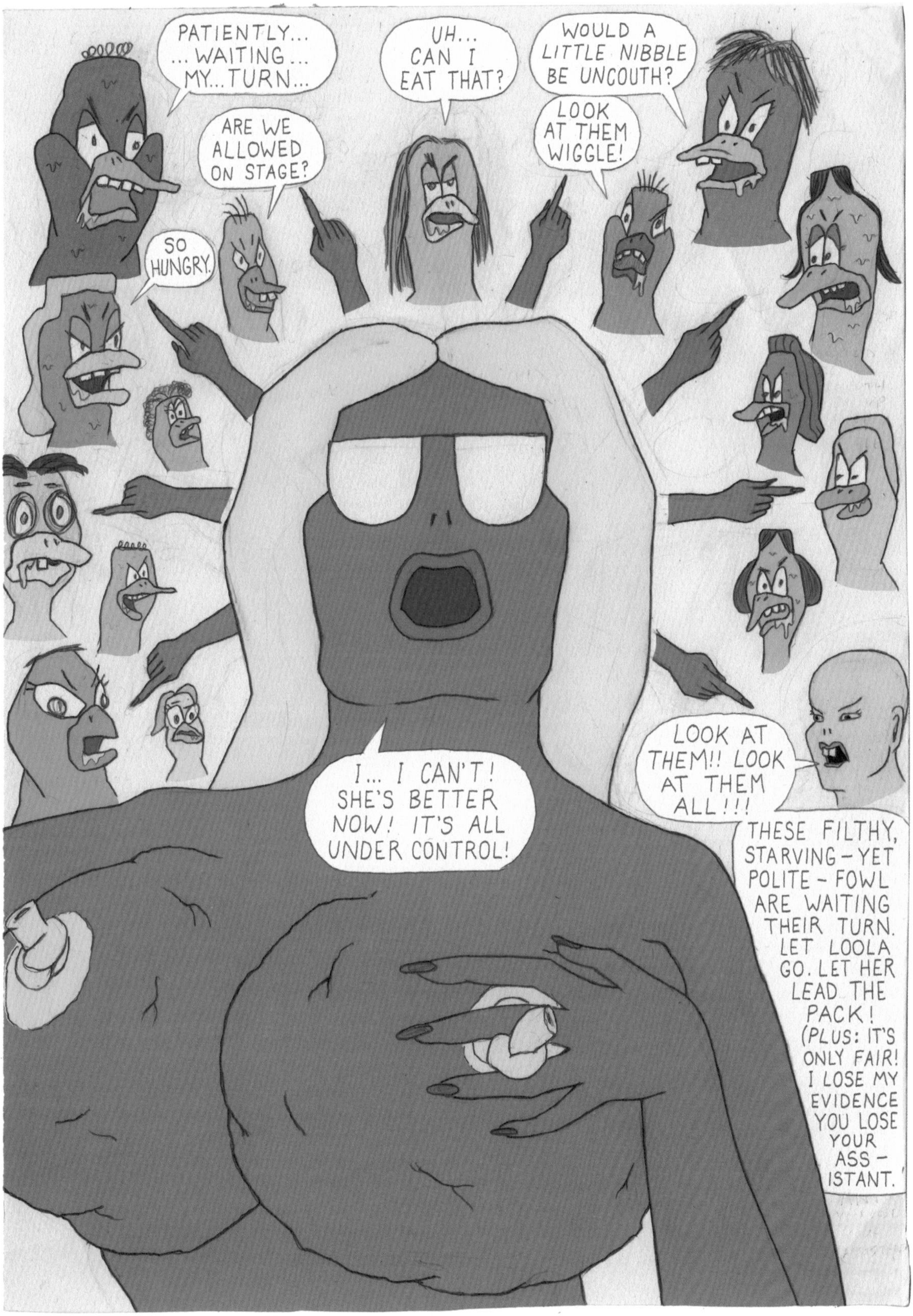
PATIENTLY... ...WAITING... MY...TURN...
UH... CAN I EAT THAT?
WOULD A LITTLE NIBBLE BE UNCOUTH?
ARE WE ALLOWED ON STAGE?
LOOK AT THEM WIGGLE!
SO HUNGRY.
I... I CAN'T! SHE'S BETTER NOW! IT'S ALL UNDER CONTROL!
LOOK AT THEM!! LOOK AT THEM ALL!!!
THESE FILTHY, STARVING - YET POLITE - FOWL ARE WAITING THEIR TURN. LET LOOLA GO. LET HER LEAD THE PACK! (PLUS: IT'S ONLY FAIR! I LOSE MY EVIDENCE YOU LOSE YOUR ASS - ISTANT.

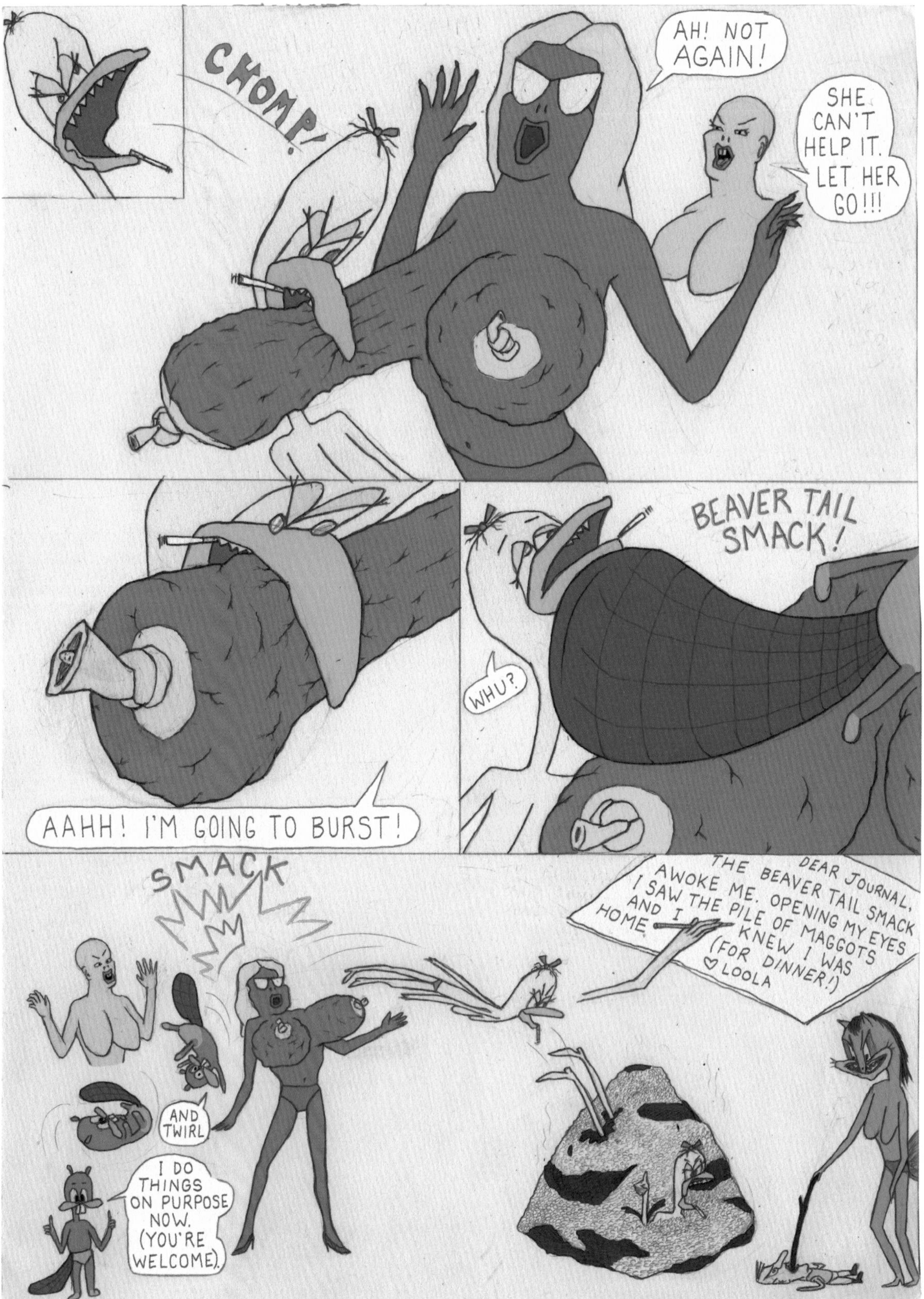
CHOMP!
AH! NOT AGAIN!
SHE CAN'T HELP IT. LET HER GO!!!
AAHH! I'M GOING TO BURST!
BEAVER TAIL SMACK!
WHU?
SMACK
DEAR JOURNAL, THE BEAVER TAIL SMACK AWOKE ME. OPENING MY EYES I SAW THE PILE OF MAGGOTS AND I KNEW I WAS HOME (FOR DINNER!) ♡ LOOLA
AND TWIRL
I DO THINGS ON PURPOSE NOW. (YOU'RE WELCOME).

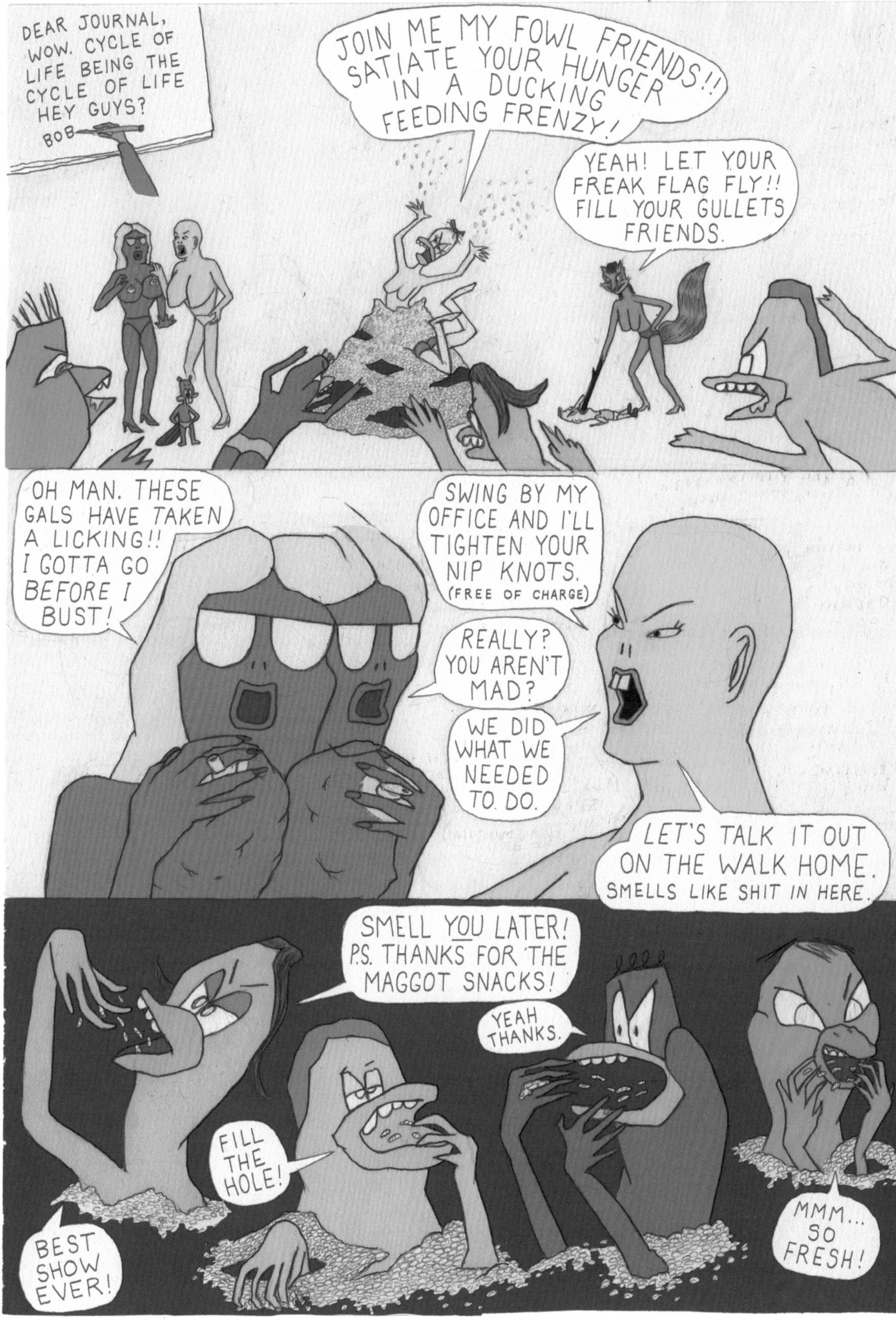
DEAR JOURNAL, WOW. CYCLE OF LIFE BEING THE CYCLE OF LIFE HEY GUYS? BOB
JOIN ME MY FOWL FRIENDS!! SATIATE YOUR HUNGER IN A DUCKING FEEDING FRENZY!
YEAH! LET YOUR FREAK FLAG FLY!! FILL YOUR GULLETS FRIENDS.
OH MAN. THESE GALS HAVE TAKEN A LICKING!! I GOTTA GO BEFORE I BUST!
SWING BY MY OFFICE AND I'LL TIGHTEN YOUR NIP KNOTS. (FREE OF CHARGE)
REALLY? YOU AREN'T MAD?
WE DID WHAT WE NEEDED TO DO.
LET'S TALK IT OUT ON THE WALK HOME. SMELLS LIKE SHIT IN HERE.
SMELL YOU LATER! P.S. THANKS FOR THE MAGGOT SNACKS!
YEAH THANKS.
FILL THE HOLE!
BEST SHOW EVER!
MMM... SO FRESH!

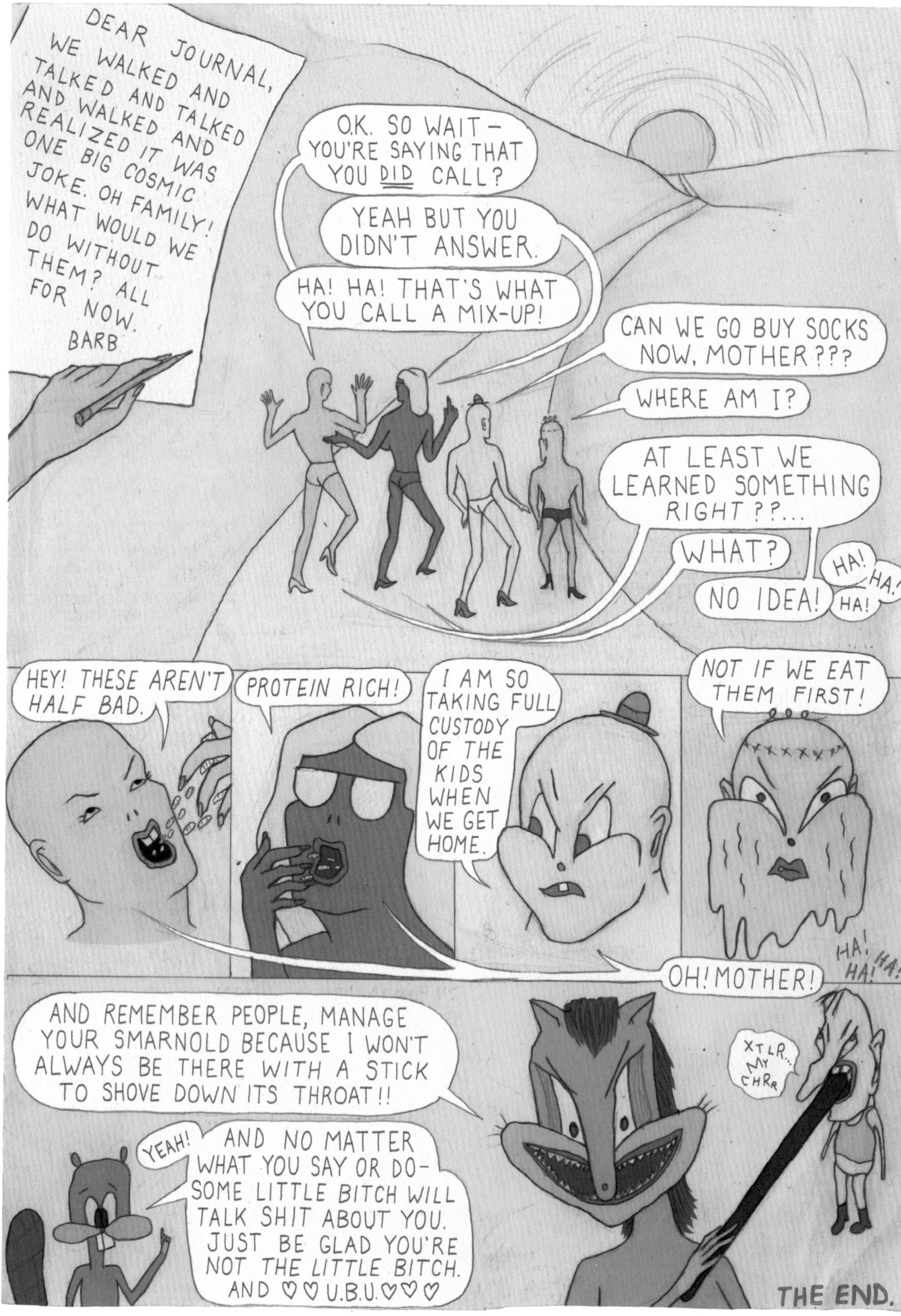
DEAR JOURNAL, WE WALKED AND TALKED AND TALKED AND WALKED AND REALIZED IT WAS ONE BIG COSMIC JOKE. OH FAMILY! WHAT WOULD WE DO WITHOUT THEM? ALL FOR NOW. BARB
O.K. SO WAIT - YOU'RE SAYING THAT YOU DID CALL?
YEAH BUT YOU DIDN'T ANSWER.
HA! HA! THAT'S WHAT YOU CALL A MIX-UP!
CAN WE GO BUY SOCKS NOW, MOTHER???
WHERE AM I?
AT LEAST WE LEARNED SOMETHING RIGHT??...
WHAT?
NO IDEA!
HA! HA! HA!
HEY! THESE AREN'T HALF BAD.
PROTEIN RICH!
I AM SO TAKING FULL CUSTODY OF THE KIDS WHEN WE GET HOME.
NOT IF WE EAT THEM FIRST!
OH! MOTHER!
HA! HA! HA!
AND REMEMBER PEOPLE, MANAGE YOUR SMARNOLD BECAUSE I WON'T ALWAYS BE THERE WITH A STICK TO SHOVE DOWN ITS THROAT!!
XTLR... MY CHRR
YEAH!
AND NO MATTER WHAT YOU SAY OR DO- SOME LITTLE BITCH WILL TALK SHIT ABOUT YOU. JUST BE GLAD YOU'RE NOT THE LITTLE BITCH. AND ♡♡ U.B.U. ♡♡♡
THE END.